Course Booklet

CCNA Discovery

Introducing Routing and Switching in the Enterprise

Version 4.0

ciscopress.com

Cisco | Networking Academy
Mind Wide Open

CCNA Discovery Course Booklet Introducing Routing and Switching in the Enterprise, Version 4.0

Cisco Networking Academy

Copyright© 2010 Cisco Systems, Inc.

Published by:
Cisco Press
800 East 96th Street
Indianapolis, IN 46240 USA

Printed in the United States of America

First Printing   October 2009

Library of Congress Cataloging-in-Publication Data is on file.

ISBN-13: 978-1-58713-256-8

ISBN-10: 1-58713-256-7

Warning and Disclaimer

Publisher
Paul Boger

Associate Publisher
Dave Dusthimer

Cisco Representative
Erik Ullanderson

**Cisco Press
Program Manager**
Anand Sundaram

Executive Editor
Mary Beth Ray

Managing Editor
Patrick Kanouse

Project Editor
Bethany Wall

Editorial Assistant
Vanessa Evans

Cover Designer
Louisa Adair

Composition
Mark Shirar

Trademark Acknowledgments

All terms mentioned in this book that are known to be trademarks or service marks have been appropriately capitalized. Cisco Press or Cisco Systems, Inc., cannot attest to the accuracy of this information. Use of a term in this book should not be regarded as affecting the validity of any trademark or service mark.

Feedback Information

At Cisco Press, our goal is to create in-depth technical books of the highest quality and value. Each book is crafted with care and precision, undergoing rigorous development that involves the unique expertise of members from the professional technical community.

Readers' feedback is a natural continuation of this process. If you have any comments regarding how we could improve the quality of this book, or otherwise alter it to better suit your needs, you can contact us through email at feedback@ciscopress.com. Please make sure to include the book title and ISBN in your message.

We greatly appreciate your assistance.

Contents at a Glance

Contents

Command Syntax Conventions

The conventions used to present command syntax in this book are the same conventions used in the IOS Command Reference. The Command Reference describes these conventions as follows:

- **Boldface** indicates commands and keywords that are entered literally as shown. In actual configuration examples and output (not general command syntax), boldface indicates commands that are manually input by the user (such as a **show** command).

- *Italic* indicates arguments for which you supply actual values.

- Vertical bars (|) separate alternative, mutually exclusive elements.

- Square brackets ([ ]) indicate an optional element.

- Braces ({ }) indicate a required choice.

- Braces within brackets ([{ }]) indicate a required choice within an optional element.

About This Course Booklet

Your Cisco Networking Academy Course Booklet is designed as a study resource you can easily read, highlight, and review on the go, wherever the Internet is not available or practical:

- The text is extracted directly, word-for-word, from the online course so you can highlight important points and take notes in the "Your Chapter Notes" section.

- Headings with the exact page correlations provide a quick reference to the online course for your classroom discussions and exam preparation.

- An icon system directs you to the online curriculum to take full advantage of the images, labs, Packet Tracer activities, and dynamic Flash-based activities embedded within the Networking Academy online course interface.

Refer to **Figure** in online course   Refer to **Lab Activity** for this chapter   Refer to **Packet Tracer Activity** for this chapter   Refer to **Interactive Graphic** in online course.   Go to the online course to take the quiz.

The Course Booklet is a faster, economical paper-based way to help you succeed with the Cisco Networking Academy online course.

Course Introduction

Welcome

Welcome to the CCNA Discovery course, Introducing Routing and Switching in the Enterprise. The goal of this course is to assist you in developing the skills necessary to use protocols to maximize enterprise LAN and WAN performance. The course provides more advanced configurations of switching and routing protocols, configuration of access control lists, and basic implementation of WAN links. It also provides detailed troubleshooting guidance for LAN, WAN, and VLAN implementations. This course prepares you with the skills required for entry-level Network Technician, Help Desk Technician and Computer Technician jobs.

More than just information

This computer-based learning environment is an important part of the overall course experience for students and instructors in the Networking Academy. These online course materials are designed to be used along with several other instructional tools and activities. These include:

- Class presentation, discussion, and practice with your instructor
- Hands-on labs that use networking equipment within the Networking Academy classroom
- Online scored assessments and grade book
- Packet Tracer 4.1 simulation tool
- Additional software for classroom activities

A global community

When you participate in the Networking Academy, you are joining a global community linked by common goals and technologies. Schools, colleges, universities and other entities in over 160 countries participate in the program. You can see an interactive network map of the global Networking Academy community at http://www.academynetspace.com.

The material in this course encompasses a broad range of technologies that facilitate how people work, live, play, and learn by communicating with voice, video, and other data. Networking and the Internet affect people differently in different parts of the world. Although we have worked with instructors from around the world to create these materials, it is important that you work with your instructor and fellow students to make the material in this course applicable to your local situation.

Keep in Touch

These online instructional materials, as well as the rest of the course tools, are part of the larger Networking Academy. The portal for the program is located at http://cisco.netacad.net. There you will obtain access to the other tools in the program such as the assessment server and student grade book), as well as informational updates and other relevant links.

Mind Wide Open®

An important goal in education is to enrich you, the student, by expanding what you know and can do. It is important to realize, however, that the instructional materials and the instructor can only facilitate the process. You must make the commitment yourself to learn new skills. Below are a few suggestions to help you learn and grow.

1. Take notes. Professionals in the networking field often keep Engineering Journals in which they write down the things they observe and learn. Taking notes is an important way to help your understanding grow over time.

2. Think about it. The course provides information both to change what you know and what you can do. As you go through the course, ask yourself what makes sense and what doesn't. Stop and ask questions when you are confused. Try to find out more about topics that interest you. If you are not sure why something is being taught, consider asking your instructor or a friend. Think about how the different parts of the course fit together.

3. Practice. Learning new skills requires practice. We believe this is so important to e-learning that we have a special name for it. We call it e-doing. It is very important that you complete the activities in the online instructional materials and that you also complete the hands-on labs and Packet Tracer® activities.

4. Practice again. Have you ever thought that you knew how to do something and then, when it was time to show it on a test or at work, you discovered that you really hadn't mastered it? Just like learning any new skill like a sport, game, or language, learning a professional skill requires patience and repeated practice before you can say you have truly learned it. The online instructional materials in this course provide opportunities for repeated practice for many skills. Take full advantage of them. You can also work with your instructor to extend Packet Tracer, and other tools, for additional practice as needed.

5. Teach it. Teaching a friend or colleague is often a good way to reinforce your own learning. To teach well, you will have to work through details that you may have overlooked on your first reading. Conversations about the course material with fellow students, colleagues, and the instructor can help solidify your understanding of networking concepts.

6. Make changes as you go. The course is designed to provide feedback through interactive activities and quizzes, the online assessment system, and through interactions with your instructor. You can use this feedback to better understand where your strengths and weaknesses are. If there is an area that you are having trouble with, focus on studying or practicing more in that area. Seek additional feedback from your instructor and other students.

Explore the world of networking

This version of the course includes a special tool called Packet Tracer 4.1®. Packet Tracer is a networking learning tool that supports a wide range of physical and logical simulations. It also provides visualization tools to help you to understand the internal workings of a network.

The Packet Tracer activities included in the course consist of network simulations, games, activities, and challenges that provide a broad range of learning experiences.

Create your own worlds

You can also use Packet Tracer to create your own experiments and networking scenarios. We hope that, over time, you consider using Packet Tracer – not only for experiencing the activities included in the course, but also to become an author, explorer, and experimenter.

The online course materials have embedded Packet Tracer activities that will launch on computers running Windows® operating systems, if Packet Tracer is installed. This integration may also work on other operating systems using Windows emulation.

CHAPTER 1

Networking in the Enterprise

Introduction

Refer to
Figure
in online course

1.1 Describing the Enterprise Network

1.1.1 Supporting the Business Enterprise

Refer to
Figure
in online course

As businesses grow and evolve, so do their networking requirements. A large business environment with many users and locations, or with many systems, is referred to as an *enterprise*. Common examples of enterprise environments include:

- Manufacturers
- Large retail stores
- Restaurant and service franchises
- Utilities and government agencies
- Hospitals
- School systems

The network that is used to support the *business enterprise* is called an *enterprise network*. Enterprise networks have many common characteristics, some of which are:

- Support for critical applications
- Support for *converged network* traffic
- Need for centralized control
- Support for diverse business requirements

An enterprise network must support the exchange of various types of network traffic, including data files, email, *IP telephony*, and video applications for multiple business units.

Refer to
Figure
in online course

Businesses increasingly rely on their network infrastructure to provide *mission-critical* services. Outages in the enterprise network prevent the business from performing its normal activities, which can cause lost revenue and lost customers. Users expect enterprise networks to be up 99.999% of the time.

To obtain this level of reliability, high-end equipment is commonly installed in the enterprise network. Enterprise class equipment is designed for reliability, with features such as redundant power supplies and *failover* capabilities. Designed and manufactured to more stringent standards than lower end devices, enterprise equipment moves large volumes of network traffic.

Purchasing and installing enterprise class equipment does not eliminate the need for proper network design. One objective of good network design is to prevent any single point of failure. This is accomplished by building redundancy into the network.

Other key factors in network design include optimizing bandwidth utilization, ensuring security and network performance.

1.1.2 Traffic Flow in the Enterprise Network

Refer to
Figure
in online course

To optimize bandwidth on an enterprise network, the network must be organized so that traffic stays localized and is not propagated onto unnecessary portions of the network. Using the three-layer *hierarchical design model* helps organize the network. This model divides the network functionality into three distinct layers: *Access Layer*, *Distribution Layer*, and *Core Layer*. Each layer is designed to meet specific functions.

The access layer provides connectivity for the users. The distribution layer is used to forward traffic from one local network to another. Finally, the core layer represents a high-speed backbone layer between dispersed end networks. User traffic is initiated at the access layer and passes through the other layers if the functionality of those layers is required.

Even though the hierarchical model has three layers, some enterprise networks use the Core Layer services offered by an ISP to reduce costs.

Refer to
Figure
in online course

The Cisco Enterprise Architectures divides the network into functional components while still maintaining the concept of Core, Distribution, and Access layers. The functional components are:

- *Enterprise Campus:* Consists of the campus infrastructure with server farms and network management

- *Enterprise Edge:* Consists of the Internet, VPN, and WAN modules connecting the enterprise with the service provider's network

- *Service Provider Edge:* Provides Internet, Public Switched Telephone Network (PSTN), and WAN services

All data that enters or exits the Enterprise Composite Network Model (*ECNM*) passes through an *edge device*. This is the point that all packets can be examined and a decision made if the packet should be allowed on the enterprise network. Intrusion detection systems (*IDS*) and intrusion prevention systems (*IPS*) can also be configured at the enterprise edge to prevent against malicious activity.

Refer to
Figure
in online course

A well-designed network not only controls traffic but also limits the size of failure domains. A *failure domain* is the area of a network impacted when a key device or service experiences problems.

The function of the device that initially fails determines the impact of a failure domain. For example, a malfunctioning switch on a network segment normally impacts only hosts on that segment. However, if the router that connects this segment to others fails, the impact is much greater.

The use of redundant links and reliable enterprise-class equipment minimize the chance of disruption in a network. Smaller failure domains reduce the impact of a failure on company productivity. They also simplify the troubleshooting process, thereby shortening the *downtime* for all users.

Refer to **Packet
Tracer Activity**
for this chapter

Packet Tracer Activity

Observe the flow of traffic through an enterprise network.

1.1.3 Enterprise LANs and WAN

Refer to
Figure
in online course

Enterprise networks incorporate both traditional LAN and WAN technologies. In a typical enterprise network, multiple local networks at a single campus interconnect at either the Distribution Layer or the Core Layer to form a LAN. These local LANs interconnect with other sites which are more geographically dispersed to form a WAN.

LANs are private and under the control of a single person or organization. The organization installs, manages, and maintains the wiring and devices that are the functional building blocks of the LAN.

Some WANs are privately owned; however, because the development and maintenance of a private WAN is expensive, only very large organizations can afford to maintain a private WAN. Most companies purchase WAN connections from a service provider or ISP. The ISP is then responsible for maintaining the *back end* network connections and network services between the LANs.

When an organization has many global sites, establishing WAN connections and service can be complex. For example, the major ISP for the organization may not offer service in every location or country in which the organization has an office. As a result, the organization must purchase services from multiple ISPs. Using multiple ISPs often leads to differences in the quality of services provided. In many emerging countries, for example, network designers will find differences in equipment availability, WAN services offered, and encryption technology for security. To support an enterprise network, it is important to have uniform standards for equipment, configuration, and services.

Refer to
Figure
in online course

Features of a LAN:

- The organization has the responsibility of installing and managing the infrastructure.

- Ethernet is the most common technology used.

- The focus of the network is in the Access and Distribution Layers.

- The LAN connects users, provides support for localized applications and server farms.

- Connected devices are usually in the same local area, such as a building or a campus.

Features of a WAN:

- Connected sites are usually geographically dispersed.

- Connectivity to the WAN requires a device such as a modem or CSU/DSU to put the data in a form acceptable to the network of the service provider.

- Services are provided by an ISP. WAN services include T1/T3, E1/E3, DSL, Cable, Frame Relay, and ATM.

- The ISP has the responsibility of installing and managing the infrastructure.

- The edge devices modify the Ethernet encapsulation to a serial WAN encapsulation.

Refer to
Interactive Graphic
in online course.

Full screen activity

1.1.4 Intranets and Extranets

Refer to
Figure
in online course

Enterprise networks contain both WAN and LAN technologies. These networks provide many of the services associated with the Internet, including:

- Email

- Web

- FTP

- Telnet/SSH

- Discussion forums

Many companies use this private network or *intranet* to provide access for local and remote employees using LAN and WAN technologies.

Intranets may have links to the Internet. If connected to the Internet, firewalls control the traffic that enters and exits the intranet.

Refer to
Figure
in online course

Intranets contain confidential information and are designed for company employees only. The intranet should be protected by a firewall. Remote employees who are not connected to the enterprise LAN must authenticate before gaining access.

In some situations, businesses extend privileged access to their network to key suppliers and customers. Common methods for doing this are:

- Direct WAN connectivity

- Remote logins to key application systems

- VPN access into a protected network

An intranet that allows external connections to suppliers and contractors is an *extranet*. An extranet is a private network (intranet) that allows controlled access to individuals and companies outside the organization. An extranet is not a public network.

1.2 Identifying Enterprise Applications

1.2.1 Traffic Flow Patterns

Refer to
Figure
in online course

A properly designed enterprise network has defined and predictable traffic flow patterns. In some circumstances traffic stays on the LAN portion of the enterprise network and at other times it traverses the WAN links.

When determining how to design the network it is important to consider the amount of traffic destined for a specific location and where that traffic most often originates. For example, traffic that should typically remain local to users on the network includes:

- File sharing

- Printing

- Internal backup and mirroring

- Intra-campus voice

Traffic types which are typically seen on the local network but are also commonly sent across the WAN include:

- System updates

- Company email

- Transaction processing

In addition to WAN traffic, external traffic is traffic that originates from or is destined to the Internet. VPN and Internet traffic is considered external traffic flow.

Controlling the flow of traffic on a network optimizes bandwidth and introduces a level of security through monitoring. By understanding traffic patterns and flows, the network administrator can predict the types and amount of traffic to expect. When traffic is detected in an area of the network where it is unexpected, that traffic can be filtered and the source of the traffic investigated.

Refer to **Interactive Graphic** in online course.

Full screen

Refer to **Figure** in online course

1.2.2 Applications and Traffic on an Enterprise Network

At one time, voice, video, and data each traveled on separate networks. Now technology supports a converged network, where voice, video, and data flow across the same medium.

This convergence presents many design and bandwidth management challenges. Enterprise networks must support the business enterprise by allowing traffic from a variety of applications, including:

- Database transaction processing
- Mainframe or data center access
- File and print sharing
- Authentication
- Web services
- Email and other communications
- VPN services
- Voice calls and voicemail
- Video and video conferencing

Network management and the control processes required for the underlying operation of the network also need support.

Refer to **Figure** in online course

When trying to determine how to manage network traffic, it is important to understand the type of traffic that is crossing the network as well as the current traffic flow. If the types of traffic are unknown, a *packet sniffer* can be used to capture traffic for analysis.

To determine traffic flow patterns, it is important to:

- Capture traffic during peak utilization times to get a good representation of the different traffic types.
- Perform the capture on different network segments, because some traffic will be local to a particular segment.

Using the information obtained from the packet sniffer, network technicians can determine traffic flows. Technicians analyze this information based on the source and destination of the traffic as well as the type of traffic being sent. This analysis can be used to make decisions on how to manage the traffic more efficiently. This can be done by reducing unnecessary traffic flows or changing flow patterns altogether by moving a server.

Sometimes, simply relocating a server or service to another network segment improves network performance. At other times, optimizing the network performance requires major redesign and intervention.

Refer to
Lab Activity
for this chapter

Lab Activity

Use a packet capture program to analyze network traffic.

1.2.3 Network Traffic Prioritization

Refer to
Figure
in online course

Not all types of network traffic have the same requirements or behave in the same manner.

Data Traffic

Most network applications utilize data traffic. Some types of online applications transmit data that is sporadic. Other types, such as data storage applications, transmit high volumes of traffic for a sustained period of time.

Some data applications are more concerned about time-sensitivity than reliability, and most data applications can tolerate delays. For this reason, data traffic usually employs Transmission Control Protocol (TCP). TCP uses acknowledgments to determine when lost packets must be retransmitted and therefore guarantees delivery. While the use of acknowledgements makes TCP a more reliable delivery protocol, it also incurs a delay.

Voice and Video Traffic

Voice traffic and video traffic are different from data traffic. Voice and video applications require an uninterrupted stream of data to ensure high quality conversations and images. The acknowledgement process in TCP introduces delays, which break these streams and degrade the quality of the application. Therefore, voice and video applications employ User Datagram Protocol (*UDP*) instead of TCP. Since UDP does not have mechanisms for retransmitting lost packets, it minimizes delays.

Refer to
Figure
in online course

In addition to understanding the delays of TCP versus UDP, it is also necessary to understand the delay, or *latency*, caused by the networking devices that must process the traffic on its path to the destination. OSI Layer 3 devices create more delay than Layer 2 devices due to the number of headers they have to process. Therefore, routers introduce a longer delay than switches.

Jitter, caused by network congestion, is the variation in time of the packets arriving at their destination.

It is important to reduce the impact of delay, latency, and jitter on time-sensitive traffic.

Quality of Service (*QoS*) is a process used to guarantee a specified data flow. QoS mechanisms sort traffic into queues, based on priority. For example, voice traffic has priority over ordinary data.

Refer to
Interactive Graphic
in online course.

Full screen activity

1.3 Supporting Remote Workers

1.3.1 Teleworking

Refer to
Figure
in online course

The development of enterprise networks and remote connection technology has changed the way we work.

Teleworking, also referred to as *telecommuting* and e-commuting, allows employees to use telecommunications technology to work from their homes or other remote locations. The remote worker using the technology is called a *teleworker* or telecommuter.

An increasing number of companies encourage their employees to consider teleworking. Teleworking provides many advantages and opportunities for both employer and employee. From the employer perspective, when employees work from home, the company does not have to provide them with dedicated physical office space. A single office space can be set up for shared use by employees who need to spend time in the physical office. This arrangement reduces real estate costs and the associated support services.

Some companies have even reduced the expense of air travel and hotel accommodations to bring their employees together by using *teleconferencing* and collaboration tools. People from all over the world can work together as if they were in the same physical location.

Refer to **Figure** in online course

Both the employer and the employee benefit from teleworking.

Employees save time and money, and reduce stress, by eliminating the daily travel to and from the office. Employees can dress casually at home, therefore saving money on business attire. Working from home allows employees to spend more time with their families.

Reduced travel for employees also has a very favorable effect on the environment. Less airplane and automobile traffic means less pollution.

Teleworkers need to be self-directed and disciplined. Some teleworkers miss the social environment of an office setting and find it difficult to work in physical isolation.

Not all jobs can take advantage of teleworking. Some positions require a physical presence in the office during a set period of time. However, more enterprises are taking advantage of technology to increase the frequency of telecommuting.

Refer to **Figure** in online course

Telecommuters need various tools to work efficiently. Some available teleworker tools include:

- Email
- Chat
- Desktop and application sharing
- FTP
- Telnet
- VoIP
- Video conferencing

Refer to **Figure** in online course

Application and screen sharing tools have improved, and it is now possible to integrate both voice and video into these applications.

New technology has enabled more sophisticated levels of online collaboration. Using the enterprise network, this technology creates an environment in which individuals from remote locations meet as though they were in the same room. By combining large video displays and high quality audio in specially-designed rooms, it appears as if all participants, regardless of their physical location, are sitting across the boardroom table from each other.

In the graphic, only the five people in the foreground are physically in the room. The other four people displayed on the screens are located in three other locations.

Refer to **Interactive Graphic** in online course.

Full Screen Activity

1.3.2 Virtual Private Networks

Refer to **Figure** in online course

One obstacle that teleworkers must overcome is the fact that most of the tools available for working remotely are not secure. Using nonsecure tools allows data to be intercepted or altered during transmission.

One solution is to always use the secure forms of applications, if they exist. For example, instead of using Telnet, use SSH. Unfortunately, secure forms of all applications may not be available. A much easier choice is to encrypt all traffic moving between the remote site and the enterprise network using Virtual Private Networks (*VPN*s).

VPNs are often described as tunnels. Consider the analogy of an underground tunnel versus an open road way between two points. Anything that uses the underground tunnel to travel between the two points is surrounded and protected from view. The underground tunnel represents the VPN encapsulation and virtual tunnel.

Refer to
Figure
in online course

When using a VPN, a virtual tunnel is created by linking the source and destination addresses. All data flow between the source and destination is encrypted and encapsulated using a secure protocol. This secure packet is transmitted across the network. When it arrives at the receiving end, it is de-encapsulated and unencrypted.

VPNs are a client/server application; therefore, telecommuters must install the VPN client on their computers in order to form a secure connection with the enterprise network.

When telecommuters are connected to the enterprise network through a VPN, they become part of that network and have access to all services and resources that they would have if they were physically attached to the LAN.

Summary

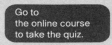

Quiz

Take the chapter quiz to check your knowledge.

Your Chapter Notes

CHAPTER 2

Exploring the Enterprise Network Infrastructure

Introduction

Refer to
Figure
in online course

2.1 Describing the Current Network

2.1.1 Enterprise Network Documentation

Refer to
Figure
in online course

One of the first tasks for a new network technician is to become familiar with the current network structure. Enterprise networks can have thousands of hosts and hundreds of networking devices, all of which are interconnected by copper, fiber-optic, and wireless technologies. End-user workstations, servers, and networking devices, such as switches and routers, must all be documented. Various types of documentation show different aspects of the network.

*Network infrastructure diagram*s, or topology diagrams, keep track of the location, function, and status of devices. Topology diagrams represent either the physical or logical network.

A *physical topology* map uses icons to document the location of hosts, networking devices, and media. It is important to maintain and update physical topology maps to aid future installation and troubleshooting efforts.

A *logical topology* map groups hosts by network usage, regardless of physical location. Host names, addresses, group information, and applications can be recorded on the logical topology map. Connections between multiple sites may be shown but do not represent actual physical locations.

Enterprise network diagrams may also include control plane information. Control plane information describes failure domains and defines the interfaces where different network technologies intersect.

Refer to
Figure
in online course

It is crucial that network documentation remain current and accurate. Network documentation is usually accurate at the installation of a network. As the network grows or changes however, the documentation is not always updated.

Network topology maps are frequently based on original floor plans. The current floor plans may have changed since the construction of the building. Blueprints can be marked up, or *redlined*, to show the changes. The modified diagram is known as an *as-built*. An as-built diagram documents how a network was actually constructed which may differ from the original plans. Always ensure that the current documentation reflects the as-built floor plan and all network topology changes.

Network diagrams are commonly created using graphical drawing software. In addition to being a drawing tool, many network diagramming tools are linked to a database. This feature allows the network support staff to develop detailed documentation by recording information about hosts and networking devices, including manufacturer, model number, purchase date, warranty period, and more. Clicking a device in the diagram opens an entry form with device data listed.

Refer to
Figure
in online course

In addition to network diagrams, several other important types of documentation are used in the enterprise network.

Business Continuity Plan:

The Business Continuity Plan (**BCP**) identifies the steps to be taken to continue business operation in the event of a natural or man-made disaster.

Business Security Plan:

The Business Security Plan (**BSP**) includes physical, system, and organizational control measures. The overall security plan must include an IT portion that describes how an organization protects its network and information assets.

Network Maintenance Plan:

The Network Maintenance Plan (**NMP**) ensures business continuity by keeping the network up and running efficiently. Network maintenance must be scheduled during specific time periods, usually nights and weekends, to minimize the impact on business operations.

Service Level Agreement:

A Service Level Agreement (**SLA**) is a contractual agreement between the customer and a service provider or ISP, specifying items such as network availability and service response time.

Refer to
Interactive Graphic
in online course.

Full Screen Activity

2.1.2 Network Operations Center (NOC)

Refer to
Figure
in online course

Most enterprise networks have a Network Operations Center (**NOC**) that allows for central management and monitoring of all network resources. The NOC is sometimes referred to as a **Data Center**.

Employees in a typical enterprise NOC provide support for both local and remote locations, often managing both local and wide area networking issues. Larger NOCs may be multi-room areas of a building where network equipment and support staff are concentrated.

The NOC usually has:

- Raised floors to allow for cabling and power to run under the floor to the equipment

- High performance UPS systems and air conditioning equipment to provide a safe operating environment for equipment

- Fire suppression systems integrated into the ceiling

- Network monitoring stations, servers, backup systems, and data storage

- Access layer switches and distribution layer routers, if it serves as a Main Distribution Facility (MDF) for the building or campus where it is located

Refer to
Figure
in online course

In addition to providing network support and management, many NOCs also provide centralized resources such as servers and data storage.

Servers in the NOC are usually clustered together, creating a server farm. The **server farm** is frequently considered as a single resource but, in fact, provides two functions: backup and **load balancing**. If one server fails or becomes overloaded, another server takes over.

The servers in the farm may be rack-mounted and interconnected by very high-speed switches (Gigabit Ethernet or higher). They may also be blade servers mounted in a chassis and connected by a high-speed backplane within the chassis.

Another important aspect of the enterprise NOC is high-speed, high-capacity data storage. This data storage, or network attached storage (*NAS*), groups large numbers of disk drives that are directly attached to the network and can be used by any server. A NAS device is typically attached to an Ethernet network and is assigned its own IP address.

A more sophisticated version of NAS is Storage Area Network (*SAN*). A SAN is a high-speed network that interconnects different types of data storage devices over a LAN or WAN.

Refer to **Figure** in online course

Equipment in the enterprise NOC is usually mounted in racks. In large NOCs, racks are usually floor-to-ceiling mounted and may be attached to each other. When mounting equipment in a rack, ensure there is adequate ventilation and access from front and back. Equipment must also be attached to a known good ground.

The most common rack width is 19 inches (48.26 cm). Most equipment is designed to fit this width. The vertical space that the equipment occupies is measured in Rack Units (*RU*s). A Unit equals 1.75 inches (4.4cm). For example, a 2U chassis is 3.5 inches (8.9 cm) high. The lower the RU number the less space a device needs therefore more devices can fit into the rack.

Another consideration is equipment with many connections, like switches. They may need to be positioned near patch panels and close to where the cabling is gathered into cable trays.

Refer to **Figure** in online course

In an enterprise NOC, thousands of cables may enter and exit the facility. *Structured cabling* creates an organized cabling system that is easily understood by installers, network administrators, and any other technicians who work with cables.

Cable management serves many purposes. First, it presents a neat and organized system that aids in isolating cabling problems. Second, best cabling practices protect the cables from physical damage and *EMI*, which greatly reduces the number of problems experienced.

To assist in troubleshooting:

- All cables should be labelled at both ends, using a standard convention that indicates source and destination.

- All cable runs should be documented on the physical network topology diagram.

- All cable runs, both copper and fiber, should be tested end-to-end by sending a signal down the cable and measuring loss.

Cabling standards specify a maximum distance for all cable types and network technologies. For example, the IEEE specifies that, for Fast Ethernet over unshielded twisted pair (UTP), the cable run from switch to host cannot be greater than 100 meters (approximately 328 ft). If the cable run is greater than the recommended length problems could occur with data communications, especially if the terminations at the ends of the cable are poorly completed.

Documentation of the cable plan and testing are critical to network operations.

2.1.3 Telecommunication Room Design and Considerations

Refer to **Figure** in online course

The NOC is the central nervous system of the enterprise. In practice, however, most users connect to a switch in a *telecommunications room*, which is some distance from the NOC. The telecommunications room is also referred to as a wiring closet or intermediate distribution facility (*IDF*). It contains the Access Layer networking devices and ideally maintains environmental conditions similar to the NOC, such as air conditioning and UPS.

Users working with wired technology connect to the network through Ethernet switches or hubs. Users working with wireless technology connect through an access point (*AP*). Access Layer devices such as switches and APs are a potential vulnerability in network security. Physical and remote access to this equipment should be limited to authorized personnel only. Network personnel can also implement port security and other measures on switches, as well as various wireless security measures on APs.

Securing the telecommunications room has become even more important because of the increasing occurrence of identity theft. New privacy legislation results in severe penalties if confidential data from a network falls into the wrong hands. Modern networking devices offer capabilities to help prevent these attacks and protect data and user integrity.

Refer to
Figure
in online course

Many IDFs connect to a Main Distribution Facility (*MDF*) using an ***extended star*** design. The MDF is usually located in the NOC or centrally located within the building.

MDFs are typically larger than IDFs. They house high-speed switches, routers, and server farms. The central MDF switches may have enterprise servers and disk drives connected using gigabit copper links.

IDFs contain lower-speed switches, APs, and hubs. The switches in the IDFs typically have large numbers of Fast Ethernet ports for users to connect at the Access Layer.

The switches in the IDF usually connect to the switches in the MDF with Gigabit interfaces. This arrangement creates backbone connections, or uplinks. These backbone links, also called vertical cabling, may be copper or fiber-optic. Copper Gigabit or Fast Ethernet links are limited to a maximum of 100 meters and should use CAT5e or CAT6 UTP cable. Fiber-optic links can run much greater distances. Fiber-optic links commonly interconnect buildings and because they do not conduct electricity, they are immune to lightning strikes, EMI, RFI, and differential grounds.

Refer to
Figure
in online course

In addition to providing basic network access connectivity, it is becoming more common to provide power to end-user devices directly from the Ethernet switches in the telecommunications room. These devices include IP phones, access points, and surveillance cameras.

These devices are powered using the IEEE 802.3af standard, Power over Ethernet, or *PoE*. PoE provides power to a device over the same twisted pair cable that carries data. This allows an IP phone, for instance, to be located on a desk without the need for a separate power cord or a power outlet. In order to support PoE devices such as the IP phone, the connecting switch must have PoE capability.

PoE can also be provided by power injectors or PoE patch panels for those switches which do not support PoE. Panduit and other suppliers produce PoE patch panels that allow non PoE capable switches to participate in PoE environments. Legacy switches connect into the PoE patch panel which then connects to the PoE capable device.

Refer to
Interactive Graphic
in online course.

Activity

Place the MDF and IDFs in an appropriate location in the campus diagram and identify appropriate cables to connect them.

2.2 Supporting the Enterprise Edge

2.2.1 Service Delivery at the Point-of-Presence

Refer to
Figure
in online course

At the outer edge of the enterprise network is the Point-of-Presence (*POP*) which provides an entry point for services to the enterprise network. Externally-provided services coming in through the POP include Internet access, wide area connections, and telephone services (PSTN).

The POP contains a point of demarcation, or the *demarc*. The demarc provides a boundary that designates responsibility for equipment maintenance and troubleshooting between the service provider (*SP*) and customer. Equipment from the service provider up to the point of demarcation is the responsibility of the provider; anything past the demarc point is the responsibility of the customer.

In an enterprise, the POP provides links to outside services and sites. The POP may provide a direct link to one or more ISPs, which allows internal users the required access to the Internet. The remote sites of an enterprise are also interconnected through the POPs. The service provider establishes the wide area links between these remote sites.

The location of the POP and the point of demarcation vary in different countries. While they are often located within the MDF of the customer, they may also be located at the ISP.

2.2.2 Security Considerations at the Enterprise Edge

Refer to
Figure
in online course

Large enterprises usually consist of multiple sites that interconnect. Multiple locations may have edge connections at each site connecting the enterprise to other individuals and organizations.

The edge is the point of entry for outside attacks and is a point of vulnerability. Attacks at the edge can affect thousands of users. For example, Denial of Service (*DoS*) attacks prevent access to resources for legitimate users inside or outside the network, affecting productivity for the entire enterprise.

All traffic in or out of the organization goes through the edge. Edge devices must be configured to defend against attacks and provide filtering based on website, IP address, traffic pattern, application, and protocol.

An organization can deploy a *firewall*, and security appliances with intrusion detection system (IDS) and intrusion prevention system (IPS) at the edge to protect the network.

External network administrators require access for internal maintenance and software installation. Virtual private networks (VPNs), access control lists (ACLs), user IDs, and passwords provide that access. VPNs also allow remote workers access to internal resources.

2.2.3 Connecting the Enterprise Network to External Services

Refer to
Figure
in online course

The network connection services commonly purchased by an enterprise include leased lines, *T1/E1* or business class, Frame Relay, and ATM. Physical cabling brings these services to the enterprise using copper wires, as in the case of T1/E1, or fiber-optic cable for higher-speed services.

The POP must contain certain pieces of equipment to obtain whichever WAN service is required. For example, to obtain T1/E1 service, the customer may require a *punchdown block* to terminate the T1/E1 circuit, as well as a Channel Service Unit / Data Service Unit (*CSU/DSU*) to provide the proper electrical interface and signaling for the service provider. This equipment may be owned and maintained by the service provider or may be owned and maintained by the customer. Regardless of ownership, all equipment located within the POP at the customer site is referred to as Customer Premise Equipment (*CPE*).

Refer to
Interactive Graphic
in online course.

Activity

Specify the components, in the correct sequence needed to connect a service from the edge to the internal network.

2.3 Reviewing Routing and Switching

2.3.1 Router Hardware

Refer to
Figure
in online course

One important device in the *Distribution Layer* of an enterprise network is a router. Without the routing process, packets could not leave the local network.

The router provides access to other private networks as well as to the Internet. All hosts on a local network specify the IP address of the local router *interface* in their IP configuration. This router interface is the *default gateway*.

Routers play a critical role in networking by interconnecting multiple sites within an enterprise network, providing redundant paths, and connecting ISPs on the Internet. Routers can also act as a translator between different media types and protocols. For example, a router can re-encapsulate packets from an Ethernet to a Serial encapsulation.

Routers use the network portion of the destination IP address to route packets to the proper destination. They select an alternate path if a link goes down or traffic is congested.

Routers also serve other beneficial functions:

- Provide broadcast containment

- Connect remote locations

- Group users logically by application or department

- Provide enhanced security (using NAT and ACLs)

With the enterprise and the ISP, the ability to route efficiently and recover from network link failures is critical to delivering packets to their destination.

Refer to
Figure
in online course

Routers come in many shapes and sizes called *form factor*s. Network administrators in an enterprise environment should be able to support a variety of routers and switches, from a small desktop to a rack-mounted or blade model.

Routers can also be categorized as fixed configuration or modular. With the fixed configuration, the desired router interfaces are built-in. Modular routers come with multiple slots that allow a network administrator to change the interfaces on the router. As an example, a Cisco 1841 router comes with two Fast Ethernet RJ-45 interfaces built-in, and two slots that can accommodate many different network interface modules.

Routers come with a variety of different interfaces, such as Fast Ethernet, Gigabit Ethernet, Serial, and Fiber-Optic. Router interfaces use the controller/interface or controller/slot/interface conventions. For example, using the controller/interface convention, the first Fast Ethernet interface on a router is numbered as Fa0/0 (controller 0 and interface 0). The second is Fa0/1. The first serial interface on a router uses controller/slot/interface is S0/0/0.

Refer to
Figure
in online course

Two methods exist for connecting a PC to a network device for configuration and monitoring tasks: *out-of-band* and *in-band* management.

Out-of-band management is used for initial configuration or when a network connection is unavailable. Configuration using out-of-band management requires:

- Direct connection to console or AUX port

- Terminal emulation client

In-band management is used to monitor and make configuration changes to a network device over a network connection. Configuration using in-band management requires:

- At least one network interface on the device to be connected and operational
- Telnet, SSH, or HTTP to access a Cisco device

2.3.2 Basic Router CLI Show Commands

Refer to **Figure** in online course

Here are some of the most commonly used IOS commands to display and verify the operational status of the router and related network functionality. These commands are divided into several categories.

General Use:

- `show running-config`
- `show startup-config`
- `show version`

Routing Related:

- `show ip protocols`
- `show ip route`

Interface Related:

- `show interfaces`
- `show ip interface brief`
- `show protocols`

Connectivity Related:

- `show cdp neighbors`
- `show sessions`
- `show ssh`
- `ping`
- `traceroute`

Refer to **Interactive Graphic** in online course. Full Screen Activty

2.3.3 Basic Router Configuration Using CLI

Refer to **Figure** in online course

A basic router configuration includes the hostname for identification, passwords for security, and assignment of IP addresses to interfaces for connectivity. Verify and save configuration changes using the `copy running-config startup-config` command. To clear the router configuration, use the `erase startup-config` command and then the `reload` command.

Configuration Management:

- `enable`

- configure terminal

- copy running-config startup-config

- erase startup-config

- reload

Global Settings:

- hostname

- banner motd

- enable password

- enable secret

Line Settings:

- line con

- line aux

- line vty

- login and password

Interface Settings:

- interface type/number

- description

- ip address

- no shutdown

- clock rate

- encapsulation

Routing Settings:

- router

- network

- ip route

Refer to **Packet Tracer Activity** for this chapter

Packet Tracer Activity

Practice basic router configuration and verification commands.

2.3.4 Switch Hardware

Refer to **Figure** in online course

Although all three layers of the hierarchical design model contain switches and routers, the Access Layer generally has more switches. The main function of switches is to connect hosts such as end user workstations, servers, IP phones, web cameras, access points and routers. This means that there are many more switches in an organization than routers.

Switches come in many form factors:

- Small standalone models sit on a desk or mount on a wall.

Refer to
Figure
in online course

- Integrated routers include a switch built into the chassis that is rack mounted.

- High-end switches mount into a rack and are often a chassis and blade design to allow more blades to be added as the number of users increases.

High-end enterprise and service provider switches support ports of varying speeds, from 100 MB to 10 GB.

An enterprise switch in an MDF connects other switches from IDFs using Gigabit fiber or copper cable. An IDF switch typically needs both RJ-45 Fast Ethernet ports for device connectivity and at least one Gigabit Ethernet port (copper or fiber) to uplink to the MDF switch. Some high-end switches have modular ports that can be changed if needed. For example, it might be necessary to switch from multimode fiber to single mode fiber, which would require a different port.

Like routers, switch ports are also designated using the controller/port or controller/slot/port conventions. For example, using the controller/port convention, the first Fast Ethernet port on a switch is numbered as Fa0/1 (controller 0 and port 1). The second is Fa0/2. The first port on a switch that uses controller/slot/port is Fa0/0/1. Gigabit ports are designated as Gi0/1, Gi0/2 etc.

Port density on a switch is an important factor. In an enterprise environment where hundreds or thousands of users need switch connections, a switch with a 1RU height and 48-ports has a higher port density than a 1RU 24-port switch.

2.3.5 Basic Switch CLI Commands

Switches make use of common IOS commands for configuration, to check for connectivity and to display current switch status. These commands can be divided into several categories, as follows:

Refer to
Figure
in online course

General Use:

- `show running-config`

- `show startup-config`

- `show version`

Interface / Port Related:

- `show interfaces`

- `show ip interface brief`

- `show port-security`

- `show mac-address-table`

Connectivity Related:

- `show cdp neighbors`

- `show sessions`

- `show ssh`

- `ping`

- `traceroute`

Refer to
Interactive Graphic
in online course.

The same in-band and out-of-band management techniques that apply to routers also applies to switch configuration.

Full screen activity

Refer to
Figure
in online course

A basic switch configuration includes the hostname for identification, passwords for security, and assignment of IP addresses for connectivity. In-band access requires the switch to have an IP address.

Verify and save the switch configuration using the `copy running-config startup-config` command. To clear the switch configuration, use the `erase startup-config` command and then the `reload` command. It may also be necessary to erase any VLAN information using the command `delete flash:vlan.dat`.

Configuration Management:

- `enable`

- `configure terminal`

- `copy running-config startup-config`

- `erase startup-config`

- `delete flash:vlan.dat`

- `reload`

Global Settings:

- `hostname`

- `banner motd`

- `enable password`

- `enable secret`

- `ip default-gateway`

Line Settings:

- `line con`

- `line vty`

- `login and password`

Interface Settings:

- `interface type/number (vlan1)`

- `ip address`

- `speed / duplex`

- `switchport port-security`

Refer to **Packet Tracer Activity** for this chapter

Packet Tracer Activity

Configure a switch in a switching environment.

Refer to **Lab Activity** for this chapter

Lab Activity

Connect and configure a multi-router network.

Summary

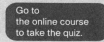

Quiz

Take the chapter quiz to check your knowledge.

Your Chapter Notes

CHAPTER 3

Switching in an Enterprise Network

Introduction

Refer to
Figure
in online course

3.1 Describing Enterprise Level Switching

3.1.1 Switching and Network Segmentation

Refer to
Figure
in online course

Although both routers and switches are used to create an enterprise network, the network design of most enterprises relies heavily on switches. Switches are cheaper per port than routers and provide fast forwarding of frames at *wire speed*.

A switch is a very adaptable Layer 2 device. In its simplest role, it replaces a hub as the central point of connection for multiple hosts. In a more complex role, a switch connects to one or more other switches to create, manage, and maintain redundant links and *VLAN* connectivity. A switch processes all types of traffic in the same way, regardless of how it is used.

A switch moves traffic based on MAC addresses. Each switch maintains a MAC address table in high-speed memory, called content addressable memory (*CAM*). The switch recreates this table every time it is activated, using both the source MAC addresses of incoming frames and the port number through which the frame entered the switch.

Refer to
Figure
in online course

The switch deletes entries from the MAC address table if they are not used within a certain period of time. The name given to this period of time is the *aging timer*; removal of an entry is called aging out.

As a *unicast* frame enters a port, the switch finds the source MAC address in the frame. It then searches the MAC table, looking for an entry that matches the address.

If the source MAC address is not in the table, the switch adds a MAC address and port number entry and sets the aging timer. If the source MAC address already exists, the switch resets the aging timer.

Next, the switch checks the table for the destination MAC address. If an entry exists, the switch forwards the frame out the appropriate port number. If the entry does not exist, the switch *floods* the frame out every active port except the port upon which it was received.

Refer to
Figure
in online course

In an enterprise, high availability, speed and throughput of the network are critical. The size of *broadcast* and *collision domain*s affect the flow of traffic. In general, larger broadcast and collision domains impact these mission-critical variables.

If a switch receives a broadcast frame, the switch floods it out every active interface, just as it does for an unknown destination MAC address. All devices that receive this broadcast make up the broadcast domain. As more switches are connected together, the size of the broadcast domain increases.

Collision domains create a similar problem. The more devices participating in a collision domain, the more collisions occur.

Hubs create large collision domains. Switches, however, use a feature called *microsegmentation* to reduce the size of collision domains to a single switch port.

Refer to
Figure
in online course

When a host connects to a switch port, the switch creates a dedicated connection. When two connected hosts communicate with each other, the switch consults the switching table and establishes a virtual connection, or *microsegment*, between the ports.

The switch maintains the virtual circuit (*VC*) until the session terminates. Multiple virtual circuits are active at the same time. Microsegmentation improves bandwidth utilization by reducing collisions and by allowing multiple simultaneous connections.

Switches can support either symmetric or *asymmetric* switching. Switches that have ports of all the same speeds are termed symmetric. Many switches, however, have two or more high-speed ports. These high-speed, or *uplink ports*, connect to areas that have a higher demand for bandwidth. Typically, these areas include:

- Connections to other switches
- Links to servers or server farms
- Connections to other networks

Connections between ports of different speeds use asymmetric switching. If necessary a switch stores information in memory to provide a buffer between ports of different speeds. Asymmetric switches are common in the enterprise environment.

Refer to
Interactive Graphic
in online course.

Activity

Determine how the switch forwards a frame based on the Destination MAC addresses and the information in the switch MAC table.

Note: A multicast frame begins with the hexadecimal characters 01:00:5E.

3.1.2 Multilayer Switching

Refer to
Figure
in online course

Traditionally, networks have been composed of separate Layer 2 and Layer 3 devices. Each device uses a different technique for processing and forwarding traffic.

Layer 2

Layer 2 switches are hardware-based. They forward traffic at wire-speeds, using the internal circuits that physically connect each incoming port to every other port. The forwarding process uses the MAC address and the existence of the destination MAC address in the MAC table. A Layer 2 switch limits the forwarding of traffic to within a single network segment or subnet.

Layer 3

Routers are software-based and use *microprocessor*s to execute routing based on IP addresses. Layer 3 routing allows traffic to be forwarded between different networks and subnets. As a packet enters a router interface, the router uses software to find the destination IP address and select the best path toward the destination network. The router then switches the packet to the correct output interface.

Refer to
Figure
in online course

Layer 3 switching, or *multilayer switching*, combines hardware-based switching and hardware-based routing in the same device.

A multilayer switch combines the features of a Layer 2 switch and a Layer 3 router. Layer 3 switching occurs in special application-specific integrated circuit (*ASIC*) hardware. The frame and packet forwarding functions use the same ASIC circuitry.

Multilayer switches often save, or *cache*, source and destination routing information from the first packet of a conversation. Subsequent packets do not have to execute a routing lookup, because they find the routing information in memory. This caching feature adds to the high performance of these devices.

3.1.3 Types of Switching

Refer to
Figure
in online course

When switching was first introcuded, a switch could support one of two major methods to forward a frame from one port to another. The two methods are *store and forward* and *cut-through switching*. Each of these methods has distinct advantages as well as some disadvantages.

Store and Forward

In this type of switching, the entire frame is read and stored in memory before being sent to the destination device. The switch checks the integrity of the bits in the frame by recalculating the cyclic redundancy check (*CRC*) value. If the calculated CRC value is the same as the CRC field value in the frame, the switch forwards the frame out the destination port. The switch does not forward frames if the CRC values do not match. The CRC value is located within the frame check sequence (*FCS*) field of an Ethernet frame.

Although this method keeps damaged frames from being switched to other network segments, it introduces the highest amount of latency. Due to the latency incurred by the store and forward method, it is typically only used in environments where errors are likely to occur, such as environments that have a high probability of EMI.

Refer to
Figure
in online course

Cut-through Switching

The other major method of switching is cut-through switching. Cut-through switching subdivides into two other methods: *fast-forward* and *fragment-free*. In both of these methods the switch forwards the frame before all of it is received. Because the switch does not calculate or check the CRC value, damaged frames can be switched.

Fast-forward is the fastest method of switching. The switch forwards the frames out the destination port as soon as it reads the destination MAC address. This method has the lowest latency but also forwards collision fragments and damaged frames. This method of switching works best in a stable network with few errors.

In fragment-free switching, the switch reads the first 64 bytes of the frame before it begins to forward it out the destination port. The shortest valid Ethernet frame is 64 bytes. Smaller frames are usually the result of a collision and are called *runt*s. Checking the first 64 bytes ensures that the switch does not forward collision fragments.

Store and forward has the highest latency and fast-forward has the lowest. Fragment-free latency is in the middle of these other methods. The fragment-free switching method works best in an environment where many collisions occur. In a properly constructed switched network, collisions are not a problem; therefore, fast-forward switching would be the preferred method.

Refer to
Figure
in online course

Today, most Cisco LAN switches rely on the store-and-forward method for switching. This is because with newer technology and faster processing times, switches are able to store and process the frames almost as quickly as cut-through switching, without the issue of errors. Additionally, many of the higher end features, such as multilayer switching, require the use of the store-and-forward method.

There are also some newer Layer 2 and Layer 3 switches that can adapt their switching method to changing network conditions.

These switches begin by forwarding traffic using the fast-forward method to achieve the lowest latency possible. Even though the switch does not check for errors before forwarding the frame, it recognized the errors and stores an error counter in memory. It compares the number of errors found to a predefined *threshold value*.

If the number of errors exceeds the threshold value, the switch has forwarded an unacceptable number of errors. In this situation, the switch modifies itself to perform store and forward switching. If the number of errors drops back below the threshold, the switch reverts back to fast-forward mode. This is known as *Adaptive Cut-through* switching.

3.1.4 Switch Security

Refer to **Figure** in online course

Keep your network secure, regardless of the switching method used. Network security often focuses on routers and blocking traffic from the outside. Switches are internal to the organization, and designed to allow ease of connectivity, therefore only limited or no security measures are applied.

Apply the following basic security features to switches to ensure that only authorized people access the devices:

- Physically secure the device
- Use secure passwords
- Enable SSH access
- Monitor access and traffic
- Disable http access
- Disable unused ports
- Enable port security
- Disable Telnet

Refer to **Lab Activity** for this chapter

Lab Activity

Enable basic switch security.

3.2 Preventing Switching Loops

3.2.1 Redundancy in a Switched Network

Refer to **Figure** in online course

Modern enterprises rely more and more on their networks for their very existence. The network is the lifeline of many organizations. Network downtime translates into potentially disastrous loss of business, income, and customer confidence.

The failure of a single network link, a single device, or a critical port on a switch causes network downtime. *Redundancy* is required in the network design in order to maintain a high degree of reliability and eliminate any single point of failure. Redundancy is accomplished by installing duplicate equipment and network links for critical areas.

Sometimes, providing complete redundancy of all links and devices in a network becomes very expensive. Network engineers are often required to balance the cost of redundancy with the need for network availability.

Refer to **Figure** in online course

Redundancy refers to having two different pathways to a particular destination. Examples of redundancy in non-networking environments include two roads into a town, two bridges to cross a river, or two doors to exit a building. If one way is blocked, another is still available.

Achieve redundancy in switches by connecting them with multiple links. Redundant links in a switched network reduce *congestion* and support high *availability* and load balancing.

Connecting switches together, however, can cause problems. For example, the broadcast nature of Ethernet traffic creates *switching loop*s. The broadcast frames go around and around in all directions, causing a *broadcast storm*. Broadcast storms use up all of the available bandwidth and can prevent network connections from being established as well as causing existing network connections to be dropped.

Refer to **Figure** in online course

Broadcast storms are not the only problem created by redundant links in a switched network. *Unicast frames* sometimes produce problems, such as multiple frame transmissions and MAC database instability.

Multiple Frame Transmissions

If a host sends a unicast frame to a destination host and the destination MAC address is not included in any of the connected switch MAC tables, then every switch floods the frame out all ports. In a looped network, the frame could be sent back to the initial switch. The process repeats, creating multiple copies of the frame on the network.

Eventually the destination host receives multiple copies of the frame. This causes three problems: wasted bandwidth, wasted CPU time, and potential duplication of transaction traffic.

MAC Database Instability

It is possible for switches in a redundant network to learn the wrong information about the location of a host. If a loop exists, one switch may associate the destination MAC address with two separate ports. This causes confusion and suboptimal of frame forwarding.

Refer to **Packet Tracer Activity** for this chapter

Packet Tracer Activity

Disable redundant links to avoid switching loops in the network provided.

3.2.2 Spanning Tree Protocol (STP)

Refer to **Figure** in online course

Spanning Tree Protocol (*STP*) provides a mechanism for disabling redundant links in a switched network. STP provides the redundancy required for reliability without creating switching loops.

STP is an open standard protocol, used in a switched environment to create a loop-free logical topology.

STP is relatively self-sufficient and requires little configuration. When switches are first powered up with STP enabled, they check the switched network for the existence of loops. Switches detecting a potential loop block some of the connecting ports, while leaving other ports active to forward frames.

Refer to **Figure** in online course

STP defines a tree that spans all the switches in an extended star switched network. Switches are constantly checking the network to ensure that there are no loops and that all ports function as required.

To prevent switching loops, STP:

- Forces certain interfaces into a standby or blocked state

- Leaves other interfaces in a forwarding state

- Reconfigures the network by activating the appropriate standby path, if the forwarding path becomes unavailable

In STP terminology, the term bridge is frequently used to refer to a switch. For example, the Root Bridge is the primary switch or focal point in the STP topology. The root bridge communicates with the other switches using Bridge Protocol Data Units (*BPDU*s). BPDUs are frames that multicast every 2 seconds to all other switches. BPDUs contain information such as:

- Identity of the source switch

- Identity of the source port

- Cumulative cost of path to root bridge

- Value of aging timers

- Value of the hello timer

Refer to
Figure
in online course

As a switch powers on, each port cycles through a series of four states: *blocking*, *listening*, *learning*, and *forwarding*. A fifth state, disabled, indicates that the administrator has shut down the switch port.

As the port cycles through these states, the LEDs on the switch change from flashing orange to steady green. It can take as long as 50 seconds for a port to cycle through all of these states and be ready to forward frames.

When a switch powers on, it first goes into a blocking state to immediately prevent the formation of a loop. It then changes to listening mode, so that it receives BPDUs from neighbor switches. After processing this information the switch determines which ports can forward frames without creating a loop. If the port can forward frames, it changes to learning mode, and then to forwarding mode.

Access ports do not create loops in a switched network and always transition to forwarding if they have a host attached. Trunking ports potentially create a looped network and transition to either a forwarding or blocking state.

Refer to
Interactive Graphic
in online course.

Activity

Select all states for which each of the Spanning Tree processes applies.

3.2.3 Root Bridges

Refer to
Figure
in online course

For STP to function, the switches in the network determine a switch that is the focal point in that network. STP uses this focal point, called a *root bridge* or *root switch*, to determine which ports to block and which ports to put into forwarding state. The root bridge sends out BPDUs containing network topology information to all other switches. This information allows the network to reconfigure itself in the event of a failure.

There is only one root bridge on each network, and it is elected based on the bridge ID (*BID*). The bridge priority value plus the MAC address creates the BID.

Bridge priority has a default value of 32,768. If a switch has a MAC address of AA-11-BB-22-CC-33, the BID for that switch would be: 32768: AA-11-BB-22-CC-33.

Refer to
Figure
in online course

The root bridge is based on the lowest BID value. Since switches typically use the same default priority value, the switch with the lowest MAC address becomes the root bridge.

As each switch powers on, it assumes that it is the root bridge, and sends out BPDUs containing its BID. For example, if S2 advertises a root ID that is a lower number than S1, S1 stops the advertisement of its root ID and accepts the root ID of S2. S2 is now the root bridge.

STP designates three types of ports: *root ports*, *designated ports*, and *blocked ports*.

Root Port

The port that provides the *least cost path* back to the root bridge becomes the root port. Switches calculate the least cost path using the bandwidth cost of each link required to reach the root bridge.

Designated Port

A designated port is a port that forwards traffic toward the root bridge but does not connect to the least cost path.

Blocked Port

A blocked port is a port that does not forward traffic.

Refer to
Figure
in online course

Before configuring STP, the network technician plans and evaluates the network in order to select the best switch to become the root of the spanning tree. If the root switch goes to the lowest MAC address, forwarding might not be optimal.

A centrally-located switch works best as the root bridge. A blocked port situated at the extreme edge of the network might cause traffic to take a longer route to get to the destination than if the switch is centrally located.

To specify the root bridge, the BID of the chosen switch is configured with the lowest priority value. The bridge priority command is used to configure the bridge priority. The range for the priority is from 0 to 65535, but values are in increments of 4096. The default value is 32768.

To set priority:

```
S3(config)#spanning-tree vlan 1 priority 4096
```
To restore priority to default:

```
S3(config)#no spanning-tree vlan 1 priority
```

Refer to
Lab Activity
for this chapter

Lab Activity

Configure the BID on a switch to control which one becomes the root bridge. Observe the spanning tree and traffic flow patterns as different switches are configured as root.

3.2.4 Spanning Tree in a Hierarchical Network

Refer to
Figure
in online course

After establishing the root bridge, root ports, designated ports, and blocked ports, STP sends BPDUs throughout the switched network at 2-second intervals. STP continues to listen to these BPDUs to ensure that no links fail and no new loops appear.

If a link failure occurs, STP recalculates by:

- Changing some blocked ports to forwarding ports
- Changing some forwarding ports to blocked ports
- Forming a new STP tree to maintain the loop-free integrity of the network

STP is not instantaneous. When a link goes down, STP detects the failure and recalculates the best paths across the network. This calculation and transition period takes about 30 to 50 seconds on each switch. During this recalculation, no user data passes through the recalculating ports.

Some user applications time out during the recalculation period, which can result in lost productivity and revenue. Frequent STP recalculations negatively impact uptime.

Refer to
Figure
in online course

A high volume, enterprise server is connected to a switch port. If that port recalculates because of STP, the server is down for 50 seconds. It would be difficult to imagine the number of transactions lost during that timeframe.

In a stable network, STP recalculations are infrequent. In an unstable network, it is important to check the switches for stability and configuration changes. One of the most common causes of frequent STP recalculations is a faulty power supply or power feed to a switch. A faulty power supply causes the device to reboot unexpectedly.

Refer to
Figure
in online course

Several enhancements to STP minimize the downtime incurred during an STP recalculation.

PortFast

STP *PortFast* causes an access port to enter the forwarding state immediately, bypassing the listening and learning states. Using PortFast on access ports that are connected to a single workstation or server allows those devices to connect to the network immediately, instead of waiting for STP to converge.

UplinkFast

STP *UplinkFast* accelerates the choice of a new root port when a link or switch fails or when STP reconfigures itself. The root port transitions to the forwarding state immediately without going through the listening and learning states, as it would do with normal STP procedures.

BackboneFast

BackboneFast provides fast convergence after a spanning tree topology change occurs. It quickly restores backbone connectivity. BackboneFast is used at the Distribution and Core Layers, where multiple switches connect.

PortFast, UplinkFast, and BackboneFast are Cisco proprietary; therefore, they can not be used if the network includes switches from other vendors. In addition, all of these features require configuration.

Refer to
Figure
in online course

There are several useful commands used to verify spanning tree operation.

`show spanning-tree` - Displays root ID, bridge ID, and port states

`show spanning-tree summary` - Displays a summary of port states

`show spanning-tree root` - Displays the status and configuration of the root bridge

`show spanning-tree detail` - Displays detailed port information

`show spanning-tree interface` - Displays STP interface status and configuration

`show spanning-tree blockedports` - Displays blocked ports

Refer to
Lab Activity
for this chapter

Lab Activity

Use various `show` commands to verify STP operation.

3.2.5 Rapid Spanning Tree Protocol (RSTP)

Refer to
Figure
in online course

When IEEE developed the original 802.1D Spanning Tree Protocol (STP), recovery time of 1 to 2 minutes was acceptable. Today, *Layer 3 switching* and advanced routing protocols provide a faster alternative path to the destination. The need to carry delay-sensitive traffic, such as voice and video, requires that switched networks converge quickly to keep up with the new technology.

Rapid Spanning Tree Protocol (*RSTP*), defined in IEEE 802.1w, significantly speeds the recalculation of the spanning tree. Unlike PortFast, UplinkFast, and BackboneFast, RSTP is not proprietary.

RSTP requires a full-duplex, point-to-point connection between switches to achieve the highest reconfiguration speed. Reconfiguration of the spanning tree by RSTP occurs in less than 1 second, as compared to 50 seconds in STP.

RSTP eliminates the requirements for features such as PortFast and UplinkFast. RSTP can revert to STP to provide services for legacy equipment.

To speed up the recalculation process, RSTP reduces the number of port states to three: *discarding*, learning and forwarding. The discarding state is similar to three of the original STP states: blocking, listening, and disabled.

RSTP also introduces the concept of *active topology*. All ports that are not discarding are part of the active topology and will immediately transition to the forwarding state.

3.3 Configuring VLANs

3.3.1 Virtual LAN

Refer to
Figure
in online course

Hosts and servers that are connected to Layer 2 switches are part of the same network segment. This arrangement poses two significant problems:

- Switches flood broadcasts out all ports, which consumes unnecessary bandwidth. As the number of devices connected to a switch increases, more broadcast traffic is generated and more bandwidth is wasted.

- Every device that is attached to a switch can forward and receive frames from every other device on that switch.

As a network design best practice, broadcast traffic is contained to the area of the network in which it is required. There are business reasons why certain hosts access each other while others do not. As an example, members of the accounting department may be the only users who need to access the accounting server. In a switched network, virtual local area networks (*VLAN*s) are created to contain broadcasts and group hosts together in communities of interest.

A VLAN is a logical broadcast domain that can span multiple physical LAN segments. It allows an administrator to group together stations by logical function, by project teams, or by applications, without regard to physical location of the users.

Refer to
Figure
in online course

The difference between a physical network and a virtual, or logical, network can be shown in the following example:

The students in a school are divided into two groups. In the first group, each student is given a red card, for identification. In the second group, each student is given a blue card. The principal announces that students with red cards can only speak to other students with red cards and that students with blue cards can only speak to other students with blue cards. The students are now logically separated into two virtual groups, or VLANs.

Using this logical grouping, a broadcast goes out only to the red card group, even though both the red card group and the blue card group are physically located within the same school.

This example also shows another feature of VLANs. Broadcasts do not forward between VLANs, they are contained within the VLAN.

Refer to
Figure
in online course

Each VLAN functions as a separate LAN. A VLAN spans one or more switches, which allows host devices to behave as if they were on the same network segment.

A VLAN has two major functions:

- A VLAN contains broadcasts.

- A VLAN groups devices. Devices located on one VLAN are not visible to devices located on another VLAN.

Traffic requires a Layer 3 device to move between VLANs.

In a switched network, a device can be assigned to a VLAN based on its location, MAC address, IP address, or the applications that the device most frequently uses. Administrators assign membership in a VLAN either statically or dynamically.

Static VLAN membership requires an administrator to manually assign each switch port to a specific VLAN. As an example, port fa0/3 may be assigned to VLAN 20. Any device that plugs into port fa0/3 automatically becomes a member of VLAN 20.

This type of VLAN membership is the easiest to configure and is also the most popular, however, it requires the most administrative support for adds, moves and changes. For example, moving a host from one VLAN to another requires either the switch port to be manually reconfigured to the new VLAN or the workstation cable to be plugged into a different switchport on the new VLAN.

Membership in a specific VLAN is totally transparent to the users. Users working on a device plugged into a switch port have no knowledge that they are members of a VLAN.

Refer to
Figure
in online course

Dynamic VLAN membership requires a VLAN management policy server (*VMPS*). The VMPS contains a database that maps MAC addresses to VLAN assignments. When a device plugs into a switch port, the VMPS searches the database for a match of the MAC address and temporarily assigns that port to the appropriate VLAN.

Dynamic VLAN membership requires more organization and configuration but creates a structure with much more flexibility than static VLAN membership. In dynamic VLAN, moves, adds, and changes are automated and do not require intervention from the administrator.

Note: Not all Catalyst switches support the use of VMPSs.

Refer to
Interactive Graphic
in online course.

Activity

Decide which problems can be solved by implementing VLANs.

3.3.2 Configuring a Virtual LAN

Refer to
Figure
in online course

Whether VLANs are created statically or dynamically, the maximum number of VLANs depends on the type of switch and the IOS. By default, VLAN1 is the *management VLAN*.

An administrator will use the IP address of the management VLAN to configure the switch remotely. When accessing the switch remotely, the network administrator can configure and maintain all VLAN configurations.

Additionally, the management VLAN is used to exchange information, such as Cisco Discovery Protocol (CDP) traffic and VLAN Trunking Protocol (VTP) traffic, with other networking devices.

When a VLAN is created, it is assigned a number and a name. The *VLAN number* is any number from the range available on the switch, except for VLAN1. Some switches support approximately 1000 VLANs; others support more than 4000. Naming a VLAN is considered a network management best practice.

Refer to
Figure
in online course

Use the following commands to create a VLAN using global configuration mode:

```
Switch(config)#vlan vlan_number
 Switch(config-vlan)#name vlan_name
Switch(config-vlan)#exit
```

Assign ports to be members of the VLAN. By default, all ports are initially members of VLAN1. Assign ports one at a time or as a range.

Use the following commands to assign individual ports to VLANs:

```
Switch(config)#interface fa0/port_number
 Switch(config-if)#switchport access vlan vlan_number
Switch(config-if)# exit
```

Use the following commands to assign a range ports to VLANs:

```
Switch(config)#interface range fa0/start_of_range - end_of_range
 Switch(config-if)#switchport access vlan vlan_number
Switch(config-if)#exit
```

Refer to
Figure
in online course

To verify, maintain, and troubleshoot VLANs, it is important to understand the key **show** commands that are available in the Cisco IOS.

The following commands are used to verify and maintain VLANs:

show vlan

- Displays a detailed list of all of the VLAN numbers and names currently active on the switch, along with the ports associated with each one

- Displays STP statistics if configured on a per VLAN basis

show vlan brief
- Displays a summarized list showing only the active VLANs and the ports associated with each one

show vlan id *id_number*
- Displays information pertaining to a specific VLAN, based on ID number

show vlan name *vlan_name*
- Displays information pertaining to a specific VLAN, based on name

Refer to
Figure
in online course

In an organization, employees are frequently added, removed, or moved to a different department or project. This constant movement requires VLAN maintenance, including removal or reassignment to different VLANs.

The removal of VLANs and the reassignment of ports to different VLANs are two separate and distinct functions. When a port is disassociated from a specific VLAN, it returns to VLAN1. When a VLAN is removed, any associated ports are deactivated because they are no longer associated with any VLAN.

To delete a VLAN:

```
Switch(config)#no vlan vlan_number
```
To disassociate a port from a specific VLAN:

```
Switch(config)#interface fa0/port_number
Switch(config-if)#no switchport access vlan vlan_number
```

Refer to
Lab Activity
for this chapter

Lab Activity

Configure, verify, and troubleshoot VLAN configuration on a Cisco switch.

3.3.3 Identifying VLANs

Refer to
Figure
in online course

Devices connected to a VLAN only communicate with other devices in the same VLAN, regardless of whether those devices are on the same switch or different switches.

A switch associates each port with a specific VLAN number. As a frame enters that port, the switch inserts the VLAN ID (*VID*) into the Ethernet frame. The addition of the VLAN ID number into the Ethernet frame is called *frame tagging*. The most commonly used frame tagging standard is *IEEE 802.1Q*.

Refer to **Figure** in online course

The 802.1Q standard, sometimes abbreviated to *dot1q*, inserts a 4-byte tag field into the Ethernet frame. This tag sits between the source address and the type/length field.

Ethernet frames have a minimum size of 64 bytes and a maximum size of 1518 bytes, however a tagged Ethernet frame can be up to 1522 bytes in size.

Frames contain fields such as:

- The destination and source MAC address
- The length of the frame
- The payload data
- The frame check sequence (FCS)

The FCS field provides error checking to ensure the integrity of all of the bits within the frame.

This tag field increases the minimum Ethernet frame from 64 to 68 bytes. The maximum size increases from 1518 to 1522 bytes. The switch recalculates the FCS because the number of bits in the frame has been modified.

If an 802.1Q-compliant port is connected to another 802.1Q-compliant port, the VLAN tagging information passes between them.

If the connecting port is not 802.1Q-compliant, the VLAN tag is removed before the frame is placed on the media.

If a non-802.1Q-enabled device or an access port receives an 802.1Q frame, the tag data is ignored, and the packet is switched at Layer 2 as a standard Ethernet frame. This allows for the placement of Layer 2 intermediate devices, such as other switches or bridges, along the 802.1Q trunk path. To process an 802.1Q tagged frame, a device must allow an MTU of 1522 or higher.

Refer to **Interactive Graphic** in online course.

Activity

Decide whether to deliver each inbound frame to the destination host based on the port configurations.

3.4 Trunking and Inter-VLAN Routing

3.4.1 Trunk Ports

Refer to **Figure** in online course

A VLAN has three major functions:

- Limits the size of broadcast domains
- Improves network performance
- Provides a level of security

To take full advantage of the benefits of VLANs, they are extended across multiple switches.

Switch ports can be configured for two different roles. A port is classified as either an *access port* or a *trunk port*.

Access Port

An access port belongs to only one VLAN. Typically, single devices such as PCs or servers connect to this type of port. If a hub connects multiple PCs to the single access port, each device connected to the hub is a member of the same VLAN.

Trunk Port

A trunk port is a point-to-point link between the switch and another networking device. Trunks carry the traffic of multiple VLANs over a single link and allow VLANs to reach across an entire network. Trunk ports are necessary to carry the traffic from multiple VLANs between devices when connecting either two switches together, a switch to a router, or a host NIC that supports 802.1Q trunking.

Without trunk ports, each VLAN requires a separate connection between switches. For example, an enterprise with 100 VLANs requires 100 connecting links. This type of arrangement does not scale well and is very expensive. Trunk links provide a solution to this problem by transporting traffic from multiple VLANs on the same link.

When multiple VLANs travel on the same link, they need VLAN identification. A trunk port supports frame tagging. Frame tagging adds VLAN information to the frame.

IEEE 802.1Q is the standardized and approved method of frame tagging. Cisco developed a proprietary frame tagging protocol called Inter-Switch Link (*ISL*). Higher-end switches, such as the Catalyst 6500 series, still support both tagging protocols; however, most LAN switches, such as the 2960, support only 802.1Q.

Switch ports are access ports by default. To configure a switch port as a trunk port, use the following commands:

```
Switch(config)#interface fa0/port_number
 Switch(config-if)#switchport mode trunk
Switch(config-if)#switchport trunk encapsulation {dot1q ¦ isl ¦ negotiate}
```

Switches that support both 802.1Q and ISL require the last configuration statement. The 2960 switch does not require that statement because it only supports 802.1Q.

The *negotiate parameter* is the default mode on many Cisco switches. This parameter automatically detects the encapsulation type of the neighbor switch.

Newer switches have the capability to detect the type of link configured at the other end. Based on the attached device, the link configures itself as either a trunk port or an access port.

```
Switch(config-if)#switchport mode dynamic {desirable ¦ auto}
```

In *desirable mode*, the port becomes a trunk port if the other end is set to either trunk, desirable, or auto.

In *auto mode*, the port becomes a trunk port if the other end is set to either trunk or desirable.

To return a trunk port to an access port, issue either of the following commands:

```
Switch(config)#interface fa0/port_number
Switch(config-if)#no switchport mode trunk
```

or

```
Switch(config-if)#switchport mode access
```

Lab Activity

Create VLANs and assign them individual ports.

Refer to **Figure** in online course

Refer to **Figure** in online course

Refer to **Figure** in online course

Refer to **Lab Activity** for this chapter

3.4.2 Extending VLANs across Switches

Refer to
Figure
in online course

Trunking enables VLANs to forward traffic between switches using only a single port.

A trunk link configured with 802.1Q on both ends allows traffic that has a 4-byte tag field added to the frame. This frame tag contains the VLAN ID.

When a switch receives a tagged frame on a trunk port, it removes the tag before sending it out an access port. The switch forwards the frame only if the access port is a member of the same VLAN as the tagged frame.

Some traffic however, needs to cross the 802.1Q configured link without VLAN ID. Traffic with no VLAN ID is called *untagged*. Examples of untagged traffic are Cisco Discovery Protocol (CDP), VTP, and certain types of voice traffic. Untagged traffic minimizes the delays associated with inspection of the VLAN ID tag.

Refer to
Figure
in online course

To accommodate untagged traffic, a special VLAN called a *native VLAN* is available. Untagged frames received on the 802.1Q trunk port will become members of the native VLAN. On Cisco Catalyst switches, VLAN 1 is the native VLAN by default.

Any VLAN can be configured as the native VLAN. Ensure that the native VLAN for an 802.1Q trunk is the same on both ends of the trunk line. If they are different, spanning-tree loops might result.

On an 802.1Q trunk, use the following command to assign the native VLAN ID on a physical interface:

```
Switch(config-if)#dot1q native vlan vlan-id
```

Refer to
Lab Activity
for this chapter

Lab Activity

Configure trunk ports to connect switches and verify connectivity across the trunk link.

3.4.3 Inter-VLAN Routing

Refer to
Figure
in online course

Although VLANs extend to span multiple switches, only members of the same VLAN can communicate.

A Layer 3 device provides connectivity between different VLANs. This arrangement enables the network administrator to strictly control the type of traffic that flows from one VLAN to another.

One method of accomplishing the inter-VLAN routing requires a separate interface connection to the Layer 3 device for each VLAN.

Refer to
Figure
in online course

Another method for providing connectivity between different VLANs requires a feature called *subinterface*s. Subinterfaces logically divide one physical interface into multiple logical pathways. Configure one pathway or subinterface for each VLAN.

To support *inter-VLAN* communication using subinterfaces requires configuration on both the switch and the router.

Switch

- Configure the switch interface as an 802.1Q trunk link.

Router

- Select a router interface with a minimum of a 100Mbps FastEthernet

- Configure subinterfaces that support 802.1Q encapsulation.

- Configure one subinterface for each VLAN.

Refer to
Figure
in online course

A subinterface allows each VLAN to have its own logical pathway and default gateway into the router.

The host from the sending VLAN forwards traffic to the router using the default gateway. The subinterface for the VLAN specifies the default gateway for all hosts in that VLAN. The router locates the destination IP address and does a routing table lookup.

If the destination VLAN is on the same switch as the source VLAN, the router forwards the traffic back down to the source switch using the subinterface parameters of the destination VLAN ID. This type of configuration is often referred to as a *router-on-a-stick*.

Refer to
Figure
in online course

If the exit interface of the router is 802.1Q-compatible, the frame retains its 4-byte VLAN tag. If the outbound interface is not 802.1Q-compatible, the router strips the tag from the frame and returns the frame to its original Ethernet format.

To configure inter-VLAN routing, use the following steps:

1. Configure a trunk port on the switch.

```
Switch(config)#interface fa0/2
Switch(config-if)#switchport mode trunk
```

2. On the router, configure a FastEthernet interface with no IP address or subnet mask.

```
Router(config)#interface fa0/1
Router(config-if)#no ip address
Router(config-if)#no shutdown
```

3. On the router, configure one subinterface with an IP address and subnet mask for each VLAN. Each subinterface has an 802.1Q encapsulation.

```
Router(config)#interface fa0/0.10
Router(config-subif)#encapsulation dot1q 10
Router(config-subif)#ip address 192.168.10.1 255.255.255.0
```

4. Use the following commands to verify the inter-VLAN routing configuration and functionality.

```
Switch#show trunk
 Router#show ip interfaces
  Router#show ip interfaces brief
Router#show ip route
```

Refer to
Lab Activity
for this chapter

Lab Activity

Configure inter-VLAN routing.

A secondary version of this lab is also available.

3.5 Maintaining VLANs on an Enterprise Network

3.5.1 VLAN Trunking Protocol (VTP)

Refer to
Figure
in online course

As networks grow in size and complexity, centralized management of the VLAN structure becomes crucial. VLAN Trunking Protocol (VTP) is a Layer 2 messaging protocol that provides a method for the distribution and management of the VLAN database from a centralized server in a network segment. Routers do not forward VTP updates.

If there is no automated way to manage an enterprise network with hundreds of VLANs, manual configuration of each VLAN on each switch is necessary. Any change to the VLAN structure requires further manual configuration. One incorrectly keyed number causes inconsistencies in connectivity throughout the entire network.

Refer to
Figure
in online course

To resolve this issue, Cisco created VTP to automate many of the VLAN configuration functions. VTP ensures that VLAN configuration is consistently maintained across the network and reduces the task of VLAN management and monitoring.

VTP is a client/server messaging protocol that adds, deletes, and renames VLANs in a single VTP domain. All switches under a common administration are part of a domain. Each domain has a unique name. VTP switches only share VTP messages with other switches in the same domain.

Two different versions of VTP exist: Version 1 and Version 2. Version 1 is the default and it is not compatible with Version 2. All switches must be configured with the same version.

Refer to
Figure
in online course

VTP has three modes: server, client, and transparent. By default, all switches are servers. It is a good practice to have at least two switches configured as servers on a network, to provide backup and redundancy.

With VTP, each switch advertises messages on its trunk ports. Messages include the management domain, configuration revision number, known VLANs, and parameters for each VLAN. These advertisement frames are sent to a multicast address so that all neighbor devices receive the frames.

Each VTP switch saves a VLAN database in NVRAM that contains a revision number. If a VTP receives an update message that has a higher revision number than the one stored in the database, the switch updates its VLAN database with this new information.

The *VTP configuration revision number* begins at zero. As changes occur, the configuration revision number increases by one. The revision number continues to increment until it reaches 2,147,483,648. When it reaches that point, the counter resets back to zero. Rebooting the switch also resets the revision number to zero.

A problem situation can occur related to the revision number if someone inserts a switch with a higher revision number into the network. Since a switch is a server by default, this results in new, but incorrect, information overwriting the legitimate VLAN information on all of the other switches.

Refer to
Figure
in online course

Another way to protect against this critical situation, is to configure a VTP password to validate the switch. In addition, when adding a switch and there is already a server switch, make sure the new switch is configured in client or transparent mode.

VTP messages come in three varieties: *summary advertisement*s, *subset advertisement*s, and *advertisement request*s.

Summary Advertisements

Catalyst switches issue summary advertisements every 5 minutes or whenever a change to the VLAN database occurs. Summary advertisements contain the current VTP domain name and the configuration revision number.

If VLANs are added, deleted, or changed, the server increments the configuration revision number and issues a summary advertisement.

When a switch receives a summary advertisement packet, it compares the VTP domain name to its own VTP domain name. If the domain name is the same, the switch compares the configuration revision number to its own number. If it is lower or equal, the switch ignores the packet. If the revision number is higher, an advertisement request is sent.

Subset Advertisements

A subset advertisement follows the summary advertisement. A subset advertisement contains a list of VLAN information.

The subset advertisement contains the new VLAN information based on the summary advertisement. If there are several VLANs, they require more than one subset advertisement.

Advertisement Requests

Catalyst switches use advertisement requests to ask for VLAN information. Advertisement requests are required if the switch has been reset or the VTP domain name has been changed. The switch receives a VTP summary advertisement with a higher configuration revision number than its own.

FULL SCREEN Activity

Activity

Identify the characteristics of server, client, and transparent VTP modes.

3.5.2 Configuring VTP

Switches are servers by default. If a switch in server mode issues an update with a higher revision number than the number currently in place, all switches will modify their databases to match the new switch.

When adding a new switch to an existing VTP domain, use the following steps:

Step 1: Configure VTP off-line (version 1)

Step 2: Verify the VTP configuration.

Step 3: Reboot the switch.

Packet Tracer Activity

Build and test a VTP domain.

Packet Tracer Activity

Add a new switch into an existing VTP domain.

3.5.3 VLAN Support for IP Telephony and Wireless

The main purpose of VLANs is to separate traffic into logical groups. Traffic from one VLAN will not impact traffic from another VLAN. A VLAN environment is ideal for traffic that is sensitive to time delays, such as voice.

Voice traffic must be given priority over normal data traffic to avoid jerky or jittery conversations. Providing a dedicated VLAN for voice traffic prevents voice traffic from having to compete with data for available bandwidth.

An IP phone usually has two ports, one for voice and one for data. Packets traveling to and from the PC and the IP phone share the same physical link to the switch and the same switch port. To segment the voice traffic, enable a separate voice VLAN on the switch.

Wireless is another type of traffic that benefits from VLANs. Wireless is, by nature, very insecure and prone to attacks by hackers. VLANs created for wireless traffic isolate some of the problems that may occur. A compromise to the integrity of the wireless VLAN has no effect on any other VLAN within the organization.

Refer to **Interactive Graphic** in online course.

Refer to **Figure** in online course

Refer to **Packet Tracer Activity** for this chapter

Refer to **Packet Tracer Activity** for this chapter

Refer to **Figure** in online course

Refer to **Figure** in online course

Most wireless deployments place the user in a VLAN on the outside of the firewall for added security. Users have to authenticate to gain entry into the internal network from the wireless network.

In addition, many organizations provide guest access to their wireless network. Guest accounts provide anyone, within a limited range, temporary wireless services such as web access, e-mail, ftp, and SSH. Guest accounts are either included in the wireless VLAN or reside in a VLAN of their own.

Refer to Packet Tracer Activity for this chapter

Packet Tracer Activity

Build an enterprise-class LAN with voice, wireless, and wired clients. Create separate VLANs that would isolate voice and wireless traffic.

Refer to Figure in online course

3.5.4 VLAN Best Practices

When carefully planned and designed, VLANs provide security, conserve bandwidth, and localize traffic on an enterprise network. All of these features combine to improve network performance.

Some best practices for configuring VLANs in an enterprise network are:

- Organizing server placement
- Disabling unused ports
- Configuring the management VLAN as a number other than 1
- Using VLAN Trunking Protocol
- Configuring VTP Domains
- Reboot any new switch entering an established network

VLANs, however, are not the answer to every problem.

If VLANs are not correctly implemented, they can overly complicate a network, resulting in inconsistent connectivity and slow network performance.

Refer to Packet Tracer Activity for this chapter

VLANs isolate certain types of traffic for reasons of security. To move traffic between VLANs requires a Layer 3 device, which increases the cost of implementation and introduces an increased level of latency into the network.

Packet Tracer Activity

Plan and build a switched network to meet client specifications.

Summary

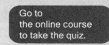

Quiz

Take the chapter quiz to check your knowledge.

Your Chapter Notes

CHAPTER 4

Addressing in an Enterprise Network

Introduction

Refer to
Figure
in online course

4.1 Using a Hierarchical IP Network Address Scheme

4.1.1 Flat and Hierarchical Networks

Refer to
Figure
in online course

Implementing switches reduces the number of collisions that occur within a local network. However, having an all-switched network often creates a single *broadcast domain*. In a single broadcast domain, or *flat network*, every device is in the same network and receives each broadcast. In small networks, a single broadcast domain is acceptable.

With large numbers of hosts, a flat network becomes less efficient. As the number of hosts increases in a switched network, so do the number of broadcasts sent and received. Broadcast packets take up a lot of bandwidth, causing traffic delays and timeouts.

Creating VLANs provides one solution to a large, flat network. Each VLAN is its own broadcast domain.

Implementing a *hierarchical network* using routers is another solution.

4.1.2 Hierarchical Network Addressing

Refer to
Figure
in online course

Enterprise networks are large, and benefit from a *hierarchical network design* and address structure. A hierarchical addressing structure logically groups networks into smaller subnetworks.

An effective hierarchical address scheme consists of a classful network address in the Core Layer that is subdivided into successively smaller subnets in the Distribution and Access Layers.

It is possible to have a hierarchical network without hierarchical addressing. Although the network still functions, the effectiveness of the network design decreases and certain routing protocol features, such as route summarization, do not work properly.

In enterprise networks with many geographically separate locations, a hierarchical network design and address structure simplifies network management and troubleshooting and also improves scalability and routing performance.

4.1.3 Using Subnetting to Structure the Network

Refer to
Figure
in online course

There are many reasons to divide the network into subnets, including:

- Physical location
- Logical grouping

- Security

- Application requirements

- Broadcast containment

- Hierarchical network design

For example, if an organization uses a 10.0.0.0 network for the enterprise, they might use an addressing scheme such as 10.**X.Y.**0, where **X** represents a geographical location and **Y** represents a building or floor within that location. This addressing scheme allows for:

- 255 different geographical locations

- 255 buildings in each location

- 254 hosts within each building

Refer to
Interactive Graphic
in online course.

Full Screen Activity

Activity

For each scenario, indicate whether a hierarchical addressing scheme using subnets should be used to structure the network.

4.2 Using VLSM

4.2.1 Subnet Mask

Refer to
Figure
in online course

To use subnetting to create a hierarchical design, it is crucial to have a clear understanding of the structure of the subnet mask.

The subnet mask indicates whether hosts are in the same network. The subnet mask is a 32-bit value that distinguishes between the network bits and the host bits. It consists of a string of 1s followed by a string of 0s. The 1 bits represent the network portion and the 0 bits represent the host portion.

- Class A addresses use a **default subnet mask** of 255.0.0.0 or a **slash notation** of /8

- Class B addresses use a default mask of 255.255.0.0 or /16

- Class C addresses use a default mask of 255.255.255.0 or /24

The /x refers to the number of bits in the subnet mask that comprise the network portion of the address.

In an enterprise network, subnet masks vary in length. LAN segments often contain varying numbers of hosts; therefore, it is not efficient to have the same subnet mask length for all subnets created.

Refer to
Interactive Graphic
in online course.

Full Screen

Activity

Enter the slash notation, number of host bits, and number of hosts possible based on the subnet mask displayed.

4.2.2 Calculating Subnets Using Binary Representation

Refer to
Figure
in online course

When one host needs to communicate with another, it determines its network address and the destination network address by applying its subnet mask to both its IPv4 address and to the destination IPv4 address. This is done to determine if the two addresses are on the same local network.

The subnet mask is a 32 bit value used to distinguish between the network bits and the host bits of the IP address. The subnet mask is made up of a string of 1s followed by a string of 0s. The 1s indicate the number of network bits and the 0s indicate the number of host bits within the IP address. The network bits are compared between the source and destination. If the resulting networks are the same, the packet can be delivered locally. If they do not match, the packet is sent to the default gateway.

For example, assume that H1, with the IP address of 192.168.1.44 and subnet mask of 255.255.255.0, or /24, needs to send a message to H2, with the IP address of 192.168.1.66 and a subnet mask of 255.255.255.0. In this instance, both hosts have a default subnet mask of 255.255.255.0, which means the network bits end on the octet boundary, the third octet. Both hosts have the same network bits of 192.168.1, and therefore are on the same network.

Refer to
Figure
in online course

While it is fairly easy to see the network and host portion of an IP address when the subnet mask ends on the network boundary, the process of determining the network bits is the same even when the network portion does not take up the entire octet. For example, H1 has an IP address of 192.168.13.21 with a subnet mask of 255.255.255.248, or /29. This means out of 32 bits, 29 of them make up the network portion. The network bits take up all of the first three octets and extend into the fourth octet. In this instance, the value of the network ID is 192.168.13.16.

If H1, with the IP address of 192.168.13.21/29 address needed to communicate with another host, H2, with the address of 192.168.13.25/29, the network portion of the two hosts must be compared to determine if the two are on the same local network. In this case, H1 has a network value of 192.168.13.16, whereas H2 has a network value of 192.168.13.24. H1 and H2 are not on the same network and require the use of a router to communicate.

Refer to
Interactive Graphic
in online course.

Full Screen

Activity

Determine if the two hosts are on the same network.

4.2.3 Basic Subnetting Process

Refer to
Figure
in online course

Using a hierarchical addressing scheme, much information can be determined by looking at only an IP address and slash notation (/x) subnet mask. For example, an IP address of 192.168.1.75 /26 shows the following information:

Decimal subnet mask

- The /26 translates to a subnet mask of 255.255.255.192.

Number of subnets created

- Assuming we started with the default /24 subnet mask, we borrowed 2 additional host bits for the network. This creates 4 subnets ($2^2 = 4$).

Number of usable hosts per subnet

- Six bits are left on the host side creating 62 hosts per subnet ($2^6 = 64 - 2 = 62$).

Network address

- Using the subnet mask to determine the placement of network bits, the value of the network address is given. In this example, the value is 192.168.1.64.

First usable host address

- A host cannot have all 0s within the host bits, because that represents the network address of the subnet. Therefore, the first usable host address within the .64 subnet is .65

Broadcast address

- A host cannot have all 1s within the host bits because that represents the broadcast address of the subnet. In this cast, the broadcast address is .127. 128 starts the network address of the next subnet.

Refer to
Lab Activity
for this chapter

Lab Activity

Design and apply an IP addressing subnet scheme for a given topology.

4.2.4 Variable Length Subnet Masks (VLSM)

Refer to
Figure
in online course

Basic subnetting is sufficient for smaller networks but does not provide the flexibility needed in larger enterprise networks.

Variable Length Subnet Masks (*VLSM*) provide for efficient use of address space. It also allows for hierarchal IP addressing which allows routers to take advantage of *route summarization*. Route summarization reduces the size of routing tables in distribution and core routers. Smaller routing tables require less CPU time for routing lookups.

VLSM is the concept of subnetting a subnet. It was initially developed to maximize addressing efficiency. With the advent of private addressing, the primary advantage of VLSM now is organization and summarization.

Not all routing protocols support VLSM. Classful routing protocols, such as RIPv1, do not include a subnet mask field with a routing update. A router with a subnet mask assigned to its interface assumes that all packets within that same class have the same subnet mask assigned.

Classless routing protocols support the use of VLSM because the subnet mask is sent with all routing update packets. Classless routing protocols include RIPv2, EIGRP, and OSPF.

Benefits of VLSM:

- Allows efficient use of address space
- Allows the use of multiple subnet mask lengths
- Breaks up an address block into smaller blocks
- Allows for route summarization
- Provides more flexibility in network design
- Supports hierarchical enterprise networks

Refer to
Figure
in online course

VLSM allows the use of different masks for each subnet. After a network address is subnetted, further division of those subnets creates *sub-subnets*.

For example, network 10.0.0.0/8 with a subnet mask of /16 subdivides into 256 subnets, each capable of addressing 16,382 hosts.

10.0.0.0/16

10.1.0.0/16

10.2.0.0/16 up to 10.255.0.0/16

Applying a subnet mask of /24 to any one of these /16 subnets, such as 10.1.0.0/16, results in a subdivision of 256 subnets. Each one of these new subnets is capable of addressing 254 hosts.

10.1.1.0/24

10.1.2.0/24

10.1.3.0/24 up to 10.1.255.0/24

Applying a subnet mask of /28 to any one of these /24 subnets, such as 10.1.3.0/28, results in a subdivision of 16 subnets. Each one of these new subnets is capable of addressing 14 hosts.

10.1.3.0/28

10.1.3.16/28

10.1.3.32/28 up to 10.1.3.240/28

Refer to
Interactive Graphic
in online course.

Full Screen

Activity

Determine the /slash format of the subnet mask necessary to accommodate the required number of hosts.

4.2.5 Implementing VLSM Addressing

Refer to
Figure
in online course

Designing an IP addressing scheme with VLSM takes practice and planning. As a practice example, a network has the following requirements:

- Atlanta HQ = 58 host addresses

- Perth HQ = 26 host addresses

- Sydney HQ = 10 host addresses

- Corpus HQ = 10 host addresses

- WAN links = 2 host addresses (each)

A subnet of /26 is required to accommodate the largest network segment of 58 hosts. Using a basic subnetting scheme is not only wasteful, but creates only four subnets. This is not enough to address each of the required seven LAN/WAN segments. A VLSM addressing scheme resolves this problem.

Refer to
Figure
in online course

When implementing a VLSM subnetting scheme, always allow for some growth in the number of hosts when planning subnet requirements.

Multiple tools exist to assist with address planning.

Refer to
Figure
in online course

VLSM Chart

One method uses a VLSM chart to identify which blocks of addresses are available and which ones are already assigned.

VLSM Circle

Another method uses a circle approach. The circle is cut into increasingly smaller segments, representing the smaller subnets.

These methods prevent assigning addresses that are already allocated. It also helps to avoid assigning address ranges that overlap.

Refer to
Interactive Graphic
in online course.

Full Screen

Activity

Create an IP addressing scheme for the specified requirements.

Refer to
Lab Activity
for this chapter

Lab Activity

Use VLSM to provide the IP addressing for a given topology.

4.3 Using Classless Routing and CIDR

4.3.1 Classful and Classless Routing

Refer to
Figure
in online course

Technology such as VLSM enables the classful IPv4 addressing system to evolve into a classless system. Classless addressing has made the exponential growth of the Internet possible.

Classful addresses consist of the three major classes of IP addresses and an associated default subnet mask:

- Class A (255.0.0.0 or /8)
- Class B (255.255.0.0 or /16)
- Class C (255.255.255.0 or /24)

A company with a Class A network address has over 16 million host addresses available, with a Class B network address, over 65,000 hosts, and with a Class C, only 254 hosts. Since there is a limited number of Class A and Class B addresses in circulation, many companies purchased multiple Class C addresses in order to obtain enough addresses to satisfy their network requirements.

As a result, purchasing multiple Class C addresses has used up the Class C address space more quickly than originally planned.

Refer to
Figure
in online course

In classful IP addresses, the value of the first octet, or the first three bits, determines whether the major network is a Class A, B, or C. Each major network has a default subnet mask of 255.0.0.0, 255.255.0.0, or 255.255.255.0 respectively.

Classful routing protocols, such as RIPv1, do not include the subnet mask in routing updates. Since the subnet mask is not included, the receiving router makes certain assumptions.

Using a classful protocol, if a router sends an update about a subnetted network, such as 172.16.1.0/24, to a router whose connecting interface is on the same major network as that in the update, such as 172.16.2.0/24 then:

- The sending router advertises the full network address but without a subnet mask. In this case, the network address is 172.16.1.0.
- The receiving router, with a configured interface of 172.16.2.0/24, adopts the subnet mask of the configured interface and applies it to the advertised network. Therefore, in the example, the receiving router assumes the subnet mask of 255.255.255.0 applies to the 172.16.1.0 network.

If the router sends an update about a subnetted network, such as 172.16.1.0/24, to a router whose connecting interface is in a different major network, such as 192.168.1.0/24:

- The sending router advertises the major classful network address only, not the subnetted address. In this case, the address advertised is 172.16.0.0.
- The receiving router assumes the default subnet mask for this network. The default subnet mask for a class B address is 255.255.0.0.

Refer to
Figure
in online course

With the rapid depletion of IPv4 addresses, the Internet Engineering Task Force (*IETF*) developed Classless Inter-Domain Routing (*CIDR*). CIDR uses IPv4 address space more efficiently and for network address aggregation or summarizing, which reduces the size of routing tables.

The use of CIDR requires a *classless routing protocol*, such as RIPv2 or EIGRP or static routing. To CIDR-compliant routers, address class is meaningless. The network subnet mask determines the network portion of the address. This is also known as the network prefix, or *prefix length*. The class of the address no longer determines the network address.

ISPs assign blocks of IP addresses to a network based on the requirements of the customer, ranging from a few hosts to hundreds or thousands of hosts. With CIDR and VLSM, ISPs are no longer limited to using prefix lengths of /8, /16 or /24.

Refer to
Figure
in online course

Classless routing protocols that can support VLSM and CIDR include interior gateway protocols (*IGPs*) RIPv2, EIGRP, OSPF, and IS-IS. ISPs also use exterior gateway protocols (*EGPs*) such as Border Gateway Protocol (*BGP*).

The difference between the classful routing protocols and classless routing protocols is that the classless routing protocols include subnet mask information with the network address information in the routing updates. Classless routing protocols are necessary when the mask cannot be assumed or determined by the value of the first octet.

In a classless protocol, if a router sends an update about a network, such as 172.16.1.0, to a router whose connecting interface is on the same major network as that in the update, such as 172.16.2.0/24 then:

- The sending router advertises all subnetworks with subnet mask information.

If the router sends an update about a subnetted network, such as 172.16.1.0/24, to a router whose connecting interface is in a different major network, such as 192.168.1.0/24 then:

- The sending router, by default, summarizes all of the subnets and advertises the major classful network along with the summarized subnet mask information. This process is often referred to as summarizing on a network boundary. While most classless routing protocols enable summarization on the network boundary by default, the process of summarizing can be disabled.

- When summarization is disabled, the sending router advertises all subnetworks with subnet mask information.

4.3.2 CIDR and Route Summarization

Refer to
Figure
in online course

The rapid growth of the Internet has caused the number of routes to networks around the world to increase dramatically. This growth results in heavy loads on Internet routers. A VLSM addressing scheme allows for route summarization, which reduces the number of routes advertised.

Route summarization groups contiguous subnets or networks using a single address. Route summarization is also known as *route aggregation* and occurs at a *network boundary* on a boundary router.

Summarization decreases the number of entries in routing updates and lowers the number of entries in local routing tables. It also reduces bandwidth utilization for routing updates and results in faster routing table lookups.

Route summarization is synonymous with the term *supernetting*. Supernetting is the opposite of subnetting. Supernetting joins multiple smaller contiguous networks together.

If the network bits are greater than the default value for that class, this represents a subnet. An example is 172.16.3.0/26. For a Class B address, any network prefix value greater than /16 is a subnet.

If the network bits are less than the default value for the class value, this represents a supernet. An example is 172.16.0.0/14. For a Class B address, any network prefix less than /16 represents a supernet.

Refer to **Figure** in online course

A border router advertises all of the known networks within an enterprise to the ISP. If there are eight different networks, the router would have to advertise all eight. If every enterprise followed this pattern, the routing table of the ISP would be huge.

Using route summarization, a router groups the networks together, if they are contiguous, and advertises them as one large group. For example, a company has a single listing in the phone book for their main office, even though you can dial individual employee extensions directly.

It is easier to perform summarization if the addressing scheme is hierarchical. Assign similar networks to the same enterprise so that grouping them using CIDR is possible.

Refer to **Interactive Graphic** in online course.

Full Screen

Activity

Determine if the IP address with the CIDR information is a subnet or a route summary.

4.3.3 Calculating Route Summarization

Refer to **Figure** in online course

To calculate a route summary requires summarizing networks into a single address. This process is performed in three steps.

Step 1

List the networks in binary format.

Step 2

Count the number of left-most matching bits to determine the mask for the summary route. This number represents the network prefix or subnet mask for the summarized route. An example is /14 or 255.252.0.0.

Step 3

Determine the summarized network address. Copy the matching bits and then add 0 bits to the end. A quicker method is to use the lowest network value.

If a contiguous hierarchical addressing scheme is not used, it may not be possible to summarize routes. If the network addresses do not have common bits from left to right, a summary mask cannot be applied.

Refer to **Interactive Graphic** in online course.

Full Screen

Activity

Select the best summary route for the contiguous address groups shown.

Refer to **Lab Activity** for this chapter

Lab Activity

Determine summarized routes to reduce the number of entries in routing tables.

4.3.4 Discontiguous Subnets

Refer to **Figure** in online course

Either an administrator configures route summarization manually or certain routing protocols perform the same function automatically. RIPv1 and EIGRP are examples of routing protocols that perform automatic summarization. It is important to control the summarization so that routers do not advertise misleading networks.

Suppose that three routers each connect to Ethernet interfaces with addresses using subnets from a Class C network, such as 192.168.3.0. The three routers also connect to each other via serial interfaces configured using another major network, such as 172.16.100.0/24. Classful routing results in each router advertising the major Class C network without a subnet mask. As a result, the middle router receives advertisements about the same network from two different directions. This scenario is called a *discontiguous* network.

Discontiguous networks cause unreliable or suboptimal routing. To avoid this condition, an administrator can:

- Modify the addressing scheme, if possible

- Use a classless routing protocol, such as RIPv2 or OSPF

- Turn automatic summarization off

- Manually summarize at the classful boundary

Refer to
Figure
in online course

Even after careful planning, it is still possible to have a situation in which a discontiguous network exists. The following traffic and routing patterns help to identify this situation:

- One router does not have any routes to the LANs attached to another router, even though it is configured to advertise them.

- A middle router has two equal-cost paths to a major network, although the subnets are separated on several network segments.

- A middle router is load balancing traffic destined for any subnet of a major network.

- A router appears to be receiving only half of the traffic.

Refer to
Lab Activity
for this chapter

Lab Activity

Configure a LAN with discontiguous networks to view the results.

4.3.5 Subnetting and Addressing Best Practices

Refer to
Figure
in online course

Properly implementing a VLSM addressing scheme is essential for creating a hierarchical network. When creating a VLSM addressing scheme, follow these basic guidelines:

- Use newer routing protocols that support VLSM and discontiguous subnets.

- Disable auto-summarization if necessary.

- Use the same routing protocol throughout the network.

- Keep the router IOS up-to-date to support the use of subnet zero.

- Avoid intermixing private network address ranges in the same internetwork.

- Avoid discontiguous subnets where possible.

- Use VLSM to maximize address efficiency.

- Assign VLSM ranges based on requirements from the largest to the smallest.

- Plan for summarization using hierarchical network design and contiguous addressing design.

- Summarize at network boundaries.

- Use /30 ranges for WAN links.

- Allow for future growth when planning for the number of subnets and hosts supported.

4.4 Using NAT and PAT

4.4.1 Private IP Address Space

Refer to
Figure
in online course

In addition to VLSM and CIDR, the use of private addressing and Network Address Translation (*NAT*) further improved the scalability of the IPv4 address space.

Private addresses are available for anyone to use in their enterprise networks because private addresses route internally, they never appear on the Internet.

RFC 1918 governs the use of the private address spacing.

- Class A: 10.0.0.0 - 10.255.255.255

- Class B: 172.16.0.0 - 172.31.255.255

- Class C: 192.168.0.0 - 192.168.255.255

Using private addressing has these benefits:

- It alleviates the high cost associated with the purchase of public addresses for each host.

- It allows thousands of internal employees to use a few public addresses.

- It provides a level of security, because users from other networks or organizations cannot see the internal addresses.

Refer to
Figure
in online course

When implementing a private addressing scheme for the internal network, apply the same hierarchical design principles that are associated with VLSM.

Although private addresses are not routed on the Internet, they are frequently routed in the internal network. Problems associated with discontiguous networks still occur when using private addresses; therefore, carefully design the addressing scheme.

Be sure that the addresses are properly distributed according to the concepts of VLSM. Also, use valid boundaries and hierarchical IP addressing best practices for effective use of address summarization.

Refer to
Interactive Graphic
in online course.

Full Screen

Activity

Determine if the IP address is public or private.

4.4.2 NAT at the Enterprise Edge

Refer to
Figure
in online course

Many organizations want the benefits of private addressing while connecting to the Internet. Organizations create huge LANs and WANs with private addressing and connect to the Internet using Network Address Translation (NAT).

NAT translates internal private addresses into one or more public addresses for routing onto the Internet. NAT changes the private IP source address inside each packet to a publicly registered IP address before sending it out onto the Internet.

Small to medium organizations connect to their ISPs through a single connection. The local boundary router configured with NAT connects to the ISP. Larger organizations may have multiple ISP connections, and the boundary router at each of these locations performs NAT.

Using NAT on boundary routers improves security. Internal private addresses translate to different public addresses each time. This hides the actual address of hosts and servers in the enterprise.

Most routers that implement NAT also block packets coming from outside the private network unless they are a response to a request from an inside host.

4.4.3 Static and Dynamic NAT

Refer to
Figure
in online course

NAT can be configured statically or dynamically.

Static NAT maps a single *inside local address* to a single global, or public address. This mapping ensures that a particular inside local address always associates with the same public address. Static NAT ensures that outside devices consistently reach an internal device. Examples include Web and FTP servers accessible to the public.

Dynamic NAT uses an available pool of Internet public addresses and assigns them to inside local addresses. Dynamic NAT assigns the first available IP address in the pool of public addresses to an inside device. That host uses the assigned global IP address throughout the length of the session. Once the session ends, the outside global address returns to the pool for use by another host.

The address that one internal host uses to connect to another internal host is the inside local address. The public address assigned to the organization is called the *inside global address*. The inside global address is sometimes used as the address of the external interface of the border router.

The NAT router manages the translations between the inside local addresses and the inside global addresses by maintaining a table that lists each address pair.

Refer to
Figure
in online course

When configuring either static or dynamic NAT.

- List any servers that require a permanent outside address.
- Determine which internal hosts require translation.
- Determine which interfaces source the internal traffic. These will become the inside interfaces.
- Determine which interface sends traffic to the Internet. This will become the outside interface.
- Determine the range of public addresses available.

Configuring Static NAT

Step 1.   Determine the public IP address that outside users should use to access the inside device/server. Administrators tend to use addresses from either the beginning or end of the range for static NAT. Map the inside, or private address to the public address.

Step 2.   Configure the inside and outside interfaces.

Configuring Dynamic NAT

Step 1.   Identify the pool of public IP addresses available for use.

Step 2.   Create an access control list (*ACL*) to identify hosts that require translation.

Step 3.   Assign interfaces as either inside or outside.

Step 4.   Link the access list with the address pool.

An important part of configuring dynamic NAT is the use of the standard access control list (ACL). The standard ACL is used to specify the range of hosts that require translation. This is done in the form of a permit or deny statement. The ACL can include an entire network, a subnet or just a specific host. The ACL can range from a single line to several permit and deny statements.

Refer to
Lab Activity
for this chapter

Lab Activity

Configure and verify static NAT.

Refer to
Lab Activity
for this chapter

Lab Activity

Configure and verify dynamic NAT.

4.4.4 Using PAT

Refer to
Figure
in online course

One of the more popular variations of dynamic NAT is known as Port Address Translation (*PAT*), also referred to as *NAT Overload*. PAT dynamically translates multiple inside local addresses to a single public address.

When a source host sends a message to a destination host, it uses an IP address and port number combination to keep track of each individual conversation. In PAT, the gateway router translates the local source address and port number combination to a single global IP address and a unique port number above 1024.

A table in the router contains a list of the internal IP address and port number combinations that are translated to the external address. Although each host translates into the same global IP address, the port number associated with the conversation is unique.

Since over 64,000 ports are available, a router is unlikely to run out of addresses.

Both enterprise and home networks take advantage of PAT functionality. PAT is built into integrated routers and is enabled by default.

Refer to
Figure
in online course

Configuring PAT requires the same basic steps and commands as configuring NAT. However, instead of translating to a pool of addresses, PAT translates to a single address. The following command translates the inside addresses to the IP address of the serial interface:

```
ip nat inside source list 1 interface serial 0/0/0 overload
```

Verfiy NAT and PAT functionality with the following commands.

```
show ip nat translations
```

This command displays active translations. If the translation is not used, it ages out after a period of time. Static NAT entries remain in the table permanently. A dynamic NAT entry requires some action from the host to a destination on the outside of the network. If configured correctly, a simple **ping** or **trace** creates an entry in the NAT table.

```
show ip nat statistics
```

This command displays translation statistics, including the number of addresses used and the number of hits and misses. The output also includes the access list that specifies internal addresses, the global address pool, and the range of addresses defined.

Refer to
Lab Activity
for this chapter

Lab Activity

Configure and verify PAT.

Summary

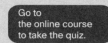

Quiz

Take the chapter quiz to check your knowledge.

Your Chapter Notes

CHAPTER 5

Routing with a Distance Vector Protocol

Introduction

Refer to
Figure
in online course

5.1 Managing Enterprise Networks

5.1.1 Enterprise Networks

Refer to
Figure
in online course

Hierarchical enterprise networks facilitate the flow of information. Information flows between mobile workers and branch offices. These branch offices connect to corporate offices in cities and countries around the world. The organization must create a hierarchy to meet the different network requirements of each part of the company.

Crucial information and services typically reside near the top of the hierarchy, in secured server farms or on storage area networks. The structure expands into many different departments that are spread across the lower part of the hierarchy.

Communication between different levels of the hierarchy requires a combination of LAN and WAN technologies. As the company grows or adds e-commerce operations, a DMZ may be required to house the various servers.

Refer to
Figure
in online course

Traffic control is essential in an enterprise network. Without it, these networks could not function.

Routers forward traffic and prevent broadcasts from clogging the main channels to crucial services. They control the flow of traffic between LANs, allowing only the required traffic to pass through the network.

Enterprise networks provide a high level of reliability and services. To ensure this, network professionals:

- Design networks to provide redundant links to use in case a primary data path fails.

- Deploy Quality of Service (QoS) to ensure critical data receives priority treatment.

- Use packet filtering to deny certain types of packets, maximize available bandwidth, and protect the network from attacks.

5.1.2 Enterprise Topologies

Refer to
Figure
in online course

Choosing the right physical topology allows a company to expand its networked services without losing reliability and efficiency. Network designers base their topology decisions upon the enterprise requirements for performance and reliability. The *star* and *mesh* topologies are normally deployed in enterprise environments.

Star Topology

One popular physical topology is the star. The center of the star corresponds to the top of the hierarchy, which could be the corporate headquarters or head office. Branch offices at multiple locations connect to the center, or hub, of the star.

A star topology provides centralized control of the network. All crucial services and technical staff can be located in one place. Star topologies are scalable. Adding a new branch office simply requires one more connection to the central point of the star. If an office adds several branches to its territory, each branch office can connect to a center hub in its own area, which then connects back to the main central point at the central office. In this way, a simple star can grow into an *extended star*, with smaller stars radiating out from the main branch offices.

Refer to **Figure** in online course

The star and extended star topologies create a single point of failure. Mesh topologies eliminate this problem.

Mesh Topologies

Each additional link provides an alternate pathway for data and adds reliability to the network. With the addition of links, the topology becomes a mesh of interconnected nodes. Each additional link adds cost and overhead. It also adds to the complexity of managing the network.

Partial Mesh

Adding redundant links only to a specific area of an enterprise creates a *partial mesh*. This topology meets uptime and reliability requirements for critical areas like server farms and SANs, while minimizing additional expenses. The other areas of the network are still vulnerable to failures. Therefore, it is essential to place the mesh where it provides the most benefit.

Full Mesh

When no downtime is acceptable, the network requires a *full mesh*. Each node in a full mesh topology connects to every other node in the enterprise. This is the most failure-proof topology, but it is also the most expensive to implement.

Refer to **Figure** in online course

The Internet is an excellent example of a meshed network. Devices on the Internet are not under the control of any one individual or organization. As a result, the topology of the Internet is constantly changing, with some links going down and others coming online. Redundant connections balance the traffic and ensure that there is a reliable path to the destination.

Enterprise networks face some of the same issues as the Internet. Therefore, processes are put in place that allow devices to adapt to these constantly changing conditions and reroute traffic as appropriate.

Refer to **Lab Activity** for this chapter

Lab Activity

Interconnect network nodes with redundant links to provide reliability at minimal cost.

5.1.3 Static and Dynamic Routing

Refer to **Figure** in online course

The physical topology of an enterprise network provides the structure for forwarding data. Routing provides the mechanism that makes it work. Finding the best path to the destination becomes very difficult in an enterprise network, because a router can have many sources of information from which to build its *routing table*.

A routing table is a data file that exists in RAM and stores information about directly connected and remote networks. The routing table associates each network with either an *exit interface* or a *next hop*.

The exit interface is the physical path that the router uses to move the data closer to the destination. The next hop is an interface on a connected router that moves the data closer to the final destination.

The table also attaches a number to each route that represents the trustworthiness or accuracy of the source of the routing information. This value is the *administrative distance*. Routers maintain information about directly connected, static, and dynamic routes.

Directly Connected Routes

Refer to **Figure** in online course

A directly connected network attaches to a router interface. Configuring the interface with an IP address and subnet mask allows the interface to become a host on the attached network. The network address and subnet mask of the interface, along with the interface type and number, appear in the routing table as a directly connected network. The routing table designates directly connected networks with a **C**.

Static Routes

Static routes are routes that a network administrator manually configures. A static route includes the network address and subnet mask of the destination network, along with the exit interface or the IP address of the next hop router. The routing table designates static routes with an S. Static routes are more stable and reliable than routes learned dynamically which results in a lower administrative distance compared to the dynamic routes.

Dynamic Routes

Dynamic routing protocols also add remote networks to the routing table. Dynamic routing protocols enable routers to share information about the reachability and status of remote networks through *network discovery*. Each protocol sends and receives data packets while locating other routers and updating and maintaining routing tables. Routes learned through a dynamic routing protocol are identified by the protocol used. For example, **R** for RIP and **D** for EIGRP. They are assigned the administrative distance of the protocol.

Refer to **Packet Tracer Activity** for this chapter

Packet Tracer Activity

Investigate a fully-converged network with connected, static, and dynamic routing.

Refer to **Figure** in online course

Typically, both static and dynamic routes are employed in an enterprise network. Static routing addresses specific network needs. Depending on the physical topology, a static route can be used to control the traffic flow.

Limiting traffic to a single point of entrance/exit creates a *stub network*. In some enterprise networks, small branch offices have only one possible path to reach the rest of the network. In this situation, It is not necessary to burden the stub router with routing updates and increased overhead by running a dynamic routing protocol, therefore static routing is beneficial

Based on their placement and function, specific enterprise routers may also require static routes. Border routers use static routes to provide secure, stable paths to the ISP. Other routers within the enterprise use either static routing or dynamic routing protocols as necessary to meet their needs.

Refer to **Figure** in online course

Routers in an enterprise network use bandwidth, memory, and processing resources to provide NAT/PAT, packet filtering, and other services. Static routing provides forwarding services without the overhead associated with most dynamic routing protocols.

Static routing provides more security than dynamic routing, because no routing updates are required. A hacker could intercept a dynamic routing update to gain information about a network.

However, static routing is not without problems. It requires time and accuracy from the network administrator, who must manually enter routing information. A simple typographical error in a static route can result in network downtime and packet loss. When a static route changes, the network may experience routing errors and problems during manual reconfiguration. For these reasons, static routing is impractical for general use in a large enterprise environment.

5.1.4 Configuring Static Routes

Refer to
Figure
in online course

The global command for configuring most static routes is **ip route**, followed by the destination network, the subnet mask, and the path used to reach it. The command is:

```
Router(config)#ip route [network-address] [subnet mask] [address of next hop OR
exit interface]
```

Using the next-hop address or the exit interface forwards traffic to the proper destination. However, these two parameters behave very differently.

Before a router forwards any packet, the routing table process determines which exit interface to use. Static routes configured with exit interfaces require a single routing table lookup. Static routes configured with the next-hop parameter must reference the routing table twice to determine the exit interface.

In an enterprise network, static routes configured with exit interfaces are ideal for point-to-point connections like those between a border router and the ISP.

Refer to
Figure
in online course

Static routes configured with a next hop interface require two steps to determine the exit interface. This is called a *recursive lookup*. In a recursive loopkup:

- The router matches the destination IP address of a packet to the static route.

- It matches the next hop IP address of the static route to entries in its routing table to determine which interface to use.

If an exit interface is disabled, static routes disappear from the routing table. The routing table re-installs the routes when the interface is re-enabled.

Refer to
Figure
in online course

Summarizing several static routes as a single entry reduces the size of the routing table and makes the lookup process more efficient. This process is called *route summarization*.

A single static route summarizes multiple static routes if:

- The destination networks summarize into a single network address.

- All of the static routes use the same exit interface or next-hop IP address.

Without summary routes, routing tables within Internet *core router*s become unmanageable. Enterprise networks encounter the same problem. Summary static routes are an indispensable solution for managing routing table size.

Refer to **Packet
Tracer Activity**
for this chapter

Packet Tracer Activity

Create static routes.

Refer to
Figure
in online course

Depending on the WAN services used in the enterprise, static routes provide a backup service when the primary WAN link fails. A feature called floating static routes can be used to provide this backup service.

By default, a static route has a lower administrative distance than the route learned from a dynamic routing protocol. A *floating static route* has a higher administrative distance than the route learned from a dynamic routing protocol. For that reason, a floating static route does not display in the routing table. The floating static route entry appears in the routing table only if the dynamic information is lost.

To create a floating static route, add an administrative distance value to the end of the **ip route** command:

```
Router(config)#ip route 192.168.4.0 255.255.255.0 192.168.9.1 200
```

The administrative distance specified must be greater than the AD assigned to the dynamic routing protocol. The router uses the primary route as long as it is active. If the primary route is down, the table installs the floating static route.

5.1.5 Default Routes

Refer to **Figure** in online course

Routing tables cannot contain routes to every possible Internet site. As routing tables grow in size, they require more RAM and processing power. A special type of static route, called a *default route*, specifies a gateway to use when the routing table does not contain a path to a destination. It is common for default routes to point to the next router in the path toward the ISP. In a complex enterprise, default routes funnel Internet traffic out of the network.

The command to create a default route is similar to the command used to create either an ordinary or a floating static route. The network address and subnet mask are both specified as 0.0.0.0, making it a *quad zero route*. The command uses either the next-hop address or the exit interface parameters.

The zeroes indicate to the router that no bits need to match in order to use this route. As long as a better match does not exist, the router uses the default static route.

The final default route, located on the border router, sends the traffic to the ISP. This route identifies the last stop within the enterprise as the *Gateway of Last Resort* for packets that cannot be matched. This information appears in the routing tables of all routers.

If the enterprise uses a dynamic routing protocol, the border router can send a default route to the other routers as part of a dynamic routing update.

Refer to **Packet Tracer Activity** for this chapter

Packet Tracer Activity

Configure a default route to forward traffic from the enterprise routers to the ISP.

5.2 Routing Using the RIP Protocol

5.2.1 Distance Vector Routing Protocols

Refer to **Figure** in online course

Dynamic routing protocols are classified into two major categories: *distance vector protocol*s and *link-state protocol*s.

Routers running distance vector routing protocols share network information with directly connected neighbors. The neighbor routers then advertise the information to their neighbors, until all routers in the enterprise learn the information.

A router running a distance vector protocol does not know the entire path to a destination; it only knows the distance to the remote network and the direction, or *vector*. Its knowledge comes through information from directly connected neighbors.

Like all routing protocols, distance vector protocols use a *metric* to determine the best route. Distance vector protocols calculate the best route based on the distance from a router to a network. An example of a metric used is hop count, which is the number of routers, or hops, between the router and the destination.

Refer to **Figure** in online course

Distance vector protocols usually require less complicated configurations and management than link-state protocols. They can run on older, less powerful routers and require lower amounts of memory and processing.

Routers using distance vector protocols broadcast or *multicast* their entire routing table to their neighbors at regular intervals. If a router learns more than one route to a destination, it calculates and advertises the route with the lowest metric.

This method of moving routing information through large networks is slow. At any given moment, some routers may not have the most current information about the network. This limits the scalability of the protocols and causes issues such as routing loops.

RIP versions 1 and 2 are true distance vector protocols, whereas EIGRP is actually a distance vector protocol with advanced capabilities. *RIPng*, the newest version of RIP was specifically designed to support IPv6.

5.2.2 Routing Information Protocol (RIP)

Refer to **Figure** in online course

Routing Information Protocol (RIP) was the first IP distance vector routing protocol to be standardized in a RFC (RFC1058 in 1988). The first version of RIP is now often called RIPv1 to distinguish it from the later improved version, RIPv2; and from the IPv6 version, RIPng.

By default RIPv1 broadcasts its routing updates out all active interfaces every 30 seconds.

RIPv1 is a classful routing protocol. It automatically summarizes subnets to the *classful boundary* and does not send subnet mask information in the update. Therefore RIPv1 does not support VLSM and CIDR. A router configured with RIPv1 either uses the subnet mask configured on a local interface, or applies the default subnet mask based on the address class. Due to this limitation, the subnets of the networks that RIPv1 advertises should not be *discontiguous* if correct routing is to occur.

For example, a router configured with interfaces as the gateways for the 172.16.1.0/24 and 172.16.4.0/24 subnets will advertise only the 172.16.0.0 Class B network with RIPv1. Another router receiving this update will therefore list the 172.16.0.0 network in its routing table. This means packets with an actual destination subnet address of 172.16.3.0 could mistakenly be forwarded to the advertising router and therefore not arrive at the correct destination subnet.

Refer to **Figure** in online course

RIP v2 has many of the features of RIPv1. It also includes important enhancements. RIPv2 is a *classless routing* protocol that supports VLSM and CIDR. A subnet mask field is included in v2 updates, which allows the use of discontiguous networks. RIPv2 also has the ability to turn off automatic summarization of routes.

Both versions of RIP send their entire routing table out all participating interfaces in updates. RIP v1 broadcasts these updates to 255.255.255.255. This requires all devices on a broadcast network like Ethernet to process the data. RIP v2 multicasts its updates to 224.0.0.9. Multicasts take up less network bandwidth than broadcasts. Devices that are not configured for RIPv2 discard multicasts at the Data Link Layer.

Attackers often introduce invalid updates to trick a router into sending data to the wrong destination or to seriously degrade network performance. Invalid information can also end up in the routing table due to poor configuration or a malfunctioning router. Encrypting routing information hides the content of the routing table from any routers that do not possess the password or authentication data. RIPv2 has an authentication mechanism, whereas RIPv1 does not.

Refer to **Figure** in online course

Although RIPv2 provides many enhancements, it is not an entirely different protocol. RIPv2 shares many of the features found in RIPv1, such as:

- Hop-count metric

- 15-hop maximum

- TTL equals 16 hops

- Default 30-second update interval

- *Route poisoning*, *poisoned reverse*, *split horizon*, and *holddown*s to avoid loops

- Updates using UDP port 520

- Administrative distance of 120

- Message header containing up to 25 routes without authentication

When a router starts up, each RIP-configured interface sends out a *request message*. This message requests that all RIP neighbors send their complete routing tables. RIP-enabled neighbors send a *response message* that includes known network entries. The receiving router evaluates each route entry based on the following criteria:

- If a route entry is new, the receiving router installs the route in the routing table.

- If the route is already in the table and the entry comes from a different source, the routing table replaces the existing entry if the new entry has a better hop count.

- If the route is already in the table and the entry comes from the same source, it replaces the existing entry even if the metric is not better.

The startup router then sends a *triggered update* out all RIP-enabled interfaces containing its own routing table. RIP neighbors are informed of any new routes.

Refer to
Figure
in online course

As long as routers send and process the correct versions of routing updates, RIPv1 and RIPv2 are completely compatible. By default, RIPv2 sends and receives only version 2 updates. If a network must use both versions of RIP, the network administrator configures RIPv2 to send and receive both versions 1 and 2. By default, RIPv1 sends version 1 updates, but receives both versions 1 and 2.

Within an enterprise, it may be necessary to use both versions of RIP. For example, part of the network may be migrating to RIPv2, whereas another part may be staying with RIPv1. Overriding the global RIP configuration with interface-specific behavior allows routers to support both versions of RIP.

To customize the global configuration of an interface, use the following interface configuration commands:

```
ip rip send version <1 ¦ 2 ¦ 1 2>
ip rip receive version <1 ¦ 2 ¦ 1 2>
```

Refer to
Interactive Graphic
in online course.

Full Screen

Activity

Select the version of RIP that is most appropriate for the situation given.

5.2.3 Configuring RIPv2

Refer to
Figure
in online course

Before configuring RIPv2, assign IP addresses and masks to all interfaces that participate in routing. Set the clock rate where necessary on serial links. After the basic configurations are complete, configure RIPv2.

The basic RIPv2 configuration consists of three commands:

```
Router(config)#router rip
```
- Enables the routing protocol

```
Router(config)#version 2
```
- Specifies the version

```
Router(config-router)#network [network address]
```
- Identify each directly connected network that should be advertised by RIP

By default, RIPv2 will summarize each network to be advertised to its classful boundary as the graphic shows.

RIPv2 updates can be configured to be authenticated.

RIPv2 propagates a default route to its neighbor routers as part of its routing updates. To accomplish this, create the default route and then add **redistribute static** to the RIPv2 configuration.

Refer to
Lab Activity
for this chapter

Lab Activity

Configuring RIPv2 with VLSM addressing scheme and a default route.

5.2.4 Problems with RIP

Various performance and security issues arise when using RIP. The first issue concerns routing table accuracy.

Refer to
Figure
in online course

Both versions of RIP automatically summarize subnets on the classful boundary. This means that RIP recognizes subnets as a single Class A, B, or C network. Enterprise networks typically use classless IP addressing and a variety of subnets, some of which are not directly connected to each other, which creates discontiguous subnets.

Unlike RIPv1, with RIPv2 the automatic summarization feature can be disabled. When disabled, RIPv2 will report all subnets with subnet mask information. This is done to ensure a more accurate routing table. To accomplish this, add the **no auto-summary** command to the RIPv2 configuration.

```
Router(config-router)#no auto-summary
```

Refer to
Figure
in online course

Another issue to consider is the broadcast nature of RIP updates. As soon as the RIP configuration lists a **network** command for a given network, RIP immediately begins to send advertisements out all interfaces that belong to that network. These updates may not be needed on all portions of a network. For example, an Ethernet LAN interface passes these updates to every device on its network segment, which produces unnecessary traffic. The routing update could also be intercepted by any device. This makes the network less secure.

The **passive-interface** command, issued in interface mode, disables routing updates on specified interfaces.

```
Router(config-router)#passive-interface interface-type interface-number
```

In complex enterprise networks running more than one routing protocol, the **passive-interface** command defines which routers learn RIP routes. When the number of interfaces advertising RIP routes is limited, security and traffic control increase.

Refer to
Figure
in online course

A network running RIP needs time to converge. Some routers may contain incorrect routes in their routing tables until all routers have updated and have the same view of the network.

Erroneous network information may cause routing updates and traffic to loop endlessly as they *count to infinity*. In the RIP routing protocol, infinity occurs when the hop count is 16.

Routing loops negatively affect network performance. RIP contains several features designed to combat this impact. These features are often used in combination:

- *Poisoned reverse*

- *Split horizon*

- *Holddown timer*

- Triggered updates

Poisoned reverse sets the metric for a route to 16, making it unreachable. Because RIP defines infinity as 16 hops, any network further away than 15 hops is unreachable. If a network is down, a router changes the metric for that route to 16 so that all other routers see it as unreachable. This feature prevents the routing protocol from sending information via poisoned routes.

Refer to
Figure
in online course

The anti-loop features of RIP add stability to the protocol, but also add to convergence time.

Split horizon prevents the formation of loops. When multiple routers advertise the same network routes to each other, routing loops may form. Split horizon dictates that a router receiving routing information on an interface cannot send an update about that same network back out the same interface.

The holddown timer stabilizes routes. The holddown timer refuses to accept route updates with a higher metric to the same destination network for a period after a route goes down. If, during the *holddown period*, the original route comes back up or the router receives route information with a lower metric, the router installs the route in the routing table and immediately begins to use it.

The default holddown time is 180 seconds, six times the regular update period. The default can be changed. However, any holddown period increases the convergence time and has a negative impact on network performance.

When a route fails, RIP does not wait for the next periodic update. Instead, RIP sends an immediate update, called a triggered update. It advertises the failed route by increasing the metric to 16, effectively poisoning the route. This update places the route in holddown status while RIP attempts to locate an alternate route with a better metric.

Refer to **Packet Tracer Activity** for this chapter

Packet Tracer Activity

Route between discontiguous networks with RIP.

5.2.5 Verifying RIP

Refer to **Figure** in online course

RIPv2 is a simple protocol to configure. However, errors and inconsistencies can occur on any network. There are many **show** commands to assist the technician in verifying a RIP configuration and troubleshooting RIP functionality.

The **show ip protocols** and **show ip route** commands are important for verification and troubleshooting on any routing protocol.

The following commands specifically verify and troubleshoot RIP:

- **show ip rip database**: Lists all the routes known by RIP

- **debug ip rip** or **debug ip rip {events}**: Displays RIP routing updates as sent and received in real time

The output of this debug command displays the source address and interface of each update, as well as the version and the metric.

Do not use the **debug** commands more than necessary. Debugging consumes bandwidth and processing power, which slows network performance.

The **ping** command can be used to test for end-to-end connectivity. The **show running-config** command provides a convenient method of verifying that all commands were entered correctly.

Refer to **Packet Tracer Activity** for this chapter

Packet Tracer Activity

Troubleshoot and correct RIPv2 problems.

5.3 Routing Using the EIGRP Protocol

5.3.1 Limitations of RIP

Refer to **Figure** in online course

The RIP distance vector routing protocol is easy to configure and requires minimal amounts of router resources in order to function.

However, the simple hop count metric used by RIP is not an accurate way to determine the best path in complex networks. Additionally, the RIP limitation of 15 hops can mark distant networks as unreachable.

RIP issues periodic updates of its routing table, which consumes bandwidth, even when no network changes have occurred. Routers must accept these updates and process them to see if they contain updated route information.

Updates passed from router to router take time to reach all areas of the network. As a result, routers may not have an accurate picture of the network. Routing loops can develop due to slow convergence time, which wastes valuable bandwidth.

These characteristics limit the usefulness of the RIP routing protocol within the enterprise environment.

5.3.2 Enhanced Interior Gateway Routing Protocol (EIGRP)

Refer to
Figure
in online course

The limitations of RIP led to the development of more advanced protocols. Networking professionals required a protocol that would support VLSM and CIDR, scale easily, and provide faster convergence in complex enterprise networks.

Cisco developed EIGRP as a *proprietary* distance vector routing protocol. It has enhanced capabilities that address many of the limitations of other distance vector protocols. EIGRP shares some of features of RIP, while employing many advanced features.

Although configuring EIGRP is relatively simple, the underlying features and options are complex. EIGRP contains many features that are not found in any other routing protocols. All of these factors makes EIGRP an excellent choice for large, multi-protocol networks that employ primarily Cisco devices.

Refer to
Figure
in online course

The two main goals of EIGRP are to provide a loop-free routing environment and rapid convergence. To achieve these goals, EIGRP uses a different method than RIP for calculating the best route. The metric used is a *composite metric* that primarily considers bandwidth and delay. This metric is more accurate than hop count in determining the distance to a destination network.

The Diffusing Update Algorithm (*DUAL*) used by EIGRP guarantees loop-free operation while it calculates routes. When a change occurs in the network topology, DUAL synchronizes all affected routers simultaneously. For these reasons, the administrative distance of EIGRP is 90, whereas the administrative distance of RIP is 120. The lower number reflects the increased reliability of EIGRP and the increased accuracy of the metric. If a router learns routes to the same destination from both RIP and EIGRP, it chooses the EIGRP route over the route learned through RIP.

EIGRP tags routes learned from another routing protocol as external. Because the information used to calculate these routes is not as reliable as the metric of EIGRP, it attaches a higher administrative distance to the routes.

Refer to
Figure
in online course

EIGRP is a good choice for complex enterprise networks that are composed primarily of Cisco routers. Its maximum hop count of 255 supports large networks. EIGRP can display more than one routing table because it can collect and maintain routing information for a variety of routed protocols, such as IP and IPX. The EIGRP routing table reports routes learned both inside and outside the local system.

Unlike other distance vector protocols, EIGRP does not send complete tables in its updates. EIGRP multicasts partial updates about specific changes to only those routers that need the information, not to all routers in the area. These are called *bounded update*s because they reflect specific parameters.

Instead of sending periodic routing updates, EIGRP sends small *hello packet*s to maintain knowledge of its neighbors. Since they are limited in size, both bounded updates and hello packets save bandwidth while keeping network information fresh.

Refer to **Interactive Graphic** in online course.

Full Screen

Activity

Identify the features appropriate to each routing protocol.

5.3.3 EIGRP Terminology and Tables

Refer to **Figure** in online course

To store network information from the updates and support rapid convergence, EIGRP maintains multiple tables. EIGRP routers keep route and topology information readily available in RAM so that they can react quickly to changes. EIGRP maintains three interconnected tables:

- *Neighbor table*
- *Topology table*
- *Routing table*

Neighbor Table

The neighbor table lists information about directly connected neighbor routers. EIGRP records the address of a newly discovered neighbor and the interface that connects to it.

When a neighbor sends a hello packet, it advertises a *hold time*. The hold time is the length of time that a router treats a neighbor as reachable. If a hello packet is not received within the hold time, the timer expires and DUAL recalculates the topology.

Since fast convergence depends on accurate neighbor information, this table is crucial to EIGRP operation.

Refer to **Figure** in online course

Topology table

The topology table lists all routes learned from each EIGRP neighbor. DUAL takes the information from the neighbor and topology tables and calculates the lowest cost routes to each network.

The topology table identifies up to four primary loop-free routes for any one destination. These *successor route*s appear in the routing table. EIGRP *load balances*, or sends packets to a destination using more than one path. It load balances using successor routes that are both *equal cost* and *unequal cost*. This feature avoids overloading any one route with packets.

Backup routes, called *feasible successor*s, appear in the topology table but not in the routing table. If a primary route fails, a feasible successor becomes a successor route. This backup occurs as long as the feasible successor has a lower reported distance than the feasible distance of the current successor distance to the destination.

Refer to **Figure** in online course

Routing Table

Whereas the topology table contains information about many possible paths to a network destination, the routing table displays only the best paths called the successor routes.

EIGRP displays information about routes in two ways:

- The routing table designates routes learned through EIGRP with a D.
- EIGRP tags dynamic or static routes learned from other routing protocols or from outside the EIGRP network as D EX or external, because they did not originate from EIGRP routers within the same AS.

Refer to
Interactive Graphic
in online course.

Full Screen

Activity

Determine which EIGRP table would be the most appropriate to find the specified information.

5.3.4 EIGRP Neighbors and Adjacencies

Refer to
Figure
in online course

Before EIGRP can exchange packets between routers, it must first discover its neighbors. EIGRP neighbors are other routers running EIGRP on shared, directly connected networks.

EIGRP routers use hello packets to discover neighbors and establish *adjacencies* with neighbor routers. By default, hello packets are multicast every 5 seconds on links greater than a T1 and every 60 seconds on T1 or slower links.

On *IP networks*, the multicast address is 224.0.0.10. The hello packet contains information about the router interfaces and the interface addresses. An EIGRP router assumes that as long as it is receiving hello packets from a neighbor, the neighbor and its routes are reachable.

The hold time is the period that EIGRP waits to receive a hello packet. Generally, the hold time is three times the duration of the *hello interval*. When the hold time expires and EIGRP declares the route as down, DUAL re-evaluates the topology and refreshes the routing table.

Information discovered through the hello protocol provides the information for the neighbor table. A sequence number records the number of the last received hello from each neighbor and timestamps the time that the packet arrived.

Refer to
Figure
in online course

When a neighbor adjacency is established, EIGRP uses various types of packets to exchange and update routing table information. Neighbors learn about new routes, unreachable routes, and rediscovered routes through exchange of these packets:

- Acknowledgement

- Update

- Query

- Reply

When a route is lost, it moves to an active state and DUAL searches for a new route to the destination. When a route is found, it is moved to the routing table and placed in a passive state.

These various packets help DUAL gather the information it requires to calculate the best route to the destination network.

Refer to
Figure
in online course

An acknowledgement packet indicates the receipt of an update, query, or reply packet. Acknowledgement packets are small hello packets without any data. These types of packets are always unicast.

An *update packet* sends information about the network topology to its neighbor. That neighbor then updates its topology table. Several updates are often required to send all the topology information to the new neighbor.

Whenever DUAL places a route in the active state, the router must send a *query packet* to each neighbor. Neighbors must send replies, even if the reply states that no information on the destination is available. The information contained in each *reply packet* helps DUAL to locate a successor route to the destination network. Queries can be multicast or unicast. Replies are always unicast.

EIGRP packet types use either a connection-oriented service similar to TCP or a connectionless service similar to UDP. Update, query, and reply packets use the TCP-like service. Acknowledgements and hello packets use the UDP-like service.

Refer to **Figure** in online course

As a routing protocol, EIGRP operates independently of the Network Layer. Cisco designed Reliable Transport Protocol (*RTP*) as a proprietary Layer 4 protocol. RTP guarantees delivery and receipt of EIGRP packets for all Network Layer protocols. Because large, complex networks may use a variety of Network Layer protocols, this protocol makes EIGRP flexible and scalable.

RTP can be used as both a reliable and best effort transport protocol, similar to TCP and UDP. Reliable RTP requires an acknowledgement packet from the receiver to the sender. Update, query, and reply packets are sent reliably; hello and acknowledgement packets are sent best effort and do not require an acknowledgement. RTP uses both unicast and multicast packets. Multicast EIGRP packets use the reserved multicast address of 224.0.0.10.

Each Network Layer protocol works through a Protocol Dependent Module (*PDM*) responsible for the specific routing task. Each PDM maintains three tables. For example, a router running IP, IPX, and AppleTalk has three neighbor tables, three topology tables, and three routing tables.

Refer to **Interactive Graphic** in online course.

Full Screen **Activity**

Match the EIGRP packet type to its definition.

5.3.5 EIGRP Metrics and Convergence

Refer to **Figure** in online course

EIGRP uses a composite metric value to determine the best path to a destination. This metric is determined from the following values:

- Bandwidth

- Delay

- Reliability

- Load

Maximum Transmission Unit (*MTU*) is another value included in routing updates, but is not a routing metric.

The composite metric formula consists of *K values*: K1 through K5. By default, K1 and K3 are set to 1. K2, K4, and K5 are set to 0. The value of 1 designates that bandwidth and delay have equal weight in the composite metric calculation.

Bandwidth

The bandwidth metric is a static value and is displayed in kbps. Most serial interfaces use the default bandwidth value of 1544 kbps. This metric reflects the bandwidth of a T1 connection.

Sometimes the bandwidth value may not reflect the actual physical bandwidth of the interface. Bandwidth influences the metric calculation and, as a result, the EIGRP path selection. If a 56 kbps link is advertised with a 1544 kbps value, it could interfere with convergence as it struggles to cope with the traffic load.

Refer to **Figure** in online course

The other metrics used by EIGRP to calculate the cost of a link are delay, reliability, and load.

The delay metric is a static value that is based on the type of exit interface. The default value is 20,000 microseconds for Serial interfaces and 100 microseconds for Fast Ethernet interfaces.

The delay metric does not represent the actual amount of time packets take to reach the destination. Changing the delay value associated with a specific interface alters the metric but does not physically affect the network.

Reliability measures how often the link has experienced errors. Unlike delay, reliability updates automatically, depending on the link conditions. It has a value of between 0 and 255. A reliability of 255/255 represents a 100 percent reliable link.

Load reflects the amount of traffic using the link. A lower load value is more desirable than a higher value. As an example, 1/255 would be a minimally loaded link, and 255/255 would be a link that is 100 percent utilized.

Refer to **Figure** in online course

The EIGRP topology table uses metrics to maintain values for feasible distance (*FD*) and advertised distance (*AD*), or reported distance (*RD*). DUAL uses these values to determine successors and feasible successors.

Feasible distance is the best EIGRP metric along the path to the destination from the router.

Advertised distance is the best metric reported by a neighbor.

The loop-free route with the lowest feasible distance becomes a successor. There can be multiple successors for a destination, depending on the actual topology. A feasible successor is a route with an advertised distance that is less than the feasible distance of a successor.

DUAL converges quickly after a change in the topology. DUAL keeps feasible successors in the topology table and promotes the best one to the routing table as a successor route if the original . If no feasible successor exists, the original route moves into active mode, and queries are sent to find a new successor.

Refer to **Interactive Graphic** in online course.

Full Screen:

Activity

Examine the network diagram and answer questions about the feasible distance (FD), advertised distance (AD), and the successor route for specified routes.

5.4 Implementing EIGRP

5.4.1 Configuring EIGRP

Refer to **Figure** in online course

Basic EIGRP is relatively simple to configure. It has many similarities to RIPv2.

To begin the EIGRP routing process, use two steps:

Step 1

Enable the EIGRP routing process.

Enabling the EIGRP process requires an autonomous system parameter. This AS parameter can be assigned any 16-bit value and identifies all of the routers belonging to a single company or organization. Although EIGRP refers to the parameter as an autonomous system number, it actually functions as a process ID. This AS number is locally significant only and is not the same as the autonomous system number issued and controlled by the Internet Assigned Numbers Authority (*IANA*).

The AS number in the command must match on all routers that work within the EIGRP routing process.

Step 2

Include network statements for each network to be advertised.

The `network` command tells EIGRP which networks and interfaces participate in the EIGRP process.

Refer to **Figure** in online course

To configure EIGRP to advertise only certain subnets, include a *wildcard mask* after the network number. To determine the wildcard mask, subtract the subnet mask from 255.255.255.255.

Some versions of the Cisco IOS allow the subnet mask to be specified instead of using the wild-card mask. Even if the subnet mask is used, the `show running-config` command displays the wildcard mask in its output.

Two additional commands complete the typical basic EIGRP configuration.

Add `eigrp log-neighbor-changes` command to view changes in neighbor adjacencies. This feature helps the administrator monitor the stability of the EIGRP network.

On serial links that do not match the default EIGRP bandwidth of 1.544 Mbps, add the `bandwidth` command followed by the actual speed of the link expressed in kbps. Inaccurate bandwidth interferes with choosing the best route.

Refer to
Figure
in online course

Once EIGRP is enabled, any router configured with EIGRP and the correct autonomous system number can enter the EIGRP network. This means routers with different or conflicting route information can affect and possibly corrupt the routing tables. To prevent this, it is possible to enable authentication within the EIGRP configuration. Once neighbor authentication is configured, the router authenticates the source of all routing updates before accepting them.

EIGRP authentication requires the use of a pre-shared key. EIGRP allows an administrator to manage the keys though a keychain. The configuration of EIGRP authentication consists of two steps: creating the key and enabling authentication to use the key.

Key Creation

To create the key perform the following commands:

`key chain` *name-of-chain*

- Global configuration command.
- Specifies the name of the keychain and enters the configuration mode for the keychain.

`key` *key-id*

- Identifies the key number and enters the configuration mode for that key-id.

`key-string` *text*

- Identifies the key string or password. This must be configured to match on all EIGRP routers.

Enabling Authentication

The key is used to enable MD5 authentication for EIGRP with the following interface configuration commands:

`ip authentication mode eigrp md5`

- Specifies that MD5 authentication is required for the exchange of EIGRP packets.

`ip authentication key-chain eigrp` *AS name-of-chain*

- AS specifies the autonomous system of the EIGPR configuration.

Name-of-chain parameter specifies the keychain that was previously configured.

Refer to
Lab Activity
for this chapter

Lab Activity

Configure EIGRP with MD5 authentication.

5.4.2 EIGRP Route Summarization

Refer to
Figure
in online course

Like RIP, EIGRP automatically summarizes subnetted networks on the classful boundary. EIGRP creates only one entry in the routing table for the summary route. A best path or successor route is associated with the summary route. As a result, all traffic destined for the subnets travels across that one path.

In an enterprise network, the path chosen to reach the summary route may not be the best choice for the traffic that is trying to reach each individual subnet. The only way that all routers can find the best routes for each individual subnet is for neighbors to send subnet information.

When default summarization is disabled, updates include subnet information. The routing table installs entries for each of the subnets and also an entry for the summary route. The summary route is called the *parent route* and the subnet routes are called the *child routes*.

EIGRP installs a Null0 summary route in the routing table for each parent route. The *Null0 interface* indicates that this is not an actual path, but a summary for advertising purposes. If a packet matches one of the child routes, it forwards out the correct interface. If the packet matches the summary route but does not match one of the child routes, it is discarded.

Using default summarization results in smaller routing tables. Turning off the summarization produces larger updates and larger tables. Consideration of the overall network performance and traffic patterns determines if auto summarization is appropriate.

Use the `no auto-summary` command to disable the default summarization.

Refer to
Figure
in online course

With auto summarization disabled, all subnets are advertised. An administrator may have a situation in which some of the subnets need to be summarized and some do not. The decision to summarize depends on the placement of the subnets. As an example, four contiguous subnets terminating on the same router are good candidates for summarization.

Manual summarization provides a more precise control of EIGRP routes. Using this feature, the administrator determines which subnets on which interfaces are advertised as summary routes.

Manual summarization is done on a per-interface basis and gives the network administrator complete control. A manually summarized route appears in the routing table as an EIGRP route sourced from a logical, not physical, interface:

```
D 192.168.0.0/22 is a summary, Null0
```

Packet Tracer Activity

Configure and verify EIGRP and EIGRP summary routes.

Refer to **Packet Tracer Activity** for this chapter

Lab Activity

Configure automatic and manual route summarization with EIGRP.

Refer to **Lab Activity** for this chapter

5.4.3 Verifying EIGRP Operation

Refer to
Figure
in online course

Although EIGRP is a relatively simple protocol to configure, it employs sophisticated technologies to overcome the limitations of distance vector routing protocols. It is important to understand these technologies in order to properly verify and troubleshoot a network configuration that utilizes EIGRP. Some of the verification commands available include:

```
show ip protocols
```

- Verifies that EIGRP is advertising the correct networks

- Displays the autonomous system number and administrative distance `show ip route`

- Verifies that the EIGRP routes are in the routing table
- Designates EIGRP routes with a **D** or a **D EX**
- Has a default administrative distance of 90 for internal routes

`show ip eigrp neighbors detail`

- Verifies the adjacencies EIGRP forms
- Displays the IP addresses and interfaces of neighbor routers

`show ip eigrp topology`

- Displays successors and all feasible successors
- Displays feasible distance and reported distance

`show ip eigrp interfaces detail`

- Verifies the interfaces using EIGRP

`show ip eigrp traffic`

- Displays the number and types of EIGRP packets sent and received

One of the primary uses of these show commands is to verify the successful formation of EIGRP adjacencies and the successful exchange of EIGRP packets between routers. EIGRP cannot work without forming adjacencies, therefore this should be verified prior to any other troubleshooting efforts.

Refer to
Figure
in online course

If adjacencies appear normal but problems still exist, an administrator should begin troubleshooting using debug commands to view real-time information on the EIGRP activities occurring on a router.

`debug eigrp packet`

- displays transmission and receipt of all EIGRP packets

`debug eigrp fsm`

- displays feasible successor activity to determine whether routes are discovered, installed, or deleted by EIGRP

Debugging operations use large amounts of bandwidth and router processing power, particularly when debugging a very complex protocol like EIGRP. These commands provide details that can pinpoint the source of a lost EIGRP route or missing adjacency; however, the use of these commands can also degrade network performance.

Refer to
Interactive Graphic
in online course.

Full Screen Activity

Match the output requirements with the appropriate command.

Refer to **Packet
Tracer Activity**
for this chapter

Packet Tracer Activity

Explore the various EIGRP verification and troubleshooting commands.

Refer to
Figure
in online course

5.4.4 Issues and Limitations of EIGRP

Although EIGRP is a powerful and sophisticated routing protocol, several considerations limit its use:

- Does not work in a multi-vendor environment because it is a Cisco proprietary protocol

- Works best with a flat network design

- Must share the same autonomous system among routers and cannot be subdivided into groups

- Can create very large routing tables, which requires large update packets and large amounts of bandwidth

- Uses more memory and processor power than RIP

- Works inefficiently when left on the default settings

- Requires administrators with advanced technical knowledge of the protocol and the network

EIGRP offers the best of distance vector routing, while using additional features typically associated with link-state routing protocols, including bounded updates and neighbor adjacencies. Successful implementation of the many features of EIGRP requires careful configuration, monitoring, and troubleshooting.

Summary

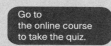

Quiz

Take the chapter quiz to check your knowledge.

Your Chapter Notes

CHAPTER 6

Routing with a Link-State Protocol

Introduction

Refer to
Figure
in online course

6.1 Routing Using the OSPF Protocol

6.1.1 Link-State Protocol Operation

Refer to
Figure
in online course

Enterprise networks and ISPs use *link-state protocol*s because of their hierarchical design and ability to scale for large networks. Distance vector routing protocols are usually not the right choice for a complex enterprise network.

Open Shortest Path First (*OSPF*) is an example of a link-state routing protocol. OSPF is an *open standard* routing protocol, developed by the Internet Engineering Task Force (*IETF*) to support IP traffic.

OSPF is a classless interior gateway protocol (*IGP*). It divides the network into different sections, which are referred to as areas. This division allows for greater scalability. Working with multiple areas allows the network administrator to selectively enable route summarization and to isolate routing issues within a single area.

Link-state routing protocols, such as OSPF, do not send frequent periodic updates of the entire routing table. Instead, after the network converges, a link-state protocol sends an update only when a change in the topology occurs, such as a link going down. In addition, OSPF performs a full update every 30 minutes.

Refer to
Figure
in online course

Link-state routing protocols like OSPF work well for larger hierarchical networks where fast convergence is important.

Compared with distance vector protocols, link-state routing protocols:

- Requires more complex network planning and configuration

- Requires increased router resources

- Requires more memory for storing multiple tables

- Requires more CPU and processing power for the complex routing calculations

With the high performance of routers available today, however, these requirements are usually not a problem.

Routers running RIP receive updates from their immediate neighbors, but with no details about the network as a whole. Routers running OSPF generate a complete map of the network from their own viewpoint. This map allows them to quickly determine loop-free alternate paths in the case of a network link failure.

OSPF does not automatically summarize at major network boundaries. Additionally, Cisco's implementation of OSPF uses bandwidth to determine the cost of a link. This cost metric is used by OSPF to determine the best path. A link with higher bandwidth results in a lower cost. The lowest cost route to a destination is the most desirable path.

The router trusts a metric based on bandwidth more than one based on hop count to establish the shortest path. The administrative distance of OSPF is 110, lower than RIP, because of the trustworthiness, or accuracy, of the metric.

Refer to **Interactive Graphic** in online course.

Full Screen Activity

6.1.2 OSPF Metrics and Convergence

Refer to **Figure** in online course

OSPF bases the cost metric for an individual link on its bandwidth or speed. The metric for a particular destination network is the sum of all link costs in the path. If there are multiple paths to the network, the path with the lowest overall cost is the preferred path and is placed in the routing table.

The equation used to calculate the cost of an OSPF link is:

Cost = 100,000,000 / bandwidth of link in bps

The configured bandwidth on an interface provides the bandwidth value for the equation. Determine the bandwidth of an interface using the `show interfaces` command.

Using this equation presents a problem with link speeds 100 Mbps or greater, such as Fast Ethernet and Gigabit Ethernet. Regardless of the difference in speed between these two links, they both calculate to a value of 1, therefore will be treated equally even though they are very different. To compensate for this, configure the interface cost value manually with the `ip ospf cost` command.

Refer to **Figure** in online course

OSPF routers within a single area advertise information about the status of their *link*s to their neighbors. Messages called Link State Advertisements (*LSA*s) are used to advertise this status information.

Once an OSPF router receives LSAs describing all of the links within an area, it uses the *SPF algorithm*, also called *Dijkstra's Algorithm*, to generate a topological tree, or map of the network. Each router running the algorithm identifies itself as the root of its own *SPF tree*. Starting from the root, the SPF tree identifies the shortest path to each destination and the total cost of each path.

The OSPF link-state or *topology database* stores the SPF tree information. The router installs the shortest path to each network in the routing table.

Convergence occurs when all routers:

- Receive information about every destination on the network
- Process this information with the SPF algorithm
- Update their routing tables

Refer to **Interactive Graphic** in online course.

Full Screen

Activity

Identify the best path that packets can take from H1 to H2 in an OSPF network based on link cost.

6.1.3 OSPF Neighbors and Adjacencies

Refer to **Figure** in online course

With OSPF, link state updates are sent when network changes occur. But how does a router know when a neighboring router fails? OSPF routers establish and maintain neighbor relationships, or adjacencies, with other connected OSPF routers. Adjacency is an advanced form of neighborship between routers that are willing to exchange routing information. When routers initiate an adjacency with neighbors, an exchange of link-state updates begins. Routers reach a FULL state of adjacency when they have synchronized views on their link-state database.

The router goes through several state changes before becoming fully adjacent with its neighbor.

- Init
- 2-Way
- Exstart
- Exchange
- Loading
- Full

The OSPF Hello protocol is used to initially establish and maintain adjacencies. The hello protocol sends very small hello packets to directly connected OSPF routers on the multicast address of 224.0.0.5. The packets are sent every 10 seconds on Ethernet and broadcast links and every 30 seconds for non-broadcast links. Router settings are also included in the hello packets. The settings include the hello interval, *dead interval*, and network type, as well as the authentication type and authentication data if configured. For any two routers to form an adjacency, all settings must match. The router records neighbor adjacencies discovered in an OSPF adjacencies database.

Refer to **Figure** in online course

Full is the normal state for an OSPF router. If a router is stuck in another state, this is an indication of a problem such as mismatched settings. The only exception to this is the 2-way state. In a broadcast environment, a router will only achieve a full state with a designated router (*DR*) and a backup designated router (*BDR*). All other neighbors will be viewed in the 2-way state.

The purpose of the DR and BDR is to reduces the number of updates sent, unnecessary traffic flow, and processing overhead on all routers. This is accomplished by requiring all routers to accept updates from the DR only. On broadcast network segments there is only one DR and BDR. All other routers must have a connection to the DR and BDR. When a link fails, the router with information about the link sends the information to the DR, using the multicast address 224.0.0.6. The DR is responsible for distributing the change to all other OSPF routers, using multicast 224.0.0.5. In addition to reducing the number of updates sent across the network, this process also ensures that all routers receive the same information at the same time from a single source.

The BDR ensures that there is no single point of failure. Like the DR, the BDR listens to 224.0.0.6 and receives all updates that are sent to the DR. If the DR fails, the BDR immediately takes over as DR, and a new BDR is elected. Any router not elected as the DR or BDR is known as a *DROther*.

Refer to **Figure** in online course

Within a local network, the router with the highest *router ID* is elected the DR. The second highest is elected as the BDR.

The router ID is an IP address that is determined by:

Step 1.   The value configured with the `router-id` command

Step 2.   If no value is set with the `router-id` command, the highest configured IP address on any *loopback interface*

Step 3.   If no loopback interface is configured, the highest IP address on any active physical interface

The router ID can be viewed using the following `show` commands:

`show ip protocols`, `show ip ospf`, or `show ip ospf interface` commands.

In some cases, an administrator may want specific routers to be the DR and BDR. These might be routers with more processing power or lighter traffic load. An administrator can force the DR and BDR election by configuring a priority using the interface configuration command:

`ip ospf priority` *number*

By default, OSPF routers have a priority value of 1. If the priority value is changed on a router, the highest priority setting will win the election for DR, regardless of highest router ID. The highest value that can be set for router priority is 255. A value of 0 signifies that the router is ineligible to be DR or BDR.

Refer to
Figure
in online course

Not all link types require a DR and BDR. Link types identified by OSPF include:

Broadcast Networks

- Ethernet

Point-to-point (***PPP***) Networks

- Serial

- T1/E1

Non-Broadcast Multi-Access (***NBMA***) Networks

- Frame Relay

- ATM

On broadcast multi-access networks, such as Ethernet, the number of neighbor relationships can become large, and therefore a DR election is required.

On point-to-point networks, the establishment of full adjacencies is not an issue because, by definition, there can only be two routers on the link. The DR election is not necessary and does not apply.

On NBMA networks, OSPF can run in two modes:

- Simulated broadcast environment: An administrator can define the network type as broadcast and the network simulates a broadcast model by electing a DR and a BDR. In this environment, it is generally recommended that the administrator choose the DR and BDR by configuring the priority of the router. This ensures that the DR and BDR have full connectivity to all other neighboring routers. Neighboring routers are also statically defined using the `neighbor` command in the OSPF configuration mode.

- Point-to-multipoint environment: In this environment, each non-broadcast network is treated as a collection of point-to-point links and a DR is not elected. This environment also requires that neighboring routers are statically defined.

Full Screen

Refer to
Interactive Graphic
in online course.

Activity

Identify the correct DR and BDR for each network shown.

Refer to
Figure
in online course

6.1.4 OSPF Areas

All OSPF networks begin with ***Area 0***, also called the backbone area. As the network is expanded, other areas can be created that are adjacent to Area 0. These other areas can be assigned any number, up to 65,535.

OSPF has a two-layer hierarchical design. Area 0, also referred to as the backbone area, exists at the top and all other areas are located at the next level. All non-backbone areas must directly connect to area 0. This group of areas creates an OSPF Autonomous System (*AS*).

The operation of OSPF within an area is different from operation between that area and the backbone area. Summarization of network information usually occurs between areas. This helps to decrease the size of routing tables in the backbone. Summarization also isolates changes and unstable, or *flapping*, links to a specific area in the routing domain. When using summarization, when there is a change in the topology, only those routers in the affected area receive the LSA and run the SPF algorithm.

A router that connects an area to the backbone area is called an Area Border Router (*ABR*). A router that connects an area to a different routing protocol, such as EIGRP, or redistributes static routes into the OSPF area is called an Autonomous System Border Router (*ASBR*).

> Refer to
> **Interactive Graphic**
> in online course.

Full Screen

Activity

Match each term to the best description.

6.2 Implementing Single-Area OSPF

6.2.1 Configuring Basic OSPF in a Single Area

> Refer to
> **Figure**
> in online course

Configuration of basic OSPF is not a complex task, it requires only two steps. The first step enables the OSPF routing process. The second step identifies the networks to advertise.

Step 1: Enable OSPF

```
router(config)#router ospf <process-id>
```
The process ID is chosen by the administrator and can be any number from 1 to 65535. The process ID is only locally significant and does not have to match the ID of other OSPF routers.

Step 2: Advertise networks

```
Router(config-router)#network <network-address> <wildcard-mask> area <area-id>
```
The **network** command has the same function as it does in other IGP routing protocols. It identifies the interfaces that are enabled to send and receive OSPF packets. This statement identifies the networks to include in OSPF routing updates.

The OSPF **network** command uses a combination of network address and *wildcard mask*. The network address, along with the wildcard mask, specifies the interface address, or range of addresses, that will be enabled for OSPF.

The *area ID* identifies the OSPF area to which the network belongs. Even if there are no areas specified, there must be an Area 0. In a single-area OSPF environment, the area is always 0.

> Refer to
> **Figure**
> in online course

The OSPF **network** statement requires the use of the wildcard mask. When used for network summarization, or supernetting, the wildcard mask is the *inverse* of the subnet mask.

To determine the wildcard mask for a network or subnet, simply subtract the decimal subnet mask for the interface from the all 255s mask (255.255.255.255).

As an example, an administrator wants to advertise the 10.10.10.0/24 subnet in OSPF. The subnet mask for this Ethernet interface is /24 or 255.255.255.0. Subtract the subnet mask from the all 255s mask to get the wildcard mask.

All 255s mask: 255.255.255.255

Subnet mask: -255.255.255.0

_____

Wildcard mask: 0 . 0 . 0 .255

The resulting OSPF **network** statement is:

```
Router(config-router)#network 10.10.10.0 0.0.0.255 area 0
```
Full Screen

Refer to
Interactive Graphic
in online course.

Activity

Determine the subnet mask and wildcard mask required to advertise the specified network addresses in OSPF.

Refer to
Lab Activity
for this chapter

Lab Activity

Configure basic single area point-to-point OSPF and verify connectivity.

6.2.2 Configuring OSPF Authentication

Refer to
Figure
in online course

Like other routing protocols, the default configuration of OSPF exchanges information between neighbors in plain text. This poses potential security threats to a network. A hacker on a network could use packet sniffing software to capture and read OSPF updates and determine network information.

To eliminate this potential security problem, configure OSPF authentication between routers. When authentication is enabled in an area, routers will only share information if the authentication information matches.

With *simple password authentication*, configure each router with a password, called a *key*. This method provides only a basic level of security because the key passes between routers in plain text form. It is just as easy to view the key as it is the plain text.

A more secure method of authentication is Message Digest 5 (MD5). It requires a key and a *key ID* on each router. The router uses an algorithm that processes the key, the OSPF packet, and the key ID to generate an encrypted number. Each OSPF packet includes that encrypted number. A packet sniffer cannot be used to obtain the key because it is never transmitted.

Refer to
Lab Activity
for this chapter

Lab Activity

Configure single-area point-to-point OSPF authentication using MD5.

6.2.3 Tuning OSPF Parameters

Refer to
Figure
in online course

In addition to performing the basic configuration of OSPF, administrators often need to modify, or tune, certain OSPF parameters.

An example is when a network administrator needs to specify which routers become the DR and the BDR. Setting the interface priority or the router ID on specific routers accomplishes this requirement.

The router selects the DR based on the highest value of any one of the following parameters, in the sequence listed:

Step 1.   Interface Priority:The interface priority is set with the **priority** command.

Step 2.   Router ID:The router ID is set with the OSPF `router-id configuration` command.

Step 3.   Highest Loopback Address:The loopback interface with the highest IP address is used as the router ID by default. OSPF favors loopback interfaces since they are logical interfaces and not physical interfaces. Logical interfaces are always up.

Step 4.   Highest Physical Interface Address:The router uses the highest active IP address from one of its interfaces as the router ID. This option poses a problem if interfaces go down or are reconfigured.

After changing the ID of a router or interface priority, reset neighbor adjacencies. Use the `clear ip ospf process` command. This command ensures that the new values take effect.

Lab Activity

Configure OSPF loopback addresses in a multi-access topology to control DR/BDR election.

Bandwidth is another parameter that often requires modification. On Cisco routers, the bandwidth value on most serial interfaces defaults to 1.544 Mbps, the speed of a T1. This bandwidth value determines the cost of the link but does not actually affect the speed of the link.

In some circumstances, an organization receives a *fractional T1* from the service provider. One-fourth of a full T1 connection is 384 Kbps and is an example of a fractional T1. The IOS assumes a T1 bandwidth value on serial links even though the interface is actually only sending and receiving at 384 Kbps. This assumption results in improper path selection, because the routing protocol determines that the link is faster than it is.

When a serial interface is not actually operating at the default T1 speed, the interface requires manual modification. Configure both sides of the link to have the same value.

In OSPF, modification using the `bandwidth interface` command or the `ip ospf cost interface` command achieves the same result. Both commands specify an accurate value for use by OSPF to determine the best route.

The `bandwidth` command modifies the bandwidth value used to calculate the OSPF cost metric. To directly modify the cost of an interface, use the `ip ospf cost` command.

Another parameter related to the OSPF cost metric is the *reference bandwidth*, which is used to calculate interface cost, also referred to as the link cost.

The bandwidth value calculation of each interface uses the equation 100,000,000/bandwidth. 100,000,000, or 10^8, is known as the reference bandwidth.

A problem exists with links of higher speeds, such as Gigabit Ethernet and 10Gbit Ethernet links. Using the default reference bandwidth of 100,000,000 results in interfaces with bandwidth values of 100 Mbps and higher having the same OSPF cost of 1.

To obtain more accurate cost calculations, it may be necessary to adjust the reference bandwidth value. The reference bandwidth is modified using the OSPF command `auto-cost reference-bandwidth`.

When this command is necessary, use it on all routers so that the OSPF routing metric remains consistent. The new reference bandwidth is specified in terms of Mbps. To set the reference bandwidth to 10-Gigabit speed, use the value of 10,000.

Lab Activity

Configure OSPF link cost in a point-to-point topology to influence routing decisions.

Refer to
Lab Activity
for this chapter

Refer to
Figure
in online course

Refer to
Figure
in online course

Refer to
Lab Activity
for this chapter

6.2.4 Verifying OSPF Operation

Refer to **Figure** in online course

Once configured, OSPF has several commands available that verify proper operation.

When troubleshooting OSPF networks, the `show ip ospf neighbor` command is used to verify that the router has formed an adjacency with its neighboring routers.

If the router ID of the neighboring router is not displayed, or if it does not show a state of FULL, the two routers have not formed an OSPF adjacency. If a router is a DROther, adjacency occurs if the state is FULL or 2WAY.

If this is a multi-access Ethernet network, DR and BDR labels display after FULL/ in the State column.

Two routers may not form an OSPF adjacency if:

- The subnet masks do not match, causing the routers to be on separate networks
- OSPF hello or dead timers do not match
- OSPF network types do not match
- There is a missing or incorrect OSPF network command

Refer to **Figure** in online course

Several `show` commands are also useful in verifying OSPF operation.

`show ip protocols`

Displays information such as the router ID, the networks that OSPF is advertising, and the IP addresses of adjacent neighbors.

`show ip ospf`

Displays the router ID and details about the OSPF process, timers, and area information. It also shows the last time the SPF algorithm executed.

`show ip ospf interface`

Displays information such as router ID, network type cost, and timer settings.

`show ip route`

Verifies that each router is sending and receiving routes via OSPF.

Refer to **Interactive Graphic** in online course.

Full Screen

Activity

Use the `show ip route` output from an OSPF router to answer questions.

Refer to **Lab Activity** for this chapter

Lab Activity

Configure and verify point-to-point and multi-access OSPF networks, including tuning parameters.

6.3 Using Multiple Routing Protocols

6.3.1 Configuring and Propagating a Default Route

Refer to **Figure** in online course

Most networks connect to other networks through the Internet. OSPF provides routing information about networks within an AS. OSPF must also provide information about reaching networks outside of the AS.

Sometimes administrators configure static routes on certain routers to provide information that is not received via a routing protocol. Configuring static routes on all routers in a large network is cumbersome. An easier method is to configure a default route that points to the Internet connection for a network.

With OSPF, an administrator configures this route on an Autonomous System Boundary Router (ASBR). The ASBR is also often called the Autonomous System Border Router. The ASBR connects the OSPF network to an outside network. As soon as the default route is entered in the routing table of the ASBR, it can be configured to advertise that pathway to the rest of the OSPF network. This process informs every router within the AS of the default route and spares the administrator the work of configuring static routes on every router in the network.

Refer to
Figure
in online course

To configure a router to distribute a default route into the OSPF network, follow these two steps.

Step 1

Configure the ASBR with a default route.

```
R1(config)#ip route 0.0.0.0 0.0.0.0 serial 0/0/0
```

The default static route statement can specify an interface or the next hop IP address.

Step 2

Configure the ASBR to propagate the default route to other routers. By default, OSPF does not inject the default route into its advertisements even when the route exists in its routing table.

```
R1(config)#router ospf 1
R1(config-router)#default-information originate
```

The routing tables of the other routers in the OSPF domain should now have a gateway of last resort and an entry to the 0.0.0.0 /0 network in their routing tables. The default route injects into the OSPF domain so that it appears as an external type route (*E2*) in the routing tables of the other routers.

Refer to
Lab Activity
for this chapter

Lab Activity

Configure an OSPF default route and propagate it to other routers in the OSPF area through the routing protocol.

6.3.2 Configuring OSPF Summarization

Refer to
Figure
in online course

One method that reduces the number of routing updates and the size of the OSPF routing tables is route summarization. Routes can be summarized into OSPF or between areas within the same OSPF network.

To facilitate OSPF summarization, group together IP addresses in a network area. For example, in a single OSPF area, allocate four contiguous network segments, such as:

- 192.168.0.0/24

- 192.168.1.0/24

- 192.168.2.0/24

- 192.168.3.0/24

It is possible to summarize and advertise the four networks as one supernet of 192.168.0.0 /22. Doing this reduces the number of networks that advertise throughout the OSPF domain. It also reduces memory requirements and the number of entries in the router updates.

Additionally, summary routes reduce the issue of flapping routes. Flapping refers to a route that consistently goes up and down. By default, every time a route flaps, a link-state update is propagated throughout the entire domain. This can create a lot of traffic and processing overhead.

When a router is using a summary route, it uses a single, supernet address to represent several routes. Only one of the routes included within the summary must actually be up in order for the router to advertise the summary route. If one or more of the routes is flapping, the router will continue to advertise the more stable summary route only. It does not forward updates about the individual routes. Any packets forwarded to the flapping route while the route is down will simply be dropped at the summarizing router.

To configure an OSPF ABR router to summarize these networks to another OSPF area, issue the following command in router configuration mode:

`area` *area-id* `range` *ip-address ip-address-mask*

Specify the area in which the networks are summarized as well as the starting network number and summary mask.

Refer to **Lab Activity** for this chapter

Lab Activity

Configure OSPF summarization to reduce routing updates.

6.3.3 OSPF Issues and Limitations

Refer to **Figure** in online course

OSPF is a scalable routing protocol. It has the ability to converge quickly and operate within very large networks. There are however, some issues to consider when using it.

OSPF must maintain multiple databases and therefore requires more router memory and CPU capabilities than distance vector routing protocols.

The Dijkstra Algorithm requires CPU cycles to calculate the best path. If the OSPF network is complex and unstable, the algorithm consumes significant resources when recalculating frequently. Routers running OSPF are typically more powerful and more expensive.

To avoid excessive use of router resources, employ a strict hierarchical design to divide the network into smaller areas. All areas must maintain connectivity to Area 0. If not, they may lose connectivity to other areas.

OSPF can be challenging to configure if the network is large and the design is complex. In addition, interpreting the information contained in the OSPF databases and routing tables requires a good understanding of the technology.

During the initial discovery process, OSPF can flood the network with LSAs and severely limit the amount of data that the network can transport. Flooding in large networks with many routers and low bandwidth noticeably decreases network throughput.

Despite the issues and limitations of OSPF, it is still the most widely used link-state routing protocol within an enterprise.

6.3.4 Using Multiple Protocols in the Enterprise

Refer to **Figure** in online course

For various reasons, organizations might choose different routing protocols.

- A network administrator may choose different routing protocols for different sections of a network, based on *legacy* equipment or available resources.

- Two companies that merge may have configured their networks using different routing protocols and still need to communicate with each other.

When multiple routing protocols exist on a single router, there is the possibility of that router learning of a destination from multiple sources. There must be a predictable method for the router to choose which route to view as the most desirable pathway and place it in the routing table.

Refer to
Figure
in online course

When a router learns of a single network from multiple sources, it uses the administrative distance (*AD*) to determine which route it prefers. The Cisco IOS assigns all routing information methods an AD.

If a router learns of a particular subnet by way of RIP and OSPF, the OSPF-learned route is the one that it chooses for the routing table. Its AD is lower and, therefore, more desirable. The code at the beginning of the routing table entry indicates the source of the route, or how it was learned. Each code associates with a specific AD.

Refer to
Interactive Graphic
in online course.

Full Screen

Activity

Analyze the routing table and determine the route source, the AD, and the metric.

Use the information from the show ip route command as reference. Not all answers are used, and some answers are used more than once.

Refer to
Figure
in online course

If two networks have the same base address and subnet mask, a router views them as identical. It considers a summarized network, as well as an individual network that is part of that summary, as different networks.

The summarized network 192.168.0.0/22 and the individual network 192.168.1.0 /24 are different entries, even though the summarization includes the individual network. When this situation occurs, both networks are placed in the routing table. The decision of which route to use falls to the entry with the closest, or longest, prefix match.

As an example, a router receives a packet with a destination IP address of 172.16.0.10. Three possible routes match this packet: 172.16.0.0/12, 172.16.0.0/18, and 172.16.0.0/26. Of the three routes, 172.16.0.0/26 has the longest match. For any of these routes to be considered a match, there must be at least the number of matching bits indicated by the subnet mask of the route.

Refer to
Interactive Graphic
in online course.

Full Screen

Activity

Select one route that the packet would take to each destination network.

Summary

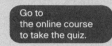

Quiz

Take the chapter quiz to check your knowledge.

Your Chapter Notes

CHAPTER 7

Implementing Enterprise WAN Links

Introduction

Refer to
Figure
in online course

7.1 Connecting the Enterprise WAN

7.1.1 WAN Devices and Technology

Refer to
Figure
in online course

As companies grow, they often expand from a single location to multiple remote locations. This expansion requires that the business network expand from a local area network (LAN) to a wide area network (WAN).

Within a LAN, a network administrator has physical control over all cabling, devices, and services. Although some larger companies maintain their own WANs, most organizations purchase WAN services from a service provider. Service providers charge for the use of their network resources. ISPs allow users to share resources among remote locations without incurring the expense of building and maintaining their own network.

Control of network resources is not the only difference between a LAN and a WAN. The technologies also differ. The most common LAN technology is Ethernet. WAN technologies are *serial transmission*s. Serial transmissions enable reliable, long-range communications at slower speeds than a LAN.

Refer to
Figure
in online course

When implementing a WAN, the WAN technology used determines the type of devices required by an organization. For example, a router used as a gateway to connect to the WAN translates the data into a format that is acceptable to the service provider network. A translation device, such as a modem, prepares the data for transmission across the service provider network.

Preparing the data for transmission on the WAN using digital lines requires a channel service unit (CSU) and a data service unit (DSU). These two devices are often combined into a single piece of equipment called the CSU/DSU. This device integrates into the interface card in the router. When using an analog connection, a modem is necessary.

When a business subscribes to WAN services through an ISP, the ISP owns and maintains most of the equipment. In certain environments, the subscriber may own and maintain some of the connection equipment. The point at which the control and responsibility of the customer ends and the control and responsibility of the service provider begins is known as the demarcation point, or demarc. For example, the demarc might exist between the router and the translating device or between the translating device and the central office (*CO*) of the service provider. Regardless of ownership, service providers use the term customer premise equipment (CPE), to describe equipment located at the customer site.

Refer to
Figure
in online course

The CO is the location where the service provider stores equipment and accepts customer connections. The physical line from the CPE connects into a router or WAN switch at the CO using copper or fiber cabling.

This connection is called the *local loop*, or last mile. From the customer perspective, it is the *first mile*, because it is the first part of the medium leading from the location of the customer.

The CSU/DSU or modem controls the rate at which data moves onto the local loop. It also provides the *clocking signal* to the router. The CSU/DSU is data communications equipment (*DCE*). The router, which is responsible for passing the data to the DCE, is data terminal equipment (*DTE*).

The DTE/DCE interface uses various Physical Layer protocols, such as X.21 and *V.35*. These protocols establish the codes and electrical parameters that the router and the CSU/DSU use to communicate with each other.

Refer to
Figure
in online course

Technology continuously develops and improves signaling standards that enable increased speed and traffic.

When choosing a WAN technology, it is important to consider the link speed. The first digital networks created for WAN implementations provided support for a 64 kbps connection across a leased line. The term digital signal level 0 (*DS0*) refers to this standard.

As technology improved, service providers supplied subscribers with specific increments of the DS0 channel. For example, in North America, a *DS1* standard, also called a T1 line, defines a single line that supports 24 DS0s, plus an 8 kbps overhead channel. This standard enables speeds of up to 1.544 Mbps. A T3 line uses a *DS3* standard, which supports 28 DS1s and speeds of up to 44.736 Mbps.

Other parts of the world use different standards. For example, Europe offers lines such as E1s, which support 32 DS0s for a speed of up to 2.048 Mbps, and E3s, which support 16 E1s for a speed of up to 34.064 Mbps.

Refer to
Interactive Graphic
in online course.

Full Screen

Activity

Match the WAN term to the definition.

7.1.2 WAN Standards

Refer to
Figure
in online course

Designing a network based on specific standards ensures that all of the different devices and technologies found in a WAN environment work together.

WAN standards describe the Physical Layer and Data Link Layer characteristics of data transportation. Data Link Layer WAN standards include parameters such as *physical addressing*, *flow control*, and *encapsulation* type, as well as how the information moves across the WAN link. The type of WAN technology employed determines the specific Data Link Layer standards used. Some examples of Layer 2 WAN protocols are:

- Link Access Procedure for Frame Relay (LAPF)
- High-level Data Link Control (*HDLC*)
- Point-to-Point Protocol (PPP)

Several organizations are responsible for managing both the Physical Layer and Data Link Layer WAN standards. These include:

- International Telecommunications Union Telecommunications Standardization Sector (ITU-T)

- International Organization for Standardization (ISO)

- Internet Engineering Task Force (IETF)

- Electronics Industry Alliance (EIA)

- Telecommunications Industry Association (TIA)

> Refer to
> **Interactive Graphic**
> in online course.

Full Screen

Activity

Determine whether the standards are part of Layer 1 or Layer 2.

7.1.3 Accessing the WAN

> Refer to
> **Figure**
> in online course

WAN links use either digital or analog technology. With analog connections, the data is encoded, or *modulated*, onto a *carrier wave*. The modulated signal then carries the information across the medium to the remote site. At the remote site, the signal is demodulated and the receiver extracts the information.

A modem encodes the information onto that carrier wave before transmission and then decodes it at the receiving end. The modem gets its name from its task of modulation and demodulation of the carrier signal.

Modems enable remote sites to communicate through the plain old telephone system (*POTS*). They also enable end users to connect to service provider networks through DSL or cable connections.

> Refer to
> **Figure**
> in online course

Companies often purchase connectivty using dedicated links between their location and the ISP. These services are often obtained using leased lines for which the companies pay monthly for these services. These lines carry large amounts of data. For example, a T1 link carries 1.544 Mbps of traffic and an E1 link carries 2.048 Mbps of traffic. Often this bandwidth is larger than the amount that the organization actually requires. A T1 can be split into 24 DS0s of 64 Kbps each. In this case, the customer is ordering part of a T1/E1, or a fractional T1 or *fractional E1*.

High-bandwidth connections are split up into several DS0s. The ISP assigns each DS0 to a different conversation or end user. Organizations purchase one or more DS0 channels. A DS0 is not a separate physical entity but rather a *time slice* of the physical bandwidth on one wire. Each fractional connection enables full use of the media by the organization for part of the total time. There are two techniques in which information from multiple channels can be allocated bandwidth on a single cable based on time: Time Division Multiplexing (*TDM*) and Statistical-Time Division Multiplexing (*STDM*).

> Refer to
> **Figure**
> in online course

Time Division Multiplexing (TDM) allocates bandwidth based on pre-assigned time slots. Each of these time slices are then assigned to individual conversations. Each time slice represents a period of time during which a conversation has complete use of the physical media. Bandwidth is allocated to each channel or time slot regardless of whether the station using the channel has data to transmit. Therefore, with standard TDM, if a sender has nothing to say, its time slice goes unused, wasting valuable bandwidth.

Statistical Time Division Multiplexing (STDM) is similar to TDM except that it keeps track of conversations that require extra bandwidth. It then dynamically reassigns unused time slices on an as-needed basis. In this way, STDM minimizes wasted bandwidth.

> Refer to
> **Interactive Graphic**
> in online course.

Full Screen Activity

Drag the data blocks into the correct order to show how TDM and STDM use bandwidth.

7.1.4 Packet and Circuit Switching

Refer to
Figure
in online course

An enterprise connects to WAN services in various ways.

Dedicated Leased Line

One type of connection is a point-to-point serial link between two routers using a dedicated leased line. This enables a one-to-one connection for the basic function of data delivery across a link. Each link requires a separate physical interface and a separate CSU/DSU. As an organization grows to multiple locations, supporting a dedicated leased line between each location becomes very expensive.

Circuit Switching

Circuit switching establishes a circuit between end nodes before forwarding any data. A standard telephone call uses this type of connection. While the circuit is in place, it provides dedicated bandwidth between the two points. Completion of the conversation releases the circuit. No other organizations use the circuit until it releases. This method provides a level of security not available in *packet switching* or cell switching technology.

With circuit switching, the service provider assigns links to different connections as the need arises. Costs are incurred for the link only when the connection is active. The cost for circuit switching varies based on usage time and can become quite expensive if the circuit is used often.

Refer to
Figure
in online course

Packet Switching

Packet switching uses bandwidth more efficiently than other types of switching. The data is segmented into packets, with an identifier on each packet. The data is then released into the service provider network. The service provider accepts the data and switches the packet from one node to another until the packet reaches its final destination. The circuit, or pathway, between the source and destination is often a preconfigured link, but it is not an exclusive link. The service provider switches packets from multiple organizations over the same links. Frame Relay is an example of packet switching technology.

Cell Switching

Cell switching is a variation of packet switching. It is capable of transferring voice, video, and data through private and public networks at speeds in excess of 155 Mbps. Asynchronous Transfer Mode (ATM) uses fixed length, 53-byte cells that have 48-bytes of data and a 5-byte header. The small, uniform size of the cells allows them to be switched quickly and efficiently between nodes. An advantage of ATM is that it prevents small messages from being held up behind larger messages. However, for networks handling mainly *segmented data*, ATM introduces a large amount of overhead and actually slows network performance.

Refer to
Figure
in online course

Virtual Circuits

When using packet switching technology, the service provider establishes virtual circuits (VCs). Virtual circuits share the link between devices with traffic from other sources. As a result, the medium is not private during the duration of a connection. There are two types of virtual circuits: switched and permanent.

Switched Virtual Circuit

A switched virtual circuit (*SVC*) is dynamically established between two points when a router requests a transmission. The circuit is set up on demand and torn down when transmission is complete, such as after a file has been downloaded. When establishing an SVC, call set-up information must be sent before transmitting any data. Call clearing information tears down the connection after it is no longer required. This process introduces delays in the network as SVCs are built up and torn down for each conversation.

Permanent Virtual Circuit

A permanent virtual circuit (*PVC*) provides a permanent path to forward data between two points. The service provider must preconfigure the PVCs and they are very seldom broken or disconnected. This eliminates the need for call setup and clearing. They speed the flow of information across the WAN. PVCs also provide the ISP with much greater control over the data-flow patterns and management of their network. PVCs are more popular than SVCs and usually service sites with high-volume, constant flows of traffic. Frame Relay typically uses PVCs.

Refer to **Interactive Graphic** in online course.

Full Screen

Activity

Identify the best WAN connection technology to support the scenario.

7.1.5 Last Mile and Long Range WAN Technologies

Refer to **Figure** in online course

ISPs use several different WAN technologies to connect their subscribers. The connection type used on the local loop, or last mile, may not be the same as the WAN connection type employed within the ISP network or between various ISPs.

Some common last mile technologies are:

- Analog dialup
- Integrated Services Digital Network (ISDN)
- Leased line
- Cable
- Digital Subscriber Line (DSL)
- Frame Relay
- Wireless

Each of these technologies provides advantages and disadvantages for the customer. Not all technologies are available in all locations.

When a service provider receives data, it must forward this data to other remote sites for final delivery to the recipient. These remote sites connect either to the ISP network or pass from ISP to ISP to the recipient. Long-range communications are usually those connections between ISPs or between branch offices in very large companies.

Many different WAN technologies exist that allow the service provider to reliably forward data over great distances. Some of these include ATM, satellite, Frame Relay, and leased lines.

Refer to **Figure** in online course

Enterprises are becoming larger and more dispersed. As a result, applications require more and more bandwidth. This growth requires technologies that support high-speed and high-bandwidth transfer of data over even greater distances.

Synchronous Optical Network (*SONET*) and Synchronous Digital Hierarchy (*SDH*) are standards that allow the movement of large amounts of data over great distances through fiber-optic cables. Both SONET and SDH encapsulate earlier digital transmission standards and support either ATM or Packet over SONET/SDH (*POS*) networking. SDH and SONET are used for moving both voice and data.

One of the newer developments for extremely long-range communications is dense wavelength division multiplexing (*DWDM*). DWDM assigns incoming optical signals to specific frequencies or wavelengths of light. It is also capable of amplifying these wavelengths to boost the signal strength. DWDM can multiplex more than 80 different wavelengths or channels of data onto a single piece of fiber. Each channel is capable of carrying a multiplexed signal at 2.5 Gbps.

De-multiplexed data at the receiving end allows a single piece of fiber to carry many different formats at the same time and at different data rates. For example, DWDM can carry IP, SONET, and ATM data concurrently.

Full Screen

Activity

Match the technology to the description.

Refer to
Interactive Graphic
in online course.

7.2 Comparing Common WAN Encapsulations

7.2.1 Ethernet and WAN Encapsulations

Refer to
Figure
in online course

Encapsulation occurs before data travels across a WAN. The encapsulation conforms to a specific format based on the technology used on the network. Before converting data into bits for transmission across the media, Layer 2 encapsulation adds addressing and control information.

Layer 2 adds header information that is specific to the type of physical network transmission. Within a LAN environment, Ethernet is the most common technology. The Data Link Layer encapsulates the packet into Ethernet frames. The frame headers contain information such as the source and destination MAC addresses, and specific Ethernet controls, like the frame size and timing information.

Similarly, the encapsulation of frames destined for transmission across a WAN link match the technology in use on the link. For example, if using Frame Relay on the link, the type of encapsulation required is Frame Relay-specific.

Refer to
Figure
in online course

The type of Data Link Layer encapsulation is separate from the type of Network Layer encapsulation. As data moves across a network, the Data Link Layer encapsulation may change continuously, whereas the Network Layer encapsulation will not. If this packet must move across the WAN on its way to the final destination, the Layer 2 encapsulation changes to match the technology in use.

Packets exit the LAN by way of the default gateway router. The router strips off the Ethernet frame and then re-encapsulates that data into the correct frame type for the WAN. Conversion of frames received on the WAN interface into the Ethernet frame format occurs before placement on the local network. The router acts as a ***media converter***, by adapting the Data Link Layer frame format to a format that is appropriate to the interface.

The encapsulation type must match on both ends of a point-to-point connection. A Data Link Layer encapsulation includes the following fields:

Flag

- Marks the beginning and end of each frame

Address

- Depends on the encapsulation type
- Not required If the WAN link is point-to-point

Control

- Used to indicate the type of frame

Protocol

- Used to specify the type of encapsulated network layer protocol

- Not present in all WAN encapsulations

Data

- Used as Layer 3 data and IP datagram

Frame Check Sequence (FCS)

- Provides a mechanism to verify that the frame was not damaged in transit

Refer to
Interactive Graphic
in online course.

Full Screen

Activity

Match the Layer 2 encapsulation term to its definition.

7.2.2 HDLC and PPP

Refer to
Figure
in online course

Two of the most common serial line Layer 2 encapsulations are HDLC and PPP.

High-level Data Link Control (HDLC) is a standard ***bit-oriented*** Data Link Layer encapsulation. HDLC uses synchronous serial transmission, which provides error-free communication between two points. HDLC defines a Layer 2 framing structure that allows for flow control and error control using acknowledgments and a windowing scheme. Each frame has the same format, whether it is a data frame or a control frame.

The standard HDLC frame does not contain a field that identifies the type of protocol carried by the frame. For that reason, standards-based HDLC cannot handle multiple protocols across a single link.

Cisco HDLC incorporates an extra field, known as the ***Type field***, which allows multiple Network Layer protocols to share the same link. Use Cisco HDLC encapsulation only when interconnecting Cisco equipment. Cisco HDLC is the default Data Link Layer encapsulation type on Cisco serial links.

Refer to
Figure
in online course

Like HDLC, Point-to-Point Protocol (PPP) is a Data Link Layer encapsulation for serial links. It uses a layered architecture to encapsulate and carry multi-protocol ***datagram***s over a point-to-point link. Because PPP is standards-based, it enables communication between equipment of different vendors.

The following interfaces can support PPP:

- Asynchronous serial

- Synchronous serial

- High-Speed Serial Interface (HSSI)

- Integrated Services Digital Network (ISDN)

PPP has two sub-protocols:

- Link Control Protocol - responsible for establishing, maintaining and terminating the point-to-point link.

- Network Control Protocol - provides interaction with different Network layer protocols.

Refer to **Figure** in online course

Link Control Protocol

PPP uses the Link Control Protocol (*LCP*) to establish, maintain, test, and terminate the point-to-point link. Additionally, LCP negotiates and configures control options on the WAN link. Some of the options that LCP negotiates include:

- Authentication
- Compression
- Error detection
- Multilink
- PPP Callback

LCP also:

- Handles varied packet sizes
- Detects common misconfiguration errors
- Determines when a link is functioning properly and when it is failing

Network Control Protocol

PPP uses the Network Control Protocol (*NCP*) component to encapsulate multiple Network Layer protocols, so that they operate on the same communications link.

Every Network Layer protocol carried on the PPP link requires a separate NCP. For example, IP uses the IP Control Protocol (*IPCP*), and IPX uses the IPX Control Protocol (*IPXCP*). NCPs include fields containing codes that indicate the Network Layer protocol.

PPP sessions progress through three phases: link establishment, authentication (optional), and Network Layer protocol.

Refer to **Figure** in online course

Link-Establishment Phase

PPP sends LCP frames to configure and test the data link. LCP frames contain a configuration option field that negotiates options such as maximum transmission unit (MTU), compression, and link-authentication. If a configuration option is missing, it assumes the default value. Link authentication and link-quality determination tests are optional parameters within the link-establishment phase. A link-quality determination test determines whether the link quality is good enough to bring up Network Layer protocols. Optional parameters, such as these, must be complete before the receipt of a configuration acknowledgment frame. Receipt of the configuration acknowledgement frame completes the Link-Establishment phase.

Authentication Phase (optional)

The authentication phase provides password protection to identify connecting routers. Authentication occurs after the two routers agree to the set parameters but before the NCP Negotiation Phase can begin.

NCP Negotiation Phase

PPP sends NCP packets to choose and configure one or more Network Layer protocols, such as IP or IPX. If LCP closes the link, it informs the Network Layer protocols so that they can take appropriate action. The `show interfaces` command reveals the LCP and NCP states.

When established, the PPP link remains active until the LCP or NCP frames close the link or until an activity timer expires. A user can also terminate the link.

Full Screen

Refer to **Interactive Graphic** in online course.

Activity

Identify the correct location of the PPP components.

7.2.3 Configuring PPP

Refer to
Figure
in online course

On Cisco routers, HDLC is the default encapsulation on serial links. To change the encapsulation and use the features and functions of PPP, use the following command:

encapsulation ppp

- Enables PPP encapsulation on a serial interface.

Once PPP is enabled, optional features such as compression and load balancing can be configured.

compress *[predictor ¦ stac]*

- Enables compression on an interface using either predictor or stacker.

ppp multilink

- Configures load balancing across multiple links.

Compressing data sent across the network can improve network performance. Predictor and stacker are software compression techniques that vary in the way compression is handled. Stacker compression is more CPU-intensive and less memory-intensive. Predictor is more memory-intensive and less CPU-intensive. For this reason, generally use stacker if the bottleneck is due to line bandwidth issues and predictor if the bottleneck is due to excessive load on the router.

Only use compression if network performance issues exist because enabling it will increase router processing times and overhead. Also, do not use compression if the majority of traffic crossing the network is already-compressed files. Compressing an already-compressed file often increases its size.

Enabling PPP multilink allows for multiple WAN links to be aggregated into one logical channel for the transport of traffic. It enables the load-balancing of traffic from different links and allows some level of redundancy in case of a line failure on a single link.

Refer to
Figure
in online course

The following commands are used to verify and troubleshoot HDLC and PPP encapsulation:

show interfaces serial

- Displays the encapsulation and the states of the Link Control Protocol (LCP).

show controllers

- Indicates the state of the interface channels and whether a cable is attached to the interface.

debug serial interface

- Verifies the incrementation of keepalive packets. If packets are not incrementing, a possible timing problem exists on the interface card or in the network.

debug ppp

- Provides information about the various stages of the PPP process, including negotiation and authentication.

Refer to
Lab Activity
for this chapter

Lab Activity

Configure and verify a PPP connection between two routers.

7.2.4 PPP Authentication

Refer to
Figure
in online course

Authentication on a PPP link is optional. If configured, authentication occurs after establishment of the link but before the Network Layer protocol configuration phase begins. Two possible types of authentication on a PPP link are Password Authentication Protocol (**PAP**) and Challenge Handshake Authentication Protocol (**CHAP**).

PAP provides a simple method for a remote device to establish its identity. PAP uses a ***two-way handshake*** to send its username and password. The called device looks up the username of the calling device and confirms that the sent password matches what it has stored in its database. If the two passwords match, authentication is successful.

PAP sends the username/password pair across the link repeatedly in clear text until acknowledgement of the authentication or termination of the connection. This authentication method does not protect the username and password from being stolen using a packet sniffer.

Additionally, the remote node is in control of the frequency and timing of the login attempts. Once authenticated, no further verification of the remote device occurs. Without ongoing verification, the link is vulnerable to ***hijacking*** of the authenticated connection and the possibility of a hacker gaining illegal authorized access to the router using a ***replay attack***.

Refer to **Figure** in online course

Another form of PPP authentication is Challenge Handshake Authentication Protocol (CHAP).

Challenge Handshake Authentication Protocol

CHAP is a more secure authentication process than PAP. CHAP does not send the password across the link. Authentication occurs both during initial link establishment and repeatedly during the time the link is active. The called device is in control of the frequency and timing of the authentication, making a hijack attack extremely unlikely.

CHAP uses a ***three-way handshake***.

Step 1.   PPP establishes the link phase.

Step 2.   Local router sends a ***challenge message*** to the remote router.

Step 3.   Remote router uses the challenge and a ***shared secret*** password to generate a one-way hash.

Step 4.   Remote router sends back one-way hash to the local router.

Step 5.   Local router checks the response against its own calculation, using the challenge and the same shared secret.

Step 6.   Local router acknowledges authentication if values match.

Step 7.   Local router immediately terminates connection if the values do not match.

CHAP provides protection against playback attack through a variable challenge value. Because the challenge is unique and random, the resulting hash value is also unique and random. The use of repeated challenges limits the time of exposure to any single attack. The local router or a third-party ***authentication server*** is in control of the frequency and timing of the challenges.

Refer to **Interactive Graphic** in online course.

Activity

Sort the characteristics as belonging to either PAP or CHAP.

7.2.5 Configuring PAP and CHAP

Refer to **Figure** in online course

To configure authentication on a PPP link, use the global configuration commands:

username *name* **password** *password*

- Global configuration command.
- Creates a local database that contains the username and password of the remote device.

- The username must match the hostname of the remote router exactly and is case sensitive.

ppp authentication {*chap* ¦ *chap pap* ¦ *pap chap* ¦ *pap*}

- Interface configuration command.

- Specifies the type of authentication on each interface, such as PAP or CHAP.

- If more than one type is specified, example **chap pap**, the router attempts the first type listed and will only attempt the second if the remote router suggests it.

For CHAP authentication, no other configuration commands are required. However, in Cisco IOS version 11.1 or later, PAP is disabled on the interface by default. This means that the router will not send its own username and password combination just because PAP authentication is enable. Therefore, additional commands are required for PAP:

ppp pap sent-username *name* password *password*

- Interface configuration command.

- Specifies the local username and password combination that should be sent to the remote router.

- This must match what the remote router has configured in the local username and password database.

Refer to
Figure
in online course

With two-way authentication configured, each router authenticates the other. Use **debug** commands on both routers to display the exchange sequence as it occurs.

debug ppp {*authentication* ¦ *packet* ¦ *error* ¦ *negotiation* ¦ *chap* }

Authentication

Displays the authentication exchange sequence

Packet

Displays PPP packets sent and received

Negotiation

Displays packets transmitted during PPP startup, where PPP options are negotiated

Error

Displays protocol errors and statistics associated with PPP connection and negotiation

Chap

Displays CHAP packet exchanges

To turn off **debug**, use the **no** format of each command.

Refer to
Lab Activity
for this chapter

Lab Activity

Configure and verify PAP and CHAP authentication on a PPP link.

7.3 Using Frame Relay

7.3.1 Overview of Frame Relay

Refer to
Figure
in online course

A common Layer 2 WAN encapsulation is Frame Relay. Frame Relay networks are multi-access networks similar to Ethernet except that they do not forward broadcast traffic. Frame Relay is a nonbroadcast multi-access network (NBMA).

Frame Relay uses packet switching technology with variable length packets. It also makes use of STDM for optimum use of the available bandwidth.

The router, or DTE device, normally connects to the service provider via a leased line. It connects via a Frame Relay switch, or DCE device, to the nearest point-of-presence of the service provider. This connection is an *access link*.

The remote router at the destination end of the network is also a DTE device. The connection between the two DTE devices is a virtual circuit (*VC*).

The virtual circuit is typically established using PVCs that the service provider preconfigures. Most service providers discourage or even disallow the use of SVCs in a Frame Relay network.

7.3.2 Frame Relay Functionality

Refer to **Figure** in online course

In an NBMA network, each virtual circuit requires a Layer 2 address for identification. In Frame Relay, this address is the data-link connection identifier (*DLCI*).

The DLCI identifies the VC that data uses to reach a particular destination. The DLCI is stored in the address field of every frame transmitted. The DLCI usually has only local significance and may be different at each end of a VC.

The Layer 2 DLCI is associated with the Layer 3 address of the device at the other end of the VC. Mapping the DLCI to a remote IP address can occur manually or dynamically using a process known as *Inverse ARP*.

Establishing a mapping of DLCI to remote IP address occurs in the following steps:

Step 1.   The local device announces its presence by sending its Layer 3 address out on the VC.

Step 2.   The remote device receives this information and maps the Layer 3 IP address to the local Layer 2 DLCI.

Step 3.   The remote device announces its IP address on the VC.

Step 4.   The local device maps the Layer 3 address of the remote device to the local DLCI on which it received the information.

Refer to **Figure** in online course

Local Management Interface (*LMI*) is a signaling standard between the DTE and the Frame Relay switch. LMI reports the status of PVCs between devices.

LMI messages provide communication and synchronization between the network and the user device. They periodically report the existence of new PVCs and the deletion of existing PVCs. They also provide information about PVC integrity. VC status messages prevent data being sent to PVCs that no longer exist.

LMI provides VC connection status information that appears in the Frame Relay map table:

Active State

- The connection is active and routers can exchange data.

Inactive State

- The local connection to the FR switch is working but the remote connection to the FR switch is not.

Deleted State

- The local connection receives no LMI messages from the FR switch or there is no service between the CPE router and the FR switch.

Refer to
Figure
in online course

When an end user subscribes to a Frame Relay service, the user negotiates certain service parameters with the provider.

One parameter is the committed information rate (*CIR*). The CIR is the minimum bandwidth rate guaranteed by the provider for data on a VC.

The service provider calculates the CIR as the average amount of data transmitted over a period of time. The calculated time interval is the committed time (*Tc*). The number of committed bits within the Tc is the committed burst (*Bc*). The cost of the Frame Relay service depends on the speed of the link and the CIR.

The CIR defines the minimum rate provided; however, if there is no congestion on the links, the service provider boosts or bursts the bandwidth up to a second agreed-upon bandwidth.

The excess information rate (*EIR*) is the average rate above the CIR that a VC can support when no network congestion exists. Any extra bits above the committed burst, up to the maximum speed of the access link, is known as the excess burst (*Be*).

Frames transmitted above the speed of the CIR are uncommitted, but are forwarded if the network supports it. These extra fames are marked as discard eligible (*DE*). If congestion occurs, the provider first drops frames with the DE bit set.

Users often pay for a lower CIR, counting on the fact that the service provider supplies higher bandwidth and bursts their traffic when there is no congestion.

Refer to
Figure
in online course

The forward explicit congestion notification (*FECN*) is a single-bit field that can be set to a value of 1 by a switch. It indicates to an end DTE device that the network is congested ahead.

The backward explicit congestion notification (*BECN*) is a single-bit field that, when set to a value of 1 by a switch, indicates that the network is congested in the opposite direction.

FECN and BECN allow higher-layer protocols to react intelligently to these congestion indicators. For example, the sending device uses BECNs to slow its transmission rate.

Refer to
Interactive Graphic
in online course.

Full Screen Activity

Activity

Match the term to the definition.

Summary

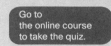

Go to
the online course
to take the quiz.

Quiz

Take the chapter quiz to check your knowledge.

Your Chapter Notes

CHAPTER 8

Filtering Traffic Using Access Control Lists

Introduction

Refer to
Figure
in online course

8.1 Using Access Control Lists

8.1.1 Traffic Filtering

Refer to
Figure
in online course

Security within an enterprise network is extremely critical. It is important to prevent access by unauthorized users and protect the network from various attacks, such as DoS attacks. Unauthorized users can modify, destroy, or steal sensitive data on servers. DoS attacks prevent valid users from accessing facilities. Both of these situations cause a business to lose time and money.

Through *traffic filtering*, an administrator controls traffic in various segments of the network. Filtering is the process of analyzing the contents of a packet to determine if the packet should be allowed or blocked.

Packet filtering can be simple or complex, denying or permitting traffic based on:

- Source IP address

- Destination IP address

- MAC addresses

- Protocols

- Application type

Packet filtering can be compared to junk email filtering. Many email applications allow the user to adjust the configuration to automatically delete email from a particular source address. Packet filtering can be done in the same way by configuring a router to identify unwanted traffic.

Traffic filtering improves network performance. By denying unwanted or restricted traffic close to its source, the traffic does not travel across a network and consume valuable resources.

Refer to
Figure
in online course

Devices most commonly used to provide traffic filtering are:

- Firewalls built into integrated routers

- Dedicated security appliances

- Servers

Some devices only filter traffic that originates from the internal network. More sophisticated security devices recognize and filter known types of attacks from external sources.

Enterprise routers recognize harmful traffic and prevent it from accessing and damaging the network. Nearly all routers filter traffic based on the source and destination IP addresses of packets. They also filter on specific applications and on protocols such as IP, TCP, HTTP, FTP, and Telnet.

8.1.2 Access Control Lists

Refer to **Figure** in online course

One of the most common methods of traffic filtering is the use of access control lists (ACLs). ACLs can be used to manage and filter traffic that enters a network, as well as traffic that exits a network.

An ACL ranges in size from one statement that allows or denies traffic from one source, to hundreds of statements that allow or deny packets from multiple sources. The primary use of ACLs is to identify the types of packets to accept or deny.

ACLs identify traffic for multiple uses such as:

- Specifying internal hosts for NAT
- Identifying or classifying traffic for advanced features such as QoS and queuing
- Restricting the contents of routing updates
- Limiting debug output
- Controlling virtual terminal access to routers

The following potential problems can result from using ACLs:

- The additional load on the router to check all packets means less time to actually forward packets.
- Poorly designed ACLs place an even greater load on the router and might disrupt network usage.
- Improperly placed ACLs block traffic that should be allowed and permit traffic that should be blocked.

8.1.3 Types and Usage of ACLs

Refer to **Figure** in online course

When creating access control lists, a network administrator has several options. The complexity of the design guidelines determines the type of ACL required.

There are three types of ACLs:

Standard ACLs

The *Standard ACL* is the simplest of the three types. When creating a standard IP ACL, the ACLs filter based on the source IP address of a packet. Standard ACLs permit or deny based on the entire protocol, such as IP. So, if a host device is denied by a standard ACL, all services from that host are denied. This type of ACL is useful for allowing all services from a specific user, or LAN, access through a router while denying other IP addresses access. Standard ACLs are identified by the number assigned to them. For access lists permitting or denying IP traffic, the identification number can range from 1 to 99 and from 1300 to 1999.

Extended ACLs

*Extended ACL*s filter not only on the source IP address but also on the destination IP address, protocol, and port numbers. Extended ACLs are used more than Standard ACLs because they are more specific and provide greater control. The range of numbers for Extended ACLs is from 100 to 199 and from 2000 to 2699.

Named ACLs

Named ACLs (***NACL***s) are either Standard or Extended format that are referenced by a descriptive name rather than a number. When configuring named ACLs, the router IOS uses a NACL subcommand mode.

Refer to
Interactive Graphic
in online course.

Activity

Indicate whether the characteristic describes a Standard, Extended, or Named ACL.

8.1.4 ACL Processing

Refer to
Figure
in online course

Access control lists consist of one or more statements. Each statement either ***permits*** or ***denies*** traffic based on specified parameters. Traffic is compared to each statement in the ACL sequentially until a match is found or until there are no more statements.

The last statement of an ACL is always an ***implicit deny***. This statement is automatically inserted at the end of each ACL even though it is not physically present. The implicit deny blocks all traffic. This feature prevents the accidental entry of unwanted traffic.

After creating an access control list, apply it to an interface for it to become effective. The ACL targets traffic that is either inbound or outbound through the interface. If a packet matches a permit statement, it is allowed to enter or exit the router. If it matches a deny statement, it goes no further. An ACL that does not have at least one permit statement blocks all traffic. This is because at the end of every ACL is an implicit deny. Therefore an ACL will deny all traffic not specifically permitted.

Refer to
Figure
in online course

An administrator applies either an inbound or outbound ACL to a router interface. The inbound or outbound direction is always from the perspective of the router. Traffic coming in an interface is inbound and traffic going out an interface is outbound.

When a packet arrives at an interface, the router checks the following parameters:

- Is there an ACL associated with the interface?

- Is the ACL inbound or outbound?

- Does the traffic match the criteria for permitting or denying?

An ACL applied outbound to an interface has no effect on traffic inbound on that same interface.

Each interface of a router can have one ACL per direction for each network protocol. For the IP protocol, one interface can have one ACL inbound and one ACL outbound at the same time.

ACLs applied to an interface add latency to the traffic. Even one long ACL can affect router performance.

Refer to
Interactive Graphic
in online course.

Activity

Determine whether the packet is permitted or denied based on source IP address, interface, and direction.

8.2 Using a Wildcard Mask

8.2.1 ACL Wildcard Mask Purpose and Structure

Refer to
Figure
in online course

Simple ACLs specify only one permitted or denied address. Blocking multiple addresses or ranges of addresses requires using either multiple statements or a wildcard mask. Using an IP network address with a wildcard mask allows much more flexibility. A wildcard mask can block a range of addresses or a whole network with one statement.

A wildcard mask uses 0s to indicate the portion of an IP address that must match exactly and 1s to indicate the portion of the IP address that does not have to match a specific number.

A wildcard mask of 0.0.0.0 requires an exact match on all 32 bits of the IP address. This mask equates to the use of the *host* parameter.

Refer to
Figure
in online course

The wildcard mask used with ACLs functions like the one used in the OSPF routing protocol. However, the purpose of each mask is different. With ACL statements, the wildcard mask specifies a host or range of addresses to be permitted or denied.

When creating an ACL statement, the IP address and wildcard mask become the comparison fields. All packets that enter or exit an interface are compared to each statement of the ACL to determine if there is a match. The wildcard mask determines how many bits of the incoming IP address match the comparison address.

As an example, the following statement permits all hosts from the 192.168.1.0 network and blocks all others:

```
access-list 1 permit 192.168.1.0 0.0.0.255
```

The wildcard mask specifies that only the first three octets must match. Therefore, if the first 24 bits of the incoming packet match the first 24 bits of the comparison field, the packet is permitted. Any packet with a source IP address in the range of 192.168.1.1 to 192.168.1.255 matches the example comparison address and mask combination. All other packets are denied by the ACL implicit **deny an**y statement.

Refer to
Interactive Graphic
in online course.

Full Screen

Activity

Determine the wildcard mask for each ACL statement objective.

8.2.2 Analyzing the Effects of the Wildcard Mask

Refer to
Figure
in online course

When creating an ACL, there are two special parameters that can be used in place of a wildcard mask: host and any.

Host parameter

To filter a single, specific host, use either the wildcard mask 0.0.0.0 after the IP address or the host parameter prior to the IP address.
```
R1(config)#access-list 9 deny 192.168.15.99 0.0.0.0
```
Is the same as:
```
R1(config)#access-list 9 deny host 192.168.15.99
```
Any parameter

To filter all hosts, use the all 1s parameter by configuring a wildcard mask of 255.255.255.255. When using a wildcard mask of 255.255.255.255 all bits are considered matches, therefore, the IP address is typically represented as 0.0.0.0. Another way to filter all hosts is to use the any parameter.
```
R1(config)#access-list 9 permit 0.0.0.0 255.255.255.255
```
Is the same as:
```
R1(config)#access-list 9 permit any
```
Consider the following example that denies a specific host and permits all others:
```
R1(config)#access-list 9 deny host 192.168.15.99
R1(config)#access-list 9 permit any
```
The permit any command permits all traffic not specifically denied in the ACL. When this is configured, no packets will reach the implicit **deny any** at the end of the ACL.

Refer to
Figure
in online course

In an enterprise network with a hierarchical IP addressing scheme, it is often necessary to filter subnet traffic.

If 3 bits are used for subnetting the 192.168.77.0 network, the subnet mask is 255.255.255.224. Subtracting the subnet mask from the all 255s mask results in a wildcard mask of 0.0.0.31. To permit the hosts on the 192.168.77.32 subnet, the ACL statement is:

```
access-list 44 permit 192.168.77.32 0.0.0.31
```

The first 27 bits of each packet match the first 27 bits of the comparison address. The overall range of addresses that this statement permits is from 192.168.77.33 to 192.168.77.63, which is the range of all addresses on the 192.168.77.32 subnet.

Refer to
Figure
in online course

Creating accurate wildcard masks for ACL statements provides the control required to fine-tune traffic flow. Filtering different subnet traffic is the most difficult concept for beginners.

The 192.168.77.0 network, with a subnet mask of 255.255.255.192 or /26, creates the following four subnets:

192.168.77.0/26

192.168.77.64/26

192.168.77.128/26

192.168.77.192/26

To create an ACL to filter any of these four subnets, subtract the subnet mask 255.255.255.192 from the all 255s mask resulting in a wildcard mask of 0.0.0.63. To permit traffic from the first two of these subnets, use two ACL statements:

```
access-list 55 permit 192.168.77.0 0.0.0.63
access-list 55 permit 192.168.77.64 0.0.0.63
```

The first two networks also summarize to 192.168.77.0/25. Subtracting the summarized subnet mask of 255.255.255.128 from the all 255s mask results in a wildcard mask of 0.0.0.127. Using this mask groups these two subnets together into one ACL statement instead of two.

```
access-list 5 permit 192.168.77.0 0.0.0.127
```

Refer to
Interactive Graphic
in online course.

Full Screen

Activity

Determine whether the IP packet is permitted or denied by analyzing the comparison address and wildcard mask.

8.3 Configuring Access Control Lists

8.3.1 Placing Standard and Extended ACLs

Refer to
Figure
in online course

Properly designed access control lists have a positive impact on network performance and availability. Plan the creation and placement of access control lists to maximize this effect.

Planning involves the following steps:

1. Determine the traffic filtering requirements

2. Decide which type of ACL best suits the requirements

3. Determine the router and the interface on which to apply the ACL

4. Determine in which direction to filter traffic

Step 1: Determine Traffic Filtering Requirements

Gather traffic filtering requirements from *stakeholders* from within each department of an enterprise. These requirements differ from enterprise to enterprise and are based on customer needs, traffic types, traffic loads, and security concerns.

Refer to
Figure
in online course

Step 2: Decide Type of ACL to Suit Requirements

The decision to use a Standard ACL or an Extended ACL depends on the filtering requirements of the situation. The choice of ACL type can affect the flexibility of the ACL, as well as the router performance, and network link bandwidth.

Standard ACLs are simple to create and implement. However, standard ACLs only filter based on the source address and will filter all traffic without regard to the type or the destination of the traffic. With routes to multiple networks, a standard ACL placed too close to the source may unintentionally block traffic that should be permitted. Therefore, it is important to place standard ACLs as close to the destination as possible.

When filtering requirements are more complex, use an Extended ACL. Extended ACLs offer more control than Standard ACLs. They filter on source and destination addresses. They also filter by looking at the network layer protocol, transport layer protocol, and port numbers if required. This increased filtering detail allows a network administrator to create ACLs that meet the specific needs of a security plan.

Place an Extended ACL close to the source address. By looking at both the source and destination address, the ACL blocks packets intended for a specific destination network before they leave the source router. The packets are filtered before they cross the network, which helps conserve bandwidth.

Refer to
Figure
in online course

Step 3: Determine Router and Interface for ACL

Place ACLs on routers in either the Access or Distribution Layer. A network administrator must have control of these routers and be able to implement a security policy. A network administrator who does not have access to a router cannot configure an ACL on it.

Selection of the appropriate interface depends on the filtering requirements, the ACL type, and the location of the designated router. It is best to filter traffic before it advances onto a lower bandwidth serial link. The interface selection is usually obvious once the router is chosen.

Step 4: Determine Direction to Filter Traffic

When determining the direction in which to apply an ACL, visualize the traffic flow from the perspective of the router.

Inbound traffic is traffic that is coming into a router interface from outside. The router compares the incoming packet to the ACL before looking up the destination network in the routing table. Packets discarded at this point save the overhead of routing lookups. This makes the inbound access control list more efficient for the router than an outbound access list.

Outbound traffic is inside the router and leaves through an interface. For an outbound packet, the router has already done a routing table lookup and has switched the packet to the correct interface. The packet is compared to the ACL just before leaving the router.

Refer to
Interactive Graphic
in online course.

Full Screen **Activity**

Determine the correct router, interface, and direction for placement of the ACL.

8.3.2 Basic ACL Configuration Process

Refer to
Figure
in online course

After capturing the requirements, planning the access control list, and determining the location, configure the ACL.

Each ACL requires a unique identifier. This identifier can be either a number or a descriptive name.

In numbered access control lists, the number identifies the type of ACL created:

- Standard IP ACLs have numbers in the ranges from 1 to 99 and from 1300 to 1999.

- Extended IP ACLs have numbers in the ranges from 100 to 199 and from 2000 to 2699.

It is also possible to create AppleTalk and IPX ACLs.

The limit for any one router interface is one ACL per protocol per direction. If a router is running IP exclusively, each interface handles a maximum of two ACLs: one inbound and one outbound. Since each ACL compares every packet passing through an interface, ACLs add to latency.

Refer to
Figure
in online course

Configuring an access control list requires two steps: creation and application.

ACL Creation

Enter global configuration mode. Using the **access-list** command, enter the access control list statements. Enter all statements with the same ACL number until the access control list is complete.

The syntax for the Standard ACL statement is:

```
access-list [access-list-number] [deny¦permit] [source address] [source-wildcard][log]
```

Since every packet is compared to every ACL statement until a match is found, the order that statements are placed within the ACL can effect the latency introduced. Therefore, order the statements so that the more common conditions appear in the ACL before the less common ones. For example, statements that find a match for the highest amount of traffic should be placed toward the beginning of the ACL.

Keep in mind, however, that once a match is found, the packet is no longer compared to any other statements within the ACL. This means that if one line permits a packet, but a line further down the ACL denies it, the packet will be permitted. For this reason, plan the ACL so that the more specific requirements appear before more general ones. In other words, deny a specific host of a network before permitting the remainder of the entire network.

Document the function of each section or statement of the ACL using the **remark** command:

```
access-list [list number] remark [text]
```

To delete an ACL, use the command:

```
no access-list [list number]
```

It is not possible to delete a single line from a standard or extended ACL. Instead, the ACL as a whole is deleted and must be replaced in its entirety.

8.3.3 Configuring Numbered Standard ACLs

Refer to
Figure
in online course

An ACL does not filter traffic until it has been applied, or assigned, to an interface.

ACL Application

Assign an ACL to one or more interfaces, specifying either inbound traffic or outbound traffic. Apply a standard ACL as close to the destination as possible.

```
R2(config-if)#ip access-group access list number [in ¦ out]
```

The following commands place access-list 5 on the R2 Fa0/0 interface filtering inbound traffic:

```
R2(config)#interface fastethernet 0/0
R2(config-if)#ip access-group 5 in
```

The default direction for an ACL applied to an interface is **out**. Even though **out** is the default, it is very important to specify the direction to avoid confusion and to ensure that traffic filters in the correct direction.

To remove an ACL from an interface while leaving the ACL intact, use the **no ip access-group** *interface* command.

Several ACL commands evaluate the proper syntax, order of statements, and placement on interfaces.

Refer to
Figure
in online course

show ip interface

- Displays IP interface information and indicates any assigned ACLs.

  show access-lists [*access list number*]

- Displays the contents of all ACLs on the router. It also displays the number of matches for each permit or deny statement since application of the ACL. To see a specific list, add the ACL name or number as an option for this command.

  show running-config

- Displays all configured ACLs on a router, even if they are not currently applied to an interface.

If using numbered ACLs, statements entered after the initial creation of the ACL are added to the end. This order may not yield the desired results. To resolve this issue, remove the original ACL and recreate it.

It is often recommended to create ACLs in a text editor. This allows the ACL to be easily edited and pasted into the router configuration. However, keep in mind when coping and pasting the ACL that it is important to remove the currently applied ACL first, otherwise all statements will be pasted to the end.

Refer to
Interactive Graphic
in online course.

Full Screen Activity

Determine the proper sequence for the ACL configuration statement to achieve the requirements.

Refer to
Lab Activity
for this chapter

Lab Activity

Configure and verify a Standard ACL.

8.3.4 Configuring Numbered Extended ACLs

Refer to
Figure
in online course

Extended ACLs provide a greater range of control than Standard ACLs. The Extended ACL permits or denies access based on source IP address, destination IP address, protocol type, and port numbers. Since Extended ACLs can be very specific, they tend to grow in size quickly. The more statements that an ACL contains, the more difficult it is to manage.

Extended ACLs use an access-list number in the ranges 100 to 199 and 2000 to 2699. The same rules that apply to Standard ACLs also apply to Extended ACLs :

- Configure multiple statements in one ACL.

- Assign the same ACL number to each statement.

- Use the **host** or **any** keywords to represent IP addresses.

A key difference in the Extended ACL syntax is the requirement to specify a protocol after the permit or deny condition. This protocol can be IP, indicating all IP traffic, or it can indicate filtering on a specific IP protocol such as TCP, UDP, ICMP, and OSPF.

Refer to
Figure
in online course

There are often many different ways to meet a set of requirements.

For example, a company has a server with the address of 192.168.3.75. It has the following requirements:

- Allow access to hosts on the 192.168.2.0 LAN.

- Allow access to host 192.168.1.66.

- Deny access to hosts on 192.168.4.0 LAN.

- Permit access to everyone else in the enterprise.

There are at least two possible solutions that satisfy these requirements. When planning the ACL, try to minimize statements where possible.

Some ways to minimize statements and reduce the processing load of the router include:

- Match high volume traffic and deny blocked traffic early in the ACL. This approach ensures that packets do not compare to later statements.

- Consolidate multiple permit and deny statements into a single statement using ranges.

- Consider denying a particular group rather than permitting a larger, opposite group.

Refer to
Interactive Graphic
in online course.

Full Screen

Activity

Based on the ACL, determine if packets are permitted or denied.

Refer to
Lab Activity
for this chapter

Lab Activity

Plan, configure, and verify an Extended ACL.

8.3.5 Configuring Named ACLs

Refer to
Figure
in online course

Cisco IOS versions 11.2 and higher can create Named ACLs (NACLs). In an NACL, a descriptive name replaces the numerical ranges required for Standard and Extended ACLs. Named ACLs offer all the functionality and advantages of Standard and Extended ACLs; only the syntax for creating them is different.

The name given to an ACL is unique. Using capital letters in the name makes it easier to recognize in router command output and troubleshooting.

A Named ACL is created with the command:

```
ip access-list {standard | extended} name
```

After issuing this command, the router switches to NACL configuration subcommand mode. After the initial naming command, enter all permit and deny statements, one at a time. NACLs use Standard or Extended ACL command syntax starting with the permit or deny statement.

Apply a Named ACL to an interface in the same manner as applying a Standard or Extended ACL.

The commands that help with evaluating Named ACLs for proper syntax, order of statements, and placement on interfaces are the same as the commands for Standard ACLs.

Refer to
Figure
in online course

Editing ACLs with older versions of IOS make it necessary to:

- Copy the ACL to a text editor.

- Remove the ACL from the router.

- Recreate and apply the edited version.

Unfortunately, this process allows all traffic to flow through the interface during the editing cycle, thereby leaving the network open to potential security breaches.

With current versions of the IOS, edit numbered and Named ACLs using the `ip access-list` command. ACLs display with the lines numbered as 10, 20, 30, and so forth. To see the line numbers, use the command:

`show access-lists`

To edit an existing line:

- Remove the line using the `no line number` command.
- Re-add the same line using its line number.

To insert a new line between existing lines 20 and 30:

- Issue the **new ACL** statement, starting with a number between the two existing lines, such as 25.

Refer to **Packet Tracer Activity** for this chapter

Issue the `show access-lists` command to display the lines re-sorted and renumbered by 10s.

Packet Tracer Activity

Configure and verify a Standard Named ACL.

Refer to **Lab Activity** for this chapter

Lab Activity

Configure and verify an Extended Named ACL.

8.3.6 Configure Router VTY Access

Refer to **Figure** in online course

Network administrators often need to configure a router located at a remote location. To log into the remote router, they use a program such as Telnet or a Secure Shell (SSH) client. Telnet transmits username and password in plain text and, therefore, is not very secure. SSH transmits the username and password information in an encrypted format.

When a network administrator connects to a remote router using Telnet, the router initiates an inbound session. Telnet and SSH are in-band network management tools and require the IP protocol and a network connection to the router.

The purpose of restricting virtual teletype terminal (VTY) access is to increase network security. Outside intruders may attempt to gain access to a router. If an access control list is not in place on the router virtual port, anyone who can determine the Telnet username and password can gain entry. If an ACL is applied to the router vty port that permits only specific IP addresses, anyone trying to telnet to the router from an IP address not permitted in the ACL will be denied access. Keep in mind, however, that this can create issues if the administrator must connect to the router from different locations using different IP addresses.

Refer to **Figure** in online course

The process used to create the VTY access control list is the same as for an interface. However, applying the ACL to a VTY line uses a different command. Instead of using the `ip access-group` command, use the `access-class` command.

Follow these guidelines when configuring access lists on VTY lines:

- Apply a numbered ACL, not a Named ACL, to the VTY lines.
- Place identical restrictions on all VTY lines, because it is not possible to control the line on which a user may connect.

VTY sessions are established between the Telnet client software and the destination router. The network administrator establishes a session with the destination router, enters a username and password, and makes configuration changes.

Refer to
Lab Activity
for this chapter

Lab Activity

Configure and verify router VTY restrictions.

Refer to **Packet Tracer Activity**
for this chapter

Packet Tracer Activity

Plan, configure, and verify Standard, Extended, and Named ACLs.

8.4 Permitting and Denying Specific Types of Traffic

8.4.1 Configuring ACLs for Application and Port Filtering

Refer to
Figure
in online course

Extended ACLs filter on source and destination IP addresses. It is often desirable to filter on even more specific packet details. OSI Layer 3 network protocol, Layer 4 transport protocols and application ports provide this capability.

Some of the protocols available to use for filtering include IP, TCP, UDP, and ICMP.

Extended ACLs also filter on destination port numbers. These port numbers describe the application or service required by the packet. Each application has a registered port number assigned.

The router must investigate the Ethernet frame to extract all of the IP addresses and port number information required for comparison with ACLs.

In addition to entering port numbers, it is necessary to specify a condition before the statement is matched. The abbreviations most commonly used are:

- **eq** - equals
- **gt** - greater than
- **lt** - less than

Consider the following example:

`R1(config)#access-list 122 permit tcp 192.168.1.0 0.0.0.255 host 192.168.2.89 eq 80`

This ACL statement permits traffic from 192.168.1.0 that is requesting HTTP access using port 80. If a user attempts to telnet or FTP into host 192.168.2.89, the user is denied due to the implicit deny statement assumed at the end of every access list.

Refer to
Figure
in online course

Filtering based on a particular application requires knowledge of the port number for that application. Applications are associated with both a port number and a name. An ACL can reference port 80 or HTTP.

If neither the port number nor the name is known for an application, try these steps for locating that information:

Step 1.   Research one of the IP addressing registry sites on the web, such as http://www.iana.org/

Step 2.   Refer to the software documentation.

Step 3.   Refer to the website of the application vendor.

Step 4.   Use a packet sniffer and capture data from the application.

Step 5.   Use the **?** option in the **access-list** command. The list includes well-known port names and numbers for the TCP protocol.

Some applications use more than one port number. For example, FTP data transmits using port 20, but the session control that makes FTP possible uses port 21. To deny all FTP traffic, deny both ports.

To accommodate multiple port numbers, Cisco IOS ACLs filter a range of ports. Use the gt, lt, or range operators in the ACL statement to accomplish this. For example, two FTP ACL statements can filter into one with the command:

```
R1(config)#access-list 181 deny tcp any 192.168.77.0 0.0.0.255 range 20 21
```

Packet Tracer Activity

Configure and verify Extended ACLs that filter on port numbers.

8.4.2 Configuring ACLs to Support Established Traffic

Refer to
Figure
in online course

ACLs are often created to protect an internal network from outside sources. However, while protecting the internal network, it should still allow internal users access to all resources. When internal users access external resources, those requested resources must pass through the ACL. For example, should an internal user wish to establish a connection with an external web server, the ACL must permit the requested html packets. Due to the ACLs use of implicit deny, resources must be specifically permitted by the ACL. Individual permit statements for all possible requested resources can result in a long ACL and leave security holes.

To resolve this issue, it is possible to create a single statement that permits internal users to establish a TCP session with external resources. Once the TCP three-way handshake is accomplished and the connection is established, all packets sent between the two devices will be permitted. To accomplish this, use the keyword: established.

```
access-list 101 permit tcp any any established
```

Using this statement, all external tcp packets will be permitted under the condition that they are responses to internal requests. Permitting the incoming responses to established communications is a form of Stateful Packet Inspection (SPI).

In addition to established traffic, it may be necessary for an internal user to ping external devices. It is not desirable, however, to allow external users to ping or trace a device on the inside network. In this case, a statement using the keywords **echo-reply** and **unreachable** can be written to permit ping responses and unreachable messages. A ping originating from external sources, however, will be denied unless specifically permitted in another statement.

Refer to
Interactive Graphic
in online course.

Activity

Determine if the packet is allowed or blocked based on source and destination address, packet type, and the ACLs.

8.4.3 Effects of NAT and PAT on ACL Placement

Refer to
Figure
in online course

Implementing NAT and PAT may create a problem when planning ACLs. Network administrators need to account for the address translation when creating and applying ACLs to interfaces where NAT occurs.

When using NAT with ACLs, it is important to know how they interact in the router.

Step 1.   If the packet comes inbound into a NAT outside interface, the router:

■ Applies the inbound ACL

- Translates the destination address from outside to inside, or global to local
- Routes the packet

    Step 2.   If the packet goes outbound through a NAT outside interface, the router:

- Translates the source address from inside to outside, or local to global
- Applies outbound ACL

Plan the ACL so that it filters either the private or public addresses, depending on the relationship with NAT. If traffic is inbound or outbound on a NAT outside interface, the addresses to filter are the public ones.

Refer to
Lab Activity
for this chapter

Lab Activity

Configure an ACL with NAT.

8.4.4 Analyzing Network ACLs and Placement

Refer to
Figure
in online course

Network administrators evaluate the effect of every statement in an ACL prior to implementation. An improperly designed ACL can immediately cause problems when it is applied to an interface. These problems range from a false sense of security to an unnecessary load on a router or even a non-functioning network.

Administrators need to examine the ACL, one line at a time, and answer the following questions:

- What service does the statement deny?
- What is the source and what is the destination?
- What port numbers are denied?
- What would happen if the ACL was moved to another interface?
- What would happen if the ACL filtered traffic in a different direction?
- Is NAT an issue?

When evaluating an Extended ACL, it is important to remember these key points:

- The keyword **tcp** permits or denies protocols like FTP, HTTP, Telnet, and so on.
- The key phrase **permit ip** is used to permit all IP, including any TCP, UDP, and ICMP protocols.

Refer to
Interactive Graphic
in online course.

Full Screen **Activity**

Create an Extended ACL based on the requirements and the network topology shown. Some components are not used.

8.4.5 Configuring ACLs with Inter-VLAN Routing

Refer to
Figure
in online course

When routing between VLANs in a network, it is sometimes necessary to control traffic from one VLAN to another using ACLs.

Apply ACLs directly to VLAN interfaces or subinterfaces on a router just as with physical interfaces.

Enterprise networks typically have servers on a different VLAN than user groups. In such cases, access to the server VLAN requires filtering.

All rules and guidelines for creation and application are the same for ACLs on subinterfaces as they are for physical interfaces.

Refer to Lab Activity for this chapter

Lab Activity

Configure and verify ACLs to filter inter-VLAN traffic.

Refer to Packet Tracer Activity for this chapter

Packet Tracer Activity

Configure and verify an Extended ACL that creates a DMZ and protects the corporate network.

8.5 Filtering Traffic Using Access Control Lists

8.5.1 Using Logging to Verify ACL Functionality

Refer to Figure in online course

After writing an ACL and applying it to an interface, a network administrator evaluates the number of matches. When the fields of an incoming packet are equal to all ACL comparison fields, this is a match. Viewing the number of matches helps to identify whether the ACL statements are having the desired effect.

By default, an ACL statement captures the number of matches and displays them at the end of each statement. View the matches using the following command:

`show access-list`

The basic match counts that are displayed with the `show access-list` command provide the number of ACL statements matched and the number of packets processed. The output does not indicate the source or destination of the packet or the protocols in use.

For additional details on packets permitted or denied, activate a process called *logging*. Logging activates for individual ACL statements. To activate this feature, add the `log` option to the end of each ACL statement to be tracked.

Use logging for a short time only to complete testing of the ACL. The process of logging events places an additional load on the router.

Refer to Figure in online course

Logging to the console uses router memory, which is a limited resource. Instead, configure a router to send logging messages to an external server. These messages, called `syslog` messages, allow the user to view them both, in real time or at a later date.

The message types include eight message severity levels. The levels range from 0, representing an emergency or an unusable system, to level 7, representing informational messages such as debugging.

ACL logging generates an informational message that contains:

- ACL number
- Packet permitted or denied
- Source and destination addresses
- Number of packets

The message generates for the first packet that matches and then at 5-minute intervals.

To turn off logging, use:

`no logging console`

To turn off all debugging, use:

```
undebug all
```

Refer to
Lab Activity
for this chapter

To turn off specific debugging, such as `ip packet`, use:

```
no debug ip packet
```

Lab Activity

Configure ACLs and verify using the `show access-lists` command and console logging.

8.5.2 Analyzing Router Logs

Refer to
Figure
in online course

Logging to the console uses router memory, which is a limited resource. Instead, configure a router to send logging, sometimes called *syslog* messages, to an external server. This method allows viewing the messages in real time and also at a later time.

Types of reported events include the status of:

- Router interfaces
- Protocols in use
- Bandwidth usage
- ACL messages
- Configuration events

It is advisable to include the option to notify a network administrator by email, pager, or cell phone when a critical event occurs.

Other configurable options include:

- Providing notification of new messages received
- Sorting and grouping messages
- Filtering messages by severity
- Removal of all or selected messages

Syslog software is available from many resources. The level of reporting and ease of use vary with the price, but there are also several free programs available on the Internet.

Syslog is a protocol supported by all network equipment, including switches, routers, firewalls, storage systems, modems, wireless devices, and UNIX hosts.

Refer to
Figure
in online course

To use a syslog server, install the software on a Windows, Linux, UNIX, or MAC OS server and configure the router to send logged events to the syslog server.

A sample of the command that specifies the IP address of the host where the syslog server is installed is:

```
logging 192.168.3.11
```

When troubleshooting a problem, always set the service timestamps for logging. Be sure the router date and time are set correctly so that log files display the proper time stamp.

Use the show clock command to check the date and time setting.

```
R1>show clock
*00:03:45.213 UTC Mon Mar 1 2007
```

To set the clock, first set the time zone. Base the time zone on Greenwich Mean Time (*GMT*) and then set the clock. Note that the `clock set` command is not used in configuration mode.

To set the time zone:

`R1(config)#clock timezone CST -6`

To set the clock:

`R1#clock set 10:25:00 Sep 10 2007`

Refer to
Lab Activity
for this chapter

Lab Activity

Configure ACLs and download a syslog server to record ACL activity.

8.5.3 ACL Best Practices

Refer to
Figure
in online course

ACLs are a very powerful filtering tool. They are active immediately after application onto an interface.

It is far better to spend extra time planning and troubleshooting before applying an ACL, than trying to troubleshoot after applying the ACL.

Always test basic connectivity before applying ACLs. If pinging a host is unsuccessful because of a bad cable or an IP configuration problem, the ACL can compound the problem and make it harder to troubleshoot.

When logging, add the **deny ip any** statement to end of ACL. This statement allows tracking the number of matches for packets denied.

Use the **reload in 30** command when working with remote routers and testing ACL functionality. If a mistake in an ACL blocks access to the router, remote connectivity may be denied. Using this command, the router reloads in 30 minutes and reverts to the startup configuration. When satisfied with how the ACL is functioning, copy the running configuration to the startup configuration.

Summary

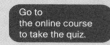

Quiz

Take the chapter quiz to check your knowledge.

Your Chapter Notes

Introduction

Refer to
Figure
in online course

9.1 Understanding the Impact of Network Failure

9.1.1 Enterprise Network Requirements

Refer to
Figure
in online course

Most enterprises rely on their networks to provide consistent and reliable access to shared resources. Network uptime is the time that the network is available and functioning as expected. Network downtime is any time that the network is not performing as required. A reduction in the performance level of the network may have a negative impact on the business.

Without a reliable network, many organizations lose access to customer databases and accounting records that employees need to perform their daily activities. Network outages also prevent customers from placing orders or obtaining the information they require. Downtime results in lost productivity, customer frustration, and often the loss of customers to competitors.

Refer to
Figure
in online course

Many different metrics are used to determine the cost of downtime to an enterprise. The actual cost to a company varies depending on the day, date, and time.

Large enterprises generally span many different time zones and have employees, customers, and suppliers accessing their network around the clock. For these organizations, any downtime is extremely costly. Many factors cause network downtime. These include:

- Weather and natural disasters
- Security breaches
- Man-made disasters
- Power surges
- Virus attacks
- Equipment failure
- Misconfiguration of devices
- Lack of resources

Refer to
Figure
in online course

A well-planned network design and implementation are crucial for meeting uptime requirements.

To ensure the proper and efficient flow of traffic, a good design includes redundancy of all critical components and data paths. This redundancy eliminates single points of failure.

The three-layer hierarchical network design model separates the functionality of the various networking devices and links. This separation ensures efficient network performance. In addition, the use of enterprise class equipment provides a high degree of reliability.

Even with proper network design, some downtime is inevitable. To keep downtime to a minimum and ensure rapid recovery requires additional considerations.

To guarantee service levels, an enterprise should have service level agreements (SLAs) with key suppliers. An SLA clearly documents network expectations in terms of level of service. These expectations include the acceptable level of downtime as well as the recovery period. SLAs often specify the penalty associated with any loss of service.

Refer to
Figure
in online course

Outages are not only associated with loss of service from ISPs. Quite often, the problem stems from the failure of a key piece of equipment that is part of the local network. To minimize this type of downtime requires warrantees on all critical pieces of equipment. Warrantees provide for rapid replacement of mission-critical components.

Business continuity plans provide a detailed plan of action in case of unexpected man-made or natural disasters such as power failures or earthquakes. Business continuity plans provide the details on how the business continues or resumes operations, with minimal disruption to its clients, after the disaster. They clearly specify how the network re-establishes functionality in the event of a catastrophic failure. One way to ensure functionality is to have a redundant backup site at another location, in case of failure at the primary site.

9.1.2 Monitoring and Proactive Maintenance

Refer to
Figure
in online course

One way of ensuring uptime is to monitor current network functionality and perform *proactive maintenance*.

The purpose of network monitoring is to watch network performance in comparison to a predetermined *baseline*. Any observed deviations from this baseline indicate potential problems with the network and require investigation. As soon as the network administrator determines the cause of degraded performance, corrective actions can be taken to prevent a serious network outage.

Several groups of tools are available for monitoring network performance levels and gathering data. These tools include:

- Network utilities
- Packet sniffing tools
- SNMP monitoring tools

Each of these groups of tools has different capabilities and provides different types of information. Using these tools in combination provides comprehensive information on current network performance.

A network administrator performs proactive maintenance on a regular basis to verify and service equipment. By doing this, the administrator can detect weaknesses prior to a critical error that could bring down the network. Like regular servicing on a car, proactive maintenance extends the life of a network device.

Refer to
Figure
in online course

Network monitoring tools, techniques, and programs rely on the availability of a complete set of accurate and current network documentation. This documentation includes:

- Physical and logical topology diagrams
- Configuration files of all network devices

■ A baseline performance level

It is best practice to determine baseline network performance levels when the network is first installed and then again after any major changes or upgrades occur. Network administrators perform baseline testing of the network under normal load levels, using the protocols and applications that are normally encountered on the network.

Many complex tools and procedures exist to determine performance baselines. Some programs perform many different tests with different types of traffic. The tests determine the network performance under very accurately defined loads and conditions. Others, such as a simple ping, are less accurate but often provide sufficient information to alert the administrator to a problem.

Refer to
Figure
in online course

Simple network utilities, like `ping` and `tracert`, provide information on the performance of the network or network link. Performing these commands at multiple times shows the difference in time required for a packet to travel between two locations. Using these commands, however, does not provide a reason for the difference in times.

Packet sniffing tools monitor the types of traffic on various parts of the network. These tools indicate if there is an excessive amount of a particular traffic type. They examine the contents of the packets, which provides a quick way of locating the source of this traffic.

These tools may also be able to remedy the situation before network congestion becomes critical. For example, traffic sniffing can detect whether a type of traffic or a particular transaction occurring on the network is unexpected. This detection might stop a potential denial of service attack before it impacts network performance.

Refer to
Figure
in online course

Simple Network Management Protocol (***SNMP***) allows monitoring of individual devices on the network. SNMP-compliant devices use agents to monitor a number of predefined parameters for specific conditions. These agents collect information and store it in a database known as the management information base (***MIB***).

SNMP polls devices at regular intervals to collect information about managed parameters. SNMP also traps certain events that exceed a predefined ***threshold*** or condition.

For example, SNMP monitors a router interface for errors. The network administrator defines a specific level of acceptable errors for that interface. If the errors exceed the threshold level, SNMP traps the condition and sends it to a network management station (***NMS***). The NMS alerts the network administrator. Some SNMP systems trigger events, such as the automatic reconfiguration of a device, to eliminate the problem. Most enterprise class network management systems use SNMP.

A number of freeware and commercial proactive network monitoring tools exist. These tools monitor traffic type, traffic load, server configurations, traffic patterns, and a multitude of other conditions. A proper ***Network Monitoring Plan*** and the use of proper tools help a network administrator evaluate the health of the network and detect any problem situations.

Refer to **Packet
Tracer Activity**
for this chapter

Packet Tracer Activity

Design a network and create a baseline.

9.1.3 Troubleshooting and the Failure Domain

Refer to
Figure
in online course

The objective of any troubleshooting effort is to return functionality quickly and with little disruption to the end users. Achieving this objective often means postponing an extensive or prolonged process for determining the cause of a problem in favor of quickly re-establishing functionality.

In some situations, putting a temporary solution into place allows investigation and correction of the problem under a less critical time constraint.

Redundancy is a key design element for enterprise networks. In a redundant environment, if one link goes down, traffic diversion to the redundant link occurs immediately. This temporary solution allows the network to maintain functionality and gives the administrator time to diagnose and correct the problem with the failed link. If problems occur with a specific device or configuration, having backup copies of the configuration files or spare devices allows quick restoration of connectivity.

Refer to **Figure** in online course

Quick solutions are not always possible or appropriate. The security of the network and the resources that it houses must always be the highest priority. If a quick fix compromises this security, take the time to investigate an alternative solution that is more appropriate.

Detail security concerns in the business continuity plan. The plan includes:

- Documentation of potential problems

- Description of the appropriate course of action in the event of problems

- Details of the security policy of the company

- Details of the security risks of the actions

When designing an enterprise network limit the size of a failure domain. The failure domain is the area of the network that is impacted by the failure or misconfiguration of a network device. The actual size of the domain depends on the device and the type of failure or misconfiguration. When troubleshooting a network, determine the scope of the issue and isolate the issue to a specific failure domain.

Refer to **Figure** in online course

If both a Layer 2 switch and a border router fail at the same time, they affect different failure domains.

The failure of a Layer 2 switch on a LAN segment only affects user in the broadcast domain. It has no affect on other regions of the network. Failure of a border router, however, prevents all users in the company from connecting to network resources outside of their local network.

The router has a larger impact on the network, it has a larger failure domain. Under normal circumstances, troubleshoot resources with the larger failure domains first.

In some circumstances, the size of the failure domain is not the deciding factor in troubleshooting. If a business critical server is connected to a failed switch, correction of this issue may take precedence over the border router.

Refer to **Interactive Graphic** in online course.

Full Screen Activity

Determine how many hosts are unable to connect to the Internet when each router fails.

9.1.4 Troubleshooting Process

Refer to **Figure** in online course

When a problem occurs on an enterprise network, troubleshooting that problem quickly and efficiently is very important to avoid extended periods of downtime. Many different structured and unstructured problem-solving techniques are available to the network technician. These include:

- *Top-down*

- *Bottom-up*

- *Divide-and-conquer*

- *Trial-and-error*

- *Substitution*

Most experienced network technicians rely on the knowledge gained from past experience and start the troubleshooting process using a trial-and-error approach. Correcting the problem in this manner saves a great deal of time.

Unfortunately, less experienced technicians cannot rely solely on previous experience. Additionally, many times the trial-and-error approach does not provide a solution. Both of these cases require a more structured approach to troubleshooting.

Refer to
Figure
in online course

When a situation requires a more structured approach, most network personnel use a layered process based on the OSI or TCP/IP models. The technician uses previous experience to determine if the issue is associated with the lower layers of the OSI model or the upper layers. The layer dictates whether a top-down or bottom-up approach is appropriate.

When approaching a problem situation, follow the generic problem-solving model, regardless of the type of troubleshooting technique used.

- Define the problem

- Gather facts

- Deduce possibilities and alternatives

- Design plan of action

- Implement solution

- Analyze results

If the first pass through this procedure does not determine and correct the problem, repeat the process as necessary.

Document the initial symptoms and all attempts at finding and correcting the cause. This documentation serves as a valuable resource should the same or similar problem occur again. It is important to document even failed attempts, to save time during future troubleshooting activities.

Refer to
Interactive Graphic
in online course.

Full Screen

Activity

Match each problem to the OSI model layer with which it is best associated.

9.2 Troubleshooting Switching and Connectivity Issues

9.2.1 Troubleshooting Basic Switching

Refer to
Figure
in online course

Switches are currently the most commonly used Access Layer networking device. Workstations, printers, and servers connect into the network through switches. Faults with the switch hardware or configuration prevent connection between these local and remote devices.

The most common problems with switches occur at the Physical Layer. If a switch is installed in an unprotected environment, it can suffer damage such as dislodged or damaged data or power cables. Ensure that switches are placed in a physically secure area.

If an end device cannot connect to the network and the link LED is not illuminated, the link or the switch port is defective or shutdown, perform the following steps:

- Ensure that the power LED is illuminated.

- Ensure that the correct type of cable connects the end device to the switch.

- Reseat the cables at both the workstation and the switch end.

- Check the configuration to ensure that the port is in a **no shutdown** state.

If a connectivity problem exists, and if the link LED is illuminated, the switch configuration is the most likely problem.

Refer to
Figure
in online course

If a switch port fails or malfunctions, the easiest way to test it is to move the physical connection to another port and see if this corrects the problem.

Ensure that switch port security has not disabled the port. Confirm this using the following commands:

```
show running-config
```

```
show port-security interface interface_id
```

If the switch security settings are disabling the port, review the security policy to see if altering the security is acceptable.

Switches function at Layer 2 and keep a record of the MAC address of all connected devices. If the MAC address in this table is not correct, the switch forwards information to the wrong port and communication does not occur.

To display the MAC address of the device connected to each switch port, use:

```
show mac-address-table
```

To clear the dynamic entries in the table, issue the command:

```
clear mac-address-table dynamic
```

The switch then repopulates the MAC address table with updated information.

Refer to
Figure
in online course

Although automatically detected on many devices, mismatched speed or duplex settings can prevent the link between the switch and end device from functioning. Some switches do not properly detect the speed and duplex of the connected device. If this is the suspected problem, lock down the values on the switch port to match the host device using the **interface speed** and **duplex** commands.

To display both the speed and duplex settings of the port, use the command:

```
show interface interface_id
```

Switching loops are another potential source of connectivity issues. STP prevents bridging loops and broadcast storms by shutting down redundant paths in a switched network. If STP bases its decisions on inaccurate information, loops may occur.

Indicators that a loop is present in a network include:

- Loss of connectivity to, from, and through affected network regions

- High CPU utilization on routers connected to affected segments

- High link utilization up to 100%

- High switch backplane utilization as compared to the baseline utilization

- Syslog messages indicating packet looping, constant address relearning, or MAC address flapping messages

- Increasing number of output drops on many interfaces

Refer to
Figure
in online course

A loop develops when the switch does not receive BPDUs or is unable to process them. This problem could be due to:

- Misconfigurations

- Defective *transceiver*s

- Hardware and cabling issues

- Overloaded processors

Overloaded processors disrupt STP and prevent the switch from processing the BPDUs. A port that is flapping causes multiple transitions to occur. These multiple transitions can overload the processors. This should be a rare occurrence in a properly configured network. To remedy this type of problem, remove as many of the redundant links as possible.

Another troubleshooting issue is suboptimal switching. Left to default values, STP does not always identify the best root bridge or root ports. Changing the priority value on a switch can force the selection of the root bridge. The root bridge should normally be at the center of the network to provide for optimum switching.

When troubleshooting STP, use the following commands:

To provide information about the STP configuration:

```
show spanning-tree
```

To provide information about the STP state of an individual port:

```
show spanning-tree interface interface_id
```
Packet Tracer Activity

Refer to **Packet
Tracer Activity**
for this chapter

Troubleshoot host connectivity on a switch.

9.2.2 Troubleshooting VLAN Configuration Issues

Refer to
Figure
in online course

If the Physical Layer is functioning correctly and communication is still not occurring between end devices, check the VLAN configuration.

If the non-functioning ports are in the same VLAN, the hosts must have IP addresses on the same network or subnet in order to communicate. If the non-functioning ports are in different VLANs, communication is only possible with the aid of a Layer 3 device, such as a router. If information is required on a specific VLAN, use the following command `show vlan id` *vlan_number* to display the ports assigned to each VLAN.

If inter-VLAN routing is required, verify the following configurations:

- One port from each VLAN connects into a router interface or subinterface.

- Both the switch port and the router interface are configured with trunking.

- Both the switch and router interface are configured with the same encapsulation.

Newer switches default to 802.1Q, but some Cisco switches support both 802.1Q and Cisco proprietary Inter-Switch Link (*ISL*) format. IEEE 802.1Q should be used whenever possible, because it is the *de facto standard* and 802.1Q and ISL are not compatible.

Refer to
Figure
in online course

When troubleshooting inter-VLAN issues, ensure that there is no IP address on the physical interface of the router. The interface must be active.

To verify the interface configuration, use:

`show ip interface brief`

The network associated with each VLAN should be visible in the routing table. If not, recheck all physical connections and trunk configuration on both ends of the link. If it is not directly connected to the VLAN subnets, check the configuration of the routing protocol to verify that there is a route to each of the VLANs. Use the command:

`show ip route`

Refer to
Figure
in online course

Access or Trunk Port

Each switch port is either an access port or a trunk port. On some switch models, other switch port modes are available and the switch automatically configures the port to the appropriate status. It is sometimes advisable to lock the port into either access or trunk status to avoid potential problems with this detection process.

Native and Management VLANs

The native VLAN and management VLAN are VLAN1 by default. Untagged frames sent across a trunk are assigned to the native VLAN of the trunk line. If the native VLAN assignment is changed on a device, each end of the 802.1Q trunk should be configured with the same native VLAN number. If one end of the trunk is configured for native VLAN10 and the other end is configured for native VLAN14, a frame sent from VLAN10 on one side is received on VLAN14 on the other. VLAN10 "leaks" into VLAN14. This can create unexpected connectivity issues and increase latency.

For smoother, quicker transitions, verify that the native VLAN assignment is the same on all devices throughout the network.

Refer to **Packet
Tracer Activity**
for this chapter

Packet Tracer Activity

Troubleshoot inter-VLAN routing issues.

9.2.3 Troubleshooting VTP

Refer to
Figure
in online course

VTP simplifies the distribution of VLAN information to multiple switches in a domain. Switches that participate in VTP operate in one of three modes: server, client, or transparent. Only the server adds, deletes, and modifies VLAN information.

When troubleshooting VTP on a network, ensure that:

- All participating devices have the same VTP domain name.
- Two VTP servers exist in every domain, in case one fails.
- All servers have the same information.
- The revision numbers are the same on all devices.
- All devices use the same VTP version.

To display the VTP version in use on a device, the VTP domain name, the VTP mode, and the VTP revision number, issue the command:

`show vtp status`

To modify the VTP version number, use:

`vtp version <1 ¦ 2>`

Refer to
Figure
in online course

VTP clients and servers use the VTP revision number to decide if they should update their VLAN information. If the revision number of the update is higher than the revision number currently in use, the client and server use the information to update the configuration.

Always check the VTP revision information and mode on any switch before allowing it to join the network. The revision number is stored in NVRAM and erasing the start-up configuration on the switch does not reset this value. To reset the revision number, either set the switch mode to transparent or change the VTP domain name.

It is also a problem if a *rogue switch* joins the domain and modifies VLAN information. To prevent this situation, it is important to configure a password on the VTP domain. To set a VTP password for the domain, use the global configuration command:

`vtp password` *password*

When configured, the authentication password must be the same on all devices in the VTP domain. If updates are not propagating to a new switch in the VTP domain, suspect the password. To verify the password, use the command:

`show vtp password`

Refer to **Packet
Tracer Activity**
for this chapter

Packet Tracer Activity

Troubleshoot and correct VTP Issues.

9.3 Troubleshooting Routing Issues

9.3.1 RIP Issues

Refer to
Figure
in online course

Many tools exist for troubleshooting routing issues. These include IOS `show` commands, `debug` commands and TCP/IP utilities such as `ping`, `traceroute` and `telnet`.

The `show` commands display a snapshot of a configuration or of a particular component. The `debug` commands are dynamic and provide real-time information on traffic movement and the interaction of protocols. Use TCP/IP utilities such as `ping` for verifying connectivity.

The `show` commands are important tools for understanding the status of a router, detecting neighboring routers, isolating problems in the network, and monitoring the network in general. Use a combination of `show` commands and `debug` commands to troubleshoot RIP routing protocol issues.

Before using the `debug` command, narrow the problems to a likely subset of causes. Use `debug` commands to isolate problems, not to monitor normal network operation.

Refer to
Figure
in online course

RIP is a fairly basic and simple protocol to configure. However, some common issues can arise when configuring RIP routers.

Compatibility issues exist between RIPv1 and RIPv2. If the RIP routes are not being advertised, check for the following problems:

- Layer 1 or Layer 2 connectivity issues
- Requirements for VLSM subnetting but using RIPv1
- RIPv1 and RIPv2 routing configurations mismatched
- Network statements missing or incorrect
- Interface IP addressing incorrect
- Outgoing interface is down

- Advertised network interface is down

- Passive interface misconfigurations

When testing with the `show ip route` command, it is a good idea to clear the routing tables using the `clear ip route *` command.

In addition to the issues identified here, it is always important is remember that RIP has a hop count limit of 15 hops. This limitation alone can be a problem in a large enterprise network.

Refer to **Packet Tracer Activity** for this chapter

Packet Tracer Activity

Troubleshoot RIP using `show` and `debug` commands.

Refer to **Lab Activity** for this chapter

Lab Activity

Troubleshoot RIPv2 routing issues.

9.3.2 EIGRP Issues

Refer to **Figure** in online course

A number of IOS `show` commands and `debug` commands are the same for troubleshooting EIGRP routing issues as they are for RIP. Commands specific to troubleshooting EIGRP include:

`show ip eigrp neighbors`

Displays neighbor IP addresses and the interface on which they were learned.

`show ip eigrp topology`

Displays the topology table of known networks with successor routes, status codes, feasible distance, and interface.

`show ip eigrp traffic`

Displays EIGRP traffic statistics for the AS configured, including hello packets sent/received, updates, and so on.

`debug eigrp packets`

Displays real-time EIGRP packet exchanges between neighbors.

`debug ip eigrp`

Displays real-time EIGRP events, such as link status changes and routing table updates.

Refer to **Figure** in online course

Certain issues commonly occur when configuring the EIGRP protocol. Possible reasons why EIGRP may not be working are:

- Layer 1 or Layer 2 connectivity issues exist.

- An interface has incorrect addressing or subnet mask.

- AS numbers on EIGRP routers are mismatched.

- The wrong network or incorrect wildcard mask is specified in the routing process.

- The link may be congested or down.

- The outgoing interface is down.

- The interface for an advertised network is down.

If auto-summarization is enabled on routers with discontiguous subnets, routes may not be advertised correctly.

Refer to **Packet Tracer Activity** for this chapter

Packet Tracer Activity

Troubleshoot common EIGRP issues using **show** and **debug** commands.

9.3.3 OSPF Issues

Refer to **Figure** in online course

The majority of problems encountered with OSPF relate to the formation of adjacencies and the synchronization of the link-state databases.

OSPF Troubleshooting Issues

- Neighbors must be part of the same OSPF area.

- Interfaces for neighbors must have compatible IP addresses and subnet masks.

- Routers in an area should have the same OSPF hello interval and dead interval.

- The routers must advertise the correct networks for interfaces to participate in the OSPF process.

- The appropriate wildcard masks must be used to advertise the correct IP address ranges.

- Authentication must be correctly configured on routers for communication to occur.

In addition to the standard **show** and **debug** commands, the following commands assist troubleshooting OSPF issues:

- `show ip ospf`

- `show ip ospf neighbor`

- `show ip ospf interface`

- `debug ip ospf events`

- `debug ip ospf packet`

Refer to **Interactive Graphic** in online course.

Full Screen **Activity**

Analyze the network topology and router output. Indicate whether the statements are true or false.

Refer to **Lab Activity** for this chapter

Lab Activity

Troubleshoot OSPF routing issues.

9.3.4 Route Redistribution Issues

Refer to **Figure** in online course

Configuring a static default route on an edge router provides a gateway of last resort for packets destined for IP addresses outside the network.

Although this configuration provides a solution for the edge router, it does not provide a way out of the internal network for other internal routers. One solution is to configure a default route on each internal router that points to the next hop or edge router. However, this method does not scale well with large networks. A better solution uses the routing protocol to propagate the default route on the edge router to other internal routers. All routing protocols, including RIP, EIGRP and OSPF, provide mechanisms to accomplish this.

With each routing protocol, configure a default quad 0 static route on the edge router.

```
ip route 0.0.0.0 0.0.0.0 S0/0/0
```

Next, configure the edge router to send or propagate its default route to the other routers. With RIP and OSPF, enter router configuration mode and use the command `default-information originate`. EIGRP redistributes default routes directly; the `redistribute static` command can also be used.

Failure to properly implement default route redistribution prevents users that are connected to internal routers from accessing external networks.

Refer to **Lab Activity** for this chapter

Lab Activity

Troubleshoot default route redistribution with EIGRP.

Refer to **Lab Activity** for this chapter

Lab Activity

Troubleshoot OSPF router configurations to determine why a default route is not being redistributed.

9.4 Troubleshooting WAN Configurations

9.4.1 Troubleshooting WAN Connectivity

Refer to **Figure** in online course

When configuring WAN interfaces, a number of potential problem areas can surface. Some of these problems are unavoidable if the network administrator only has control over one end of the link and the ISP controls the other end. In this case, the network administrator uses the configuration information provided by the ISP to ensure connectivity.

At the Physical Layer, the most common problems involve *clocking*, cable types, and loose or faulty connectors. Serial line connections link a DCE device to a DTE device. Two different types of cables exist for connecting devices: DTE and DCE. Usually the DCE device at the service provider provides that clocking signal.

Visually check each cable for loose connections or faulty connectors. If a cable cannot be correctly connected, swap the current cable with one known to work.

To display the type of cable and the detection and status of DTE, DCE, and clocking, use the following command:

`show controllers <serial_port>`

Refer to **Figure** in online course

For a serial link to come up, the encapsulation format on both ends of the link must match. The default serial line encapsulation used on Cisco routers is HDLC. Since Cisco HDLC and open standard HDLC are not compatible, do not use the Cisco default encapsulation when connecting to a non-Cisco device.

Some Layer 2 encapsulations have more than one form. For example, Cisco routers support both the proprietary Cisco Frame Relay format as well as the industry-standard *IETF format*. These formats are not compatible. The default format on Cisco devices is Cisco Frame Relay format.

To see the encapsulation in use on a serial line, use the command:

`show interfaces <serial_port>`

Layer 3 configurations can also prevent data from moving across a serial link. Although it is not necessary to use an IP address on a serial link, if one is used, both ends of the link must be on the same network or subnet.

Refer to **Figure** in online course

A process known as serial line address resolution protocol (*SLARP*) assigns an address to the end point of a serial link if the other end is already configured. SLARP assumes that each serial line is a separate IP subnet, and that one end of the line is host number 1 and the other end is host number 2. As long as one end of the serial link is configured, SLARP automatically configures an IP address for the other end.

The IP address configured on an interface and the status of the port and line protocol is viewable with the command:

`show ip interface brief`

Before Layer 3 information moves across the link, both the interface and the protocol must be up. If the interface is down, there is a problem with the interface itself.

If the interface is up but the line protocol is down, check that the proper cable is connected and is firmly attached to the port. If this step still does not correct the problem, replace the cable.

If the status of an interface is administratively down, the most probable cause is that the `no shutdown` command was not entered on the interface. Interfaces are shutdown by default.

Refer to **Figure** in online course

The PPP process involves both the LCP and NCP phases. LCP establishes the link and verifies that it is of sufficient quality to bring up the Layer 3 protocols. NCP allows Layer 3 traffic to move across the link. There is an optional authentication field between the LCP and NCP phases.

Each phase has to complete successfully before the other begins.

When troubleshooting PPP connectivity, verify that:

- LCP phase is complete
- Authentication has passed, if configured
- NCP phase is complete

Commands are available that assist in troubleshooting PPP. To show the status of the LCP and NCP phase, use:

`show interface`

To display PPP packets transmitted during the startup phase where PPP options are negotiated, use:

`debug ppp negotiation`

To display real-time PPP packet flow, use:

`debug ppp packet`

Refer to **Packet Tracer Activity** for this chapter

Packet Tracer Activity

Troubleshoot WAN connectivity issues.

9.4.2 Troubleshooting WAN Authentication

Refer to **Figure** in online course

PPP offers many advantages over the default HDLC serial line encapsulation. Among these features is the ability to use either PAP or CHAP to authenticate end devices. Authentication occurs as an optional phase after the establishment of the link with LCP but before the NCPs allow the movement of Layer 3 traffic.

If the LCP is not able to connect, negotiation of the optional parameters, including authentication, cannot occur. The absence of active NCPs indicates a failed authentication.

When troubleshooting PPP authentication, determine if authentication is the problem by examining the status of the LCP and NCPs using the `show interface` command.

If both the LCP and NCPs are open, authentication has been successful and the problem is elsewhere.

If the LCP is not open, the problem exists with the physical link between the source and destination.

If the LCP is open and the NCPs are not, authentication is suspect.

Refer to **Figure** in online course

Authentication can be either one-way or two-way. For enhanced security, use two-way or mutual authentication. Two-way authentication requires that each end device authenticate to the other.

On both ends of the link, verify that a user account exists for the remote device and that the password is correct. If uncertain, remove the old user account statement and recreate it. The configuration on both ends of the link must specify the same type of authentication.

The most common problem with authentication is either forgetting to configure an account for the remote router or misconfiguring the username and password. By default, the username is the name of the remote router. Both the username and the password are case-sensitive.

If using PAP authentication on a current version of the IOS, activate it with the command:

```
ppp pap sent-username username password password
```

Debugging the authentication process provides a quick method of determining what is wrong. To display packets involved in the authentication process as they are exchanged between end devices, use the command:

```
debug ppp authentication
```

Refer to **Packet Tracer Activity** for this chapter

Packet Tracer Activity

Troubleshoot PPP authentication using CHAP.

Refer to **Lab Activity** for this chapter

Lab Activity

Troubleshoot WAN and PPP connectivity.

9.5 Troubleshooting ACL Issues

9.5.1 Determining if an ACL is the Issue

Refer to **Figure** in online course

ACLs add a level of complexity to troubleshooting network issues. Therefore, it is important to verify basic network connectivity before applying an ACL.

When networks or hosts become unreachable and ACLs are in use, it is critical to determine if the ACL is the problem. Ask the following questions to help to isolate the problem:

- Is an ACL applied to the problem router or interface?

- Has it been applied recently?

- Did the issue exist before the ACL was applied?

- Is the ACL performing as expected?

- Is the problem with all hosts connected to the interface or only specific hosts?

- Is the problem with all protocols being forwarded or only specific protocols?

- Are the networks appearing in the routing table as expected?

One way to determine the answer to several of these questions is to enable logging. Logging shows the effect that ACLs are having on various packets. By default, the number of matches display with the **show access-list** command.

To display details about packets permitted or denied, add the **log** keyword to the end of ACL

Refer to **Figure** in online course

statements.

A number of commands help to determine if ACLs are configured and applied correctly.

To display all ACLs configured on the router, whether applied to an interface or not, use the following command:

```
show access-lists
```

To clear the number of matches for each ACL statement, use:

```
clear access-list counters
```

To display the source and destination IP address for each packet received or sent by any interface on the router, use:

```
debug ip packet
```

The **debug ip packet** command shows packets whose source or destination is a router interface. This command includes packets that are denied by an ACL at the interface. Examples of traffic that create a debug message include:

- RIP updates to or from a router interface

- Telnet from an external source to an external destination blocked by an ACL on the interface

If the packets are simply passing through and the ACL does not block a packet from this IP address, no **debug** message is generated.

Full Screen **Activity**

Refer to
Interactive Graphic
in online course.

Analyze the network topology and router command output. Indicate whether the statements regarding ACLs and their effects are true or false.

Refer to **Packet Tracer Activity** *for this chapter*

Packet Tracer Activity

Troubleshoot ACL issues using **show** and **debug** commands.

9.5.2 ACL Configuration and Placement Issues

Refer to
Figure
in online course

Issues such as slow performance and unreachable network resources result from an incorrectly configured ACL. In some cases, the ACL may permit or deny the intended traffic but can also have unintended effects on other traffic. If it appears that the ACL is the problem, there are several issues to check.

If the ACL statements are not in the most efficient order to permit the highest volume traffic early in the ACL, check the logging results to determine a more efficient order.

The implicit deny may be having unintended effects on other traffic. If so, use an explicit **deny ip any any log** command so that packets that do not match any of the previous ACL statements can be monitored.

Use logging to determine if the ACL is optimized or working as expected.

Refer to
Figure
in online course

In addition to determining whether the ACL is correctly configured, it is also important to apply the ACL to the right router or interface, and in the appropriate direction. A correctly configured ACL that is incorrectly applied is one of the most common errors when creating ACLs.

Standard ACLs filter only on the source IP address; therefore, place them as close to the destination as possible.

Placing a Standard ACL close to the source may unintentionally block traffic to networks that should be allowed.

Placing the ACL close to the destination unfortunately allows traffic to flow across one or more network segments prior to being denied. This is a waste of valuable bandwidth.

Using an Extended ACL resolves both of these issues.

Packets destined for networks other than the one being blocked are unaffected. The routers along the potential path never see the denied packets, which helps to conserve bandwidth.

Refer to **Packet Tracer Activity** for this chapter

Packet Tracer Activity

Troubleshoot the placement and direction of an ACL.

Refer to **Lab Activity** for this chapter

Lab Activity

Troubleshoot ACL configuration and placement issues.

Summary

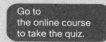

Quiz

Take the chapter quiz to check your knowledge.

Your Chapter Notes

10.0 Putting It All Together

Summary

Refer to **Lab Activity** for this chapter

Lab Activity

Use the knowledge and skills presented in this course to perform the following tasks:

- Analyze a network design and create a hierarchical addressing scheme.
- Configure switches with multiple VLANs, VTP, and port security.
- Configure routers and switches to allow inter-VLAN routing.
- Configure multiple routers using OSPF, PAT, a default route, and route summarization.
- Configure WAN links using PPP and authentication.
- Configure ACLs to control network access and to secure routers.
- Verify connectivity, device configuration, and functionality.

Refer to **Packet Tracer Activity** for this chapter

Packet Tracer Activity

Use the knowledge and skills presented in this course to troubleshoot network connectivity problems relating to:

- VLAN configuration
- OSPF configuration
- WAN interface configuration
- Access Control List configuration

Your Chapter Notes

3DES

Triple Data Encryption Standard

Procedure to secure data by first separating it into 64-bit blocks. Each block is then processed three times, each time with an independent 56-bit key. 3DES uses a total key of 168-bits to ensure strong encryption. 3DES is a variant of the 56-bit data encryption standard.

802.1Q

IEEE standard that is designed to enable traffic between virtual LANs. IEEE 802.1Q uses an internal tagging mechanism which inserts a four-byte tag field in the original Ethernet frame between the source address and type/length fields. Because the frame is altered, the trunking device recomputes the frame check sequence on the modified frame.

ABR

area border router

Routing device that connects one or more OSPF areas to a backbone network. An ABR maintains routing tables for the backbone and the attached areas of an OSPF.

access control list

See ACL.

Access Layer

Level of the hierarchical Cisco internetworking model that encompass the hosts that are the point of entry into the network. Access Layer devices include switches, hubs, workstations, servers, IP phones, web cameras, and access points.

access link

Connection between a DTE, such as a router, to the nearest point-of-presence of a service provider through a DCE, such as a modem in a Frame Relay network.

access point

See AP.

access port

Pathway to a device that does not create loops in a switched network and always transitions to forwarding if a host is attached.

ACK

acknowledgment

Notification sent between network devices when an event has occurred. For example, a destination device sends an ACK to a source device when a message is received.

acknowledgment

See ACK.

ACL

access control list

List kept by a network device, such as a router, to manage access to or from the router for a number of services. For example, an ACL can be used to prevent packets with a certain IP address or protocol from leaving a particular interface on the router.

active topology

RSTP network design that transition ports to the forwarding state if they are not discarding or are blocked.

AD

1) advertised distance

Distance that is broadcast by an upstream neighbor.

2) administrative distance

Rating of trustworthiness of a routing information source. For a Cisco router, an administrative distance is expressed as a numerical value between 0 and 255. The higher the value, the lower the trustworthiness rating.

adaptive cut-through

Type of switching when the flow reverts back to fast-forward mode when the number of errors drops below the threshold value to an acceptable level.

address

Data structure used to identify a unique entity, such as a particular process or network device. An IP address is a string of characters assigned by an administrator. A MAC address is burned into a device and cannot be changed.

address mask
Bit combination used to identify the part of an address that refers to the network or subnet, and the part that refers to the host.

adjacencies
See adjacency.

adjacency
Relationship between neighboring routers and end nodes for the purpose of exchanging routing information. Adjacency is based on the use of a common media segment.

administrative distance
See AD.

Advanced Encryption Standard
See AES.

advanced replacement
Part of a SMARTnet agreement offered as part of a customer service enhancement.

advertised distance
See AD.

advertisement request
VLAN information that a VTP client requires if the switch has been reset or the VTP domain name has been changed.

advertising
Router process in which routing or service updates containing lists of usable routes are sent at specified intervals to routers on the network .

AES
Advanced Encryption Standard

Specifications for a symmetric 128-bit block cipher that is the current cryptographic standard for the United States adopted by the National Institute of Standards and Techonology. The algorithm must be used with key sizes of 128 bits, 192 bits, or 256 bits, depending on the application security requirement.

aging timer
Period of time in which an entry must be used before a switch deletes it from the MAC address table.

AH
Authentication Header

Security protocol that provides data authentication and optional anti-replay services. AH is embedded in the data to be protected.

algorithm
Well-defined rule or mathematical process for solving a problem. In networking, an algorithm is commonly used to determine the best route for traffic from a source to a destination.

anycast
Type of IPv6 network addressing and routing scheme where data is routed to a destination considered to be the best or closest by the routing topology. An anycast address is formatted the same as an IPv6 global unicast address.

AP
access point

Access Layer device that connects to a wired network and relays data between wireless and wired devices. An AP connects wireless communication devices to form a wireless network to allow roaming.

application characterization
Collecting information about network bandwidth usage and response times of an application. Some of the considerations for application characterization include how the application works and interacts on a network, and the technical requirements.

Application Layer
Layer 7 of the OSI Reference Model. The Application Layer provides services to application processes such as email, file transfer, and terminal emulation that are outside of the OSI Reference Model. It identifies and establishes the availability of intended communication partners and the resources required to connect with them, synchronizes cooperating applications, and establishes agreement on procedures for error recovery and control of data integrity.

application-specific integrated circuit (ASIC)
See ASIC.

area
Logical set of either CLNS-, DECnet-, or OSPF-based network segments, and all attached devices. Areas are usually connected through routers, creating a single autonomous system.

Area 0
Area at the beginning of an OSPF network. An OSPF network must have at least one area, which is area 0. As the network expands, other areas are created adjacent to Area 0.

Area 0 is also known as the backbone area.

area border router
See ABR.

area ID

Identification of the OSPF area to which the network belongs.

AS

autonomous system.

Collection of networks under a common administration sharing a common routing strategy. Autonomous systems are subdivided by areas. An autonomous system must be assigned a unique 16-bit number by the IANA.

ASA

Cisco adaptive security appliance

Hardware device that integrates firewall, Unified Communications security, SSL and IPsec VPN, IPS, and content security services. An example of an ASA is a Cisco ASA 5500 series.

ASBR

autonomous system boundary router

Area border router located between an OSPF autonomous system and a non-OSPF network. An ASBR runs the OSPF routing protocol and another routing protocol, such as RIP. An ASBR must reside in a nonstub OSPF area.

as-built

Diagram that shows the original design and any changes that have been made to a network topology.

ASIC

application-specific integrated circuit

Circuit that gives precise instructions for the functionality of a device during Layer 3 switching.

asymmetric

When one function on a network takes a greater length of time than the reverse function. An example of an asymmetric function is the compression and decompression of data.

asynchronous transfer mode

See ATM.

ATM

asynchronous transfer mode

International standard for the cell relay of service types, such as voice, video, or data. In ATM, the services are conveyed in fixed-length, 53-byte cells. Fixed-length cells reduce transit delays because cell processing occurs in the hardware. ATM is designed for high-speed transmission media such as E3, SONET, and T3.

atomic transaction

Process that guarantees that either all or none of the tasks of a transaction are performed in a database system. An atomic transaction is void if it is not fully processed.

authentication

Security measure designed to control access to network resources by verifying the identity of a person or process.

Authentication Header

See AH.

authentication server

Server that controls the frequency and timing of challenges to prevent attacks on a network.

authority zone

Section of the domain-name tree for which one name server is the authority. Authority zone is associated with DNS.

auto mode

Designation of a port on a device as a trunk port if the other end is set to either trunk or desirable mode.

autonomous system

See AS.

autonomous system boundary router

See ASBR.

AutoQoS

Feature that automates consistent deployment of QoS features across Cisco routers and switches to ensure high-quality application performance. AutoQoS configures the device with QoS features and variables that are based on Cisco best-practice recommendations. A user is able to adjust parameters that are generated by Cisco AutoQoS.

availability

Condition of accessibility.

baby giant

Ethernet frame on a network that has been tagged as too large. A baby giant is dropped and logged as an error.

back end

Application that performs final or hidden functions in a process.

backbone cabling

Physical media that connects wiring closets to each other, wiring closets and the POP, and buildings that are part of the same LAN.

BackboneFast

Feature on the switches of a bridge network that provides fast convergence after a spanning tree topology change. BackboneFast is used at the Distribution and Core Layers to restore backbone connectivity. BackboneFast is Cisco proprietary.

backup designated router

See BDR.

backward explicit congestion notification

See BECN.

bandwidth

Rated throughput capacity of a given network medium or protocol. Bandwidth is the difference between the highest and lowest frequencies available for network signals.

bandwidth reservation

Process of assigning bandwidth to users and applications served by a network. Bandwidth reservation involves assigning priority to different flows of traffic based on critical and delay-sensitive characteristics. If the network becomes congested, lower-priority traffic can be dropped.

Bandwidth reservation is also known as bandwidth allocation.

banner motd

banner motd

Command used to configure a message of the day, or motd. The message is displayed at login. A banner motd is useful for conveying messages, such as an impending system shutdown, that affects all network users.

baseline

A quantitative expression of planned costs, schedules, and technical requirements for a defined project. A baseline is established to describe the 'normal' status of network or computer system performance. The status can then be compared with the baseline at any point to measure the variation from the 'normal' operation condition.

basic configuration

Minimal configuration information entered when a router, switch, or other configurable device is installed on a network. For example, the basic configuration for a LightStream 2020 ATM switch includes the IP addresses, date, and parameters for at least one trunk line. The basic configuration enables the switch to receive a full configuration from the Network Management System.

baud

Unit of signaling speed equal to the number of discrete signal elements transmitted per second. Baud is synonymous with bits per second, if each signal element represents exactly one bit.

Bc

committed burst

Maximum amount of data, in bits, that a Frame Relay internetwork is committed to accept and transmit at the CIR. Bc is a negotiated tariff metric.

BCP

business continuity plan

Steps to be taken to continue business operations when there is a natural or man-made disaster.

BDR

backup designated router

Router that is identified to take over if the designated router fails.

Be

excess burst

Number of bits that a Frame Relay internetwork will attempt to transmit after Bc is accommodated. Be data is, in general, delivered with a lower probability than Bc data because Be data can be marked as DE by the network. Be is a negotiated tariff metric.

BECN

backward explicit congestion notification

Signal in a frame travelling in the opposite direction of frames that have encountered a congested path in a Frame Relay network. The DTE that receives the frame with the BECN signal can request that higher-level protocols take appropriate flow-control action.

BGP

Border Gateway Protocol

Routing standard used to connect a SP to and from the Internet.

BGP is also known as exterior gateway protocol.

BID

bridge ID

Identification of the root bridge which is the focal point in an STP network.

Bill Of Material
See BOM.

bit-oriented
In networking, data is transmitted using individual bits, instead of the entire byte.

block cipher
Method of encrypting a group of bits together as a single unit.

blocked port
See blocking.

blocking
1) Condition in a switching system in which no paths are available to complete a circuit. 2) Condition when one activity cannot begin until another has been completed.

BOM
bill of material

Itemized list of hardware, software, and other items necessary to build a network. The BOM is used to obtain price quotations and to order equipment.

Boolean ANDing
Clears a pattern of bits; if you AND a bit with zero, it will clear it to zero, while ANDing with one will leave the bit unchanged, leaving it a "1".

bootup process
Activity of starting a computer-based device. The bootup process has three steps. First, the internal components are tested. Then, the operating system is located and started. Finally, the initial configuration is loaded. After the bootup process is complete a device is in an operational state.

border gateway
Router that communicates with routers in other autonomous systems.

Border Gateway Protocol
See BGP.

bottom-up
Troubleshooting technique that begins by examining the lower levels of a hierarchical model first.

bounded update
Feature associated with a link-state routing protocols, such as EIGRP. A bounded update contains specific parameters and is delivered only to routers that require the information.

BPDU
bridge protocol data unit

Spanning Tree Protocol hello packet that is sent out at configurable intervals to exchange information among bridges in the network.

bridge
Device that connects and passes packets between two network segments that use the same communications protocol. A bridge operates at the Data Link Layer of the OSI reference model. In general, it filters, forwards, or floods an incoming frame based on the MAC address of that frame.

bridge ID
See BID.

bridge protocol data unit
See BPDU.

broadcast
Set of devices that receive broadcast frames originating from any of the devices within the set. A broadcast domain is typically bounded by routers because routers do not forward broadcast frames.

broadcast address
Address reserved for sending a message to all stations. Generally, a broadcast address is a MAC destination address consisting of all ones.

broadcast domain
Set of devices that receive broadcast frames originating from any of the devices within the set. A broadcast domain is typically bounded by routers because routers do not forward broadcast frames.

broadcast multi-access
Type of Ethernet link identified by OSPF, which is a standard for a multi-access network that forwards broadcast traffic.

broadcast storm
Undesirable network event in which many broadcasts are sent simultaneously across all network segments. A broadcast storm uses substantial network bandwidth and typically causes network time-outs.

BSP
business security plan

Physical, system, and organizational control measures to be taken to protect network and information assets.

buffer

Storage area used for handling data in transit. A buffer is used in internetworking to compensate for differences in processing speed between network devices. Bursts of data can be stored in a buffer until the data can be handled by slower processing devices.

A buffer is also known as a packet buffer.

business case

Structured design document to justify the financial investment required to implement a technology change.

business continuity

Ability to continue business operations if there is a natural or man-made disaster.

business continuity plan

See BCP.

business enterprise

Large corporate environment with many users and locations, or with many systems.

business security plan

Physical, system, and organizational control measures to be taken to protect network and information assets.

cache

Act of storing data, or the location of stored data.

call agent

Control device that processes calls and administers gateways in IP telephony. A call agent performs functions similar to a switchboard in a traditional telephone system. Examples of call agents include the Cisco Unified Communications Manager and the Cisco Unified Communications Manager Express.

CAM

content addressable memory

MAC address table maintained by a switch. A CAM is recreated every time a switch is activated.

carrier

Electromagnetic wave or alternating current of a single frequency that is suitable for modulation by another data-bearing signal.

carrier wave

Signal on which data is modulated and then demodulated in an analog connection.

Catalyst Workgroup Switch

Series of Cisco workgroup switches that enhance the network performance of Ethernet client/server workgroups. The Catalyst Workgroup Switch integrates software enhancements for network management and provides a 100 Mbps interface to servers and dedicated Ethernet-to-desktop workstations.

CBWFQ

class-based weighted fair queueing

Network packet prioritizing technique based on the standard practice of weighted fair queuing. CBWFQ has additional QoS functionality that assigns packets to user-defined traffic classes. Each class is given a level of priority based on matching criteria including protocols, ACLs, and input interfaces.

CCITT

Consultative Committee for International Telegraph and Telephone

International organization responsible for the development of communications standards. The CCITT is now referred to as the ITU-T.

CDP

Cisco Discovery Protocol

Protocol on Cisco-manufactured equipment, including routers, access servers, bridges, and switches, that enables a device to communicate with other devices on the LAN or on the remote side of a WAN. CDP runs on LANs, Frame Relay, and ATM media.

Cell-switched networks

Data communication scheme based on fixed-length cell structure. In a cell-switched network, the fixed-length cell achieves a faster speed of transmission than those using variable-length packets. ATM is an example of a switched technology on a network that provides full bandwidth of the link when a station communicates to the switch.

central office

See CO.

Challenge Handshake Authentication Protocol

See CHAP.

challenge message

Response sent by a router to establish the identity of the sender.

channel

Communication path that can be multiplexed over a single cable.

IANA

Internet Assigned Numbers Authority

Entity that keeps records of the autonomous system numbers and is a registry for IP addresses and protocol numbers.

ICMP

Internet Control Message Protocol

Standard for network layer testing and troubleshooting. ICMP provides the ability to report diagnostic and error messages. The ping command is part of the ICMP utility.

IDF

intermediate distribution facility

Secondary communications room for a building that uses a star networking topology. An IDF has a frame that cross-connects the user cable media to individual user line circuits and may serve as a distribution point for multipair cables from the main distribution frame. The IDF is dependent on the MDF.

IDS

intrusion detection system

Combination of a sensor, console, and central engine in a single device installed on a network to protect against attacks missed by a conventional firewall. IDS inspects all inbound and outbound network activity and identifies suspicious patterns that may indicate a network or system attack. It is configured to send an alarm to network administrators when such attack is encountered.

IEEE

Professional organization whose activities include the development of communications and network standards. IEEE LAN standards are the predominant LAN standards today.

IEEE 802.1Q

IEEE standard that is designed to enable traffic between virtual LANs. IEEE 802.1Q uses an internal tagging mechanism which inserts a four-byte tag field in the original Ethernet frame between the source address and type/length fields. Because the frame is altered, the trunking device recomputes the frame check sequence on the modified frame.

IETF

Internet Engineering Task Force

Task force consisting of over 80 working groups responsible for developing Internet standards. The IETF is part of the Internet Society, or ISOC, organization.

IETF format

Task force consisting of over 80 working groups responsible for developing Internet standards. The IETF is part of the Internet Society, or ISOC, organization.

IGMP

Internet Group Management Protocol

Standard used by IP hosts to report a multicast group membership to an adjacent multicast router. IGMP can be used to access online video and gaming more efficiently.

IGP

Interior Gateway Protocol

Standard used to exchange routing information within an autonomous system. Examples of an Internet IGP includes EIGRP, OSPF, and RIP.

IKE

Internet Key Exchange

Hybrid protocol obtained from ISAKMP and Oakley standards that provides utility services for IPSec which include authentication of the IPSec peers, negotiation of IKE and IPSec security associations, and establishment of keys for encryption algorithms used by IPSec.

implicit deny

Last statement of an ACL inserted to block the accidental entry of unwanted traffic.

in-band

Management technique for connecting a computer to a network device. In-band management is used to monitor and make configuration changes to a network device over a network connection.

inbound

One of two directions a packet will travel on a network through an interface. An inbound packet is enteiring a device.

inside global address

Public-routable IP address of an inside host as it appears to the outside network. An inside global address is an IP address translated by NAT.

inside local address

Private IP address configured on a host on an inside network. An inside local address must be translated before it can travel outside the local addressing structure to the Internet.

inside local network
Privately addressed network space connected to a router interface. Inside local network is used to overcome shortages of public IP addressing.

Institute of Electrical and Electronics Engineers
See IEEE.

insured burst
Largest transfer of data above the insured rate that will be temporarily allowed on a permanent virtual circuit. An insured burst is not tagged to be dropped in the case of network congestion. An insured burst is specified in bytes or cells.

insured traffic
Data transfer at the rate specified for the PVC. Insured traffic should not be dropped by the network under normal network conditions.

interactive voice response
See IVR.

inter-area routing
Transfer of data between two or more logical areas.

interface
1) Connection between two systems or devices. 2) In routing terminology, a network connection. 3) In telephony, a shared boundary defined by common physical interconnection characteristics, signal characteristics, and meanings of interchanged signals. 4) The boundary between adjacent layers of the OSI model.

Interior Gateway Protocol
See IGP.

intermediate distribution facility
See IDF.

Intermediate System-to-Intermediate System
See IS-IS.

internal traffic
Data transmitted within a private, trusted network.

International Telecommunication Union
See ITU-T.

Internet Assigned Numbers Authority
See IANA.

Internet Control Message Protocol
See ICMP.

Internet Engineering Task Force
See IETF.

Internet Group Management Protocol
See IGMP.

Internet Key Exchange
See IKE.

Internet operating system file naming system
See IOS file naming convention.

Internet Protocol address
See IP address.

Internet Protocol address pool
See IP address pool.

Internet Protocol Control Protocol
See IPCP.

Internet Protocol multicast
See IP multicast.

Internet Protocol phone
See IP phone.

Internet Protocol security
See IPSec.

Internet Protocol telephony
See IP telephony.

Internet Protocol version 4
See IPv4.

Internet Protocol version 6
See IPv6.

internetwork
Collection of networks interconnected by routers and other devices that functions as a single network.

Internetwork Packet Exchange Control Protocol
See IPXCP.

Inter-Switch Link
See ISL.

inter-VLAN
Routing within a virtual LAN. Specific configuration to switches and routers is necessary.

intra-area routing
Transfer of data within a logical area when the source and destination are in the same area.

intranet

Networks accessible internal users of an organization. An intranet is used to share internal information and computing resources.

intrusion detection system

See IDS.

intrusion prevention system

See IPS.

inverse

Having the reverse effect.

Inverse Address Resolution Protocol

See Inverse ARP.

inverse ARP

Inverse·Address Resolution Protocol

Method of building dynamic routes in a network. Inverse ARP allows an access server to discover the network address of a device associated with a virtual circuit.

Inverse ARP is also known as Reverse ARP or RARP.

IOS file naming convention

Internet operating system file naming system

Cisco IOS software image name that represents the hardware, feature set, format, maintenance release, individual release, and T release, in that order.

IP address

Internet Protocol address

32-bit address in IPv4 that is assigned to hosts that use TCP/IP. An IP address belongs to one of five classes: A, B, C, D, or E.

It is written with four octets in the dot address format <a.b.c.d>. Each address consists of a network number, an optional subnetwork number, and a host number. The network and subnetwork numbers together are used for routing. The host number is used to address an individual host within the network or subnetwork. A subnet mask is used to extract network and subnetwork information from the IP address.

IP address pool

Internet Protocol address pool

Range of registered IP addresses to be used with NAT.

IP multicast

Internet Protocol multicast

Routing technique where one packet is sent to a multicast group identified by a single IP destination group address. IP multicast saves network bandwidth because packets are transmitted as one stream over the backbone and only split apart to the target stations by the router at the end of the path.

IP network

A network that uses the IP protocol, which is part of TCP/IP.

IP phone

Telephone that supports voice calls over an IP network.

IP Security

see IPSec.

IP telephony

Telephone that supports voice calls over an IP network.

IPCP

IP Control Protocol

Standard for establishing and configuring IP over PPP. IPCP is responsible for configuring, enabling, and disabling IP protocol modules on both ends of the point-to-point link.

IPS

intrusion prevention system

Active device in the traffic path that monitors network traffic and permits or denies flows and packets into the network. All traffic passes through an IPS for inspection. When the IPS detects malicious traffic, it sends an alert to the management station and blocks the malicious traffic immediately. IPS proactively prevents attacks by blocking the original and subsequent malicious traffic.

IPSec

IP Security

Framework of open standards that provides data confidentiality, data integrity, and data authentication between participating peers. IPSec provides security services at the IP layer. IPSec uses IKE to handle the negotiation of protocols and algorithms based on local policy and to generate the encryption and authentication keys to be used by IPSec. IPSec can protect one or more data flows between a pair of hosts, between a pair of security gateways, or between a security gateway and a host.

IPv4

Internet Protocol version 4

Current network layer standard for packet-switched internetworks. The IP address of IPv4 is 32 bits.

IPv6

Internet Protocol version 6

Network layer standard for packet-switched internetworks. IPv6 is the successor of IPv4 for general use on the Internet.

IPXCP

Internetwork Packet Exchange Control Protocol

Standard that establishes and configures IPX over PPP.

IS-IS

Intermediate System-to-Intermediate System

Standard for OSI link-state hierarchical routing based on DECnet Phase V routing. Routers exchange information based on a single metric to determine network topology.

ISL

Inter-Switch Link

Cisco protocol for tagging frames on an IEEE 802.1q network.

ITU-T

International Telecommunication Union Telecommunication Standardization Sector

International organization that develops communication standards.

ITU-T was formerly known as the Committee for International Telegraph and Telephone.

IVR

interactive voice response

A system that provides information in the form of recorded messages over telephone lines in response to user input in the form of spoken words or dual-tone multifrequencysignaling. An examples of IVR includes the ability to check a bank account balance from a telephone.

jabber

1) Error condition in which a network device continually transmits random and meaningless data onto the network. 2) Data packet that exceeds the length prescribed in the IEEE 802.3 standard.

jitter

Analog communication line distortion. Jitter can be caused by the variation of a signal from the reference timing positions, network congestion, or route changes. It can cause data loss, particularly at high speeds.

K value

Numeric value for a composite metric formula in EIGRP to determine the best path to a destination. K1 and K3 are set to 1. K2, K4, and K5 are set to 0. The value of 1 designates that bandwidth and delay have equal weight.

keepalive

Broadcast sent by one network device to inform another network device that the virtual circuit between the two is still active.

keepalive interval

Period of time that the client waits before sending a keepalive message on a TCP connection.

keepalive message

Broadcast sent by one network device to inform another network device that the virtual circuit between the two is still active.

key

Authentication code that passes between routers in plain text form.

key exchange

Method for two peers to establish a shared secret key, which only they recognize, while communicating over an unsecured channel.

key ID

Identification of code used between devices.

L2F Protocol

Layer 2 Forwarding Protocol

Layer 2 Forwarding (L2F) is a protocol developed by Cisco that supports the creation of secure virtual private dialup networks over the Internet by tunneling Layer 2 frames.

L2TP

Standard for tunneling PPP through a public network. L2TP provides a method to implement Virtual Private Dialup Network based on L2F and Point-to-point Tunneling protocols. L2TP is an Internet Engineering Task Force standard track protocol defined in RFC 2661.

LAN
local area network

High-speed, low-error data transfer system that encompasses a small geographic area. A LAN connects workstations, peripherals, terminals, and other devices in a single building or other geographically limited area. LAN standards specify cabling and signaling at the Physical Layer and the Data Link Layer of the OSI Reference Model. Examples of LAN technologies are Ethernet, FDDI, and Token Ring.

LAN switch
local area network switch

Device that forwards packets between data-link segments at a high speed. A LAN switch usually uses the MAC address to determine where to forward traffic. Some LAN switches operate at the network core, others operate at a workgroup level.

LAP
Lightweight access points

The access points used in the Cisco Unified Wireless Network architecture. LAPs are dependent on a Cisco wireless LAN controller for configuration and security information.

latency
1) Delay between the time when a device receives a frame and the time that frame is forwarded out the destination port. 2) Data latency is the time between a query and the results displaying on the screen.

Layer 2 Forwarding Protocol
See L2F Protocol.

Layer 2 Tunneling Protocol
See L2TP.

Layer 3 switching
Process on a router that uses cut-through techniques to increase the speed of packet inspection and forwarding.

LCP
Link Control Protocol

Standard that establishes, configures, and tests data-link connections for use by PPP. LCP checks the identity of the linked device, determines the acceptable packet size, searches for errors and can terminate the link if it exceeds the requirements.

learning
One of four states that a port cycles through when a switch powers on an STP network. The switch uses information learned to forward a packet.

leased line
Bandwidth on a communications line reserved by a communications carrier for the private use of a customer. A leased line is a type of dedicated line.

least cost path
Calculation of a switch to find a path that uses the least amount of bandwidth for each link required to reach the root bridge.

legacy
Older styles of hardware or software that are still being used.

Light Weight Access Point Protocol
See LWAPP.

lightweight access point
See LWAP.

link
Network communications channel that includes a circuit or transmission path and all related equipment between a sender and a receiver.

A link is also known as a line or a transmission link.

Link Control Protocol
See LCP.

link-state advertisement
See LSA.

link-state protocol
Type of standards, such as OSPF and IS-IS, used in a hierarchical network design. Link-state protocols help manage the packet-switching processes in large networks.

link-state routing algorithm
Mathematical process in which each router broadcasts or multicasts information regarding the cost of reaching each of its neighbors. A link-state routing algorithm creates a consistent view of the network and is not prone to routing loops. Examples of link-state algorithms are OSPF and IS-IS.

listening
One of four states that a port cycles through when a switch powers on an STP network. The switch listens for BPDUs from neighboring switches.

SLARP

Serial Line Address Resolution Protocol

Standard that assigns an address to the end point of a serial link if the other end is already configured. SLARP assumes that each serial line is a separate IP subnet, and that one end of the line is host number 1 and the other end is host number 2. As long as one end of the serial link is configured, SLARP automatically configures an IP address for the other end.

SMDS

switched multimegabit data service

High-speed, packet-switched, WAN technology offered by a telephone company.

SMTP

Simple Mail Transfer Protocol

Internet standards that provide electronic mail services.

SNMP

Simple Network Management Protocol

Standard that allows monitoring of individual devices on the network. SNMP-compliant devices use agents to monitor a number of predefined parameters for specific conditions. These agents collect information and store it in a MIB.

softphone

Application installed on a computer to support voice calls. An example of softphone is Cisco IP Communicator.

software phone

See softphone.

SONET

Synchronous Optical Network

Up to 2.5 Gbps, high-speed synchronous network specification developed by Bellcore and designed to run on optical fiber. STS-1 is the basic building block of SONET. Approved as an international standard in 1988.

SP

service provider

Organization, such as the local phone or cable company, that provides Internet service.

SPAN

switched port analyzer

Tool used with a Catalyst switch that enables the capture of traffic by mirroring the traffic at one switched segment onto a predefined SPAN port. A network analyzer attached to the SPAN port can monitor traffic from any of the other Catalyst switched ports.

spanning tree

Loop-free subset of a network topology.

Spanning Tree Protocol

See STP.

spanning-tree algorithm

Mathematical process that creates a hierarchical tree to bridge a network.

SPF algorithm

shortest path first algorithm

Mathematical process that uses the length of a path to determine a shortest-path spanning tree. An SPF algorithm is a link-state routing algorithm.

SPF tree

All paths from a source to each destination and the total cost of each path.

SPI

stateful packet inspection

Inspect and permit an incoming response to established communication on an internal network.

split horizon

Routing technique that controls the formation of loops by preventing information from exiting the router interface through the same interface it was received.

split tunneling

Configuration to give a VPN client access to the Internet while tunneled into a Cisco IOS Router. Split tunneling is required to give a VPN client secure access to corporate resources via IPsec as well as allow unsecured access to the Internet.

split-horizon updates

Routing technique in which information about a route is prevented from exiting the router interface through which that information was received. A split-horizon update is used to prevent routing loops.

spoof

1) Method used by a Cisco router to cause a host to handle an interface as if it were running and supporting a session. The router creates false replies to keepalive messages from the host to convince the host that the session still exists. Spoofing is used in a routing environment such as DDR. In DDR, a circuit-switched link is taken down when there is no traffic to save toll charges. 2) When a packet claims to be from an address from which it was not sent. Spoofing is designed to bypass network security mechanisms such as filters and access lists.

SPR

Shortest Path Routing

Algorithm that uses the length of a path to determine a shortest-path spanning tree. Shortest-path routing is commonly used in link-state routing algorithms.

SSH

Secure Shell

In-band protocol used to encrypt username and password information when it is sent.

SSID

Service Set Identifier

32-character code that normally appears in every packet of a Wi-Fi transmission. The SSID contains the network name for the WLAN. All devices on a WLAN use the same SSID. The SSID code can be set by the network administrator, or it can be automatically assigned.

SSL

Secure Sockets Layer is a protocol used for protecting confidential information and private documents across the Internet. SSL uses a cryptographic system that uses two keys to encrypt data: a public key or digital certificate, and a private or secret key known only to the recipient of the message.

stakeholder

Person or organization that has an interest in the success of a process.

standard ACL

Access control list that accepts or denies packets based on the source IP address. Standard ACLs are identified by the number assigned to them. The numbers range from 1 to 99 and from 1300 to 1999.

star

Structure in which devices on a network are connected to a common central switch by point-to-point links. The star topology is the most commonly used physical topology for Ethernet LANs.

stateful packet inspection

See SPI.

Static NAT

static network address translation

Method in which an internal host with a fixed private IP address is mapped with a fixed public IP address all of the time.

static network address translation

See static NAT.

static route

Path that is manually configured and entered into the routing table. A static route take precedence over routes chosen by dynamic routing protocols.

statistical time-division multiplexing

See STDM.

STDM

statistical time-division multiplexing

Technique where information from multiple logical channels is transmitted across a single physical channel. STDM dynamically allocates bandwidth only to active input channels, making better use of available bandwidth and allowing many devices to be connected.

Statistical time-division multiplexing is also known as statistical multiplexing or stat mux.

storage area network

See SAN.

storage networking

Infrastructure that uses SAN and security measures to support the network-based storage needs.

store and forward

See store and forward packet switching.

store and forward packet switching

Technique in which frames are completely processed before being forwarded out of the appropriate port. Store and forward packet switching is a process that includes the calculation of the cyclic redundancy check and the verification of the destination address.

STP

Spanning Tree Protocol

Bridge standards that use the spanning-tree algorithm and enable a bridge to dynamically work around loops in a network topology by creating a spanning tree. A bridge exchanges BPDU messages with other bridges to detect loops, and then removes the loops by shutting down selected bridge interfaces.

streaming video
Multimedia that is continually downloaded to the receiving host as an end-user is viewing the material. The end-user does not fully download the multimedia file to the computer.

Streaming media is also known as live video.

structured cabling
Using an internationally recognized standard to implement a physical network cabling design.

STS-1
Synchronous Transport Signal level 1

SONET format adopted by common carriers for high-speed digital circuits that operate at 51.84 Mbps.

STS-3c
Synchronous Transport Signal level 3, concatenated

SONET format that specifies the frame structure for the 155.52-Mbps lines used to carry Asynchronous Transfer Mode cells.

stub area
OSPF area that carries a default route, intra-area routes, and interarea routes, but does not carry external routes. Virtual links cannot be configured across a stub area, and they cannot contain an autonomous system border router.

stub network
Network that has only a single connection to a router.

STUN
serial tunnel

Router feature that allows two SDLC- or HDLC-compliant devices to connect to each other through an arbitrary multiprotocol topology, with the use of Cisco routers, rather than through a direct serial link.

subinterface
One of a number of virtual interfaces on a single physical interface.

subnet address
Portion of an IP address that is specified as the subnetwork by the subnet mask.

subnet mask
In IPv4, a 32-bit number associated with an IP address to determine where the network portion of an IP address ends and the host portion in an IP address begins.

subnetwork
System in an IP network that shares a particular subnet address. A subnetwork is arbitrarily segmented by a network administrator to provide a multilevel, hierarchical routing structure while shielding the subnetwork from the addressing complexity of attached networks.

subset advertisement
VTP message that contains new VLAN information based on the summary advertisement.

substitution
Troubleshooting technique using functioning parts to test equipment.

sub-subnet
Further division of a subnetted network address.

successor route
Equal cost, primary loop-free path with the lowest metric to the destination determined by the topology and recorded in in the routing table.

summary advertisement
Current VTP domain name and configuration revision number issued periodically by a Catalyst switch.

supernet
See supernetting.

supernetting
Process of summarizing of contiguous class addresses given out by the Internet community. An example of supernetting is when a group of class C addresses 200.100.16.0 through 200.100.31.0 is summarized into the address 200.100.16.0 with a mask of 255.255.224.0.

Also known as classless inter-domain routing.

SVC
switched virtual circuit

Route that is dynamically established on demand and is destroyed when transmission is complete. An SVC is used in situations where data transmission is sporadic.

switch
Network device that filters, forwards, and floods frames based on the destination address of each frame. A switch operates at the data-link layer of the OSI Reference Model.

switch block
Configuration where a router, or multilayer switch, is deployed in pairs, with Access Layer switches evenly divided between them. Each switch block acts independently which prevents the network from going down if a device fails.

A switch block is also known as a building or departmental switch block.

switched multimegabit data service
See SMDS.

switched port analyzer
See SPAN.

switched virtual circuit
See SVC.

switching loop
Causes duplicate frames to be sent throughout a network. A switching loop occurs when there is more than one path between two switches.

symmetric cryptography
Type of of data coding that involves algorithms that use the same key for two separate steps of the process. Examples of symmetric cryptography include encryption and decryption, and signature creation and verification.

symmetric key
Cryptographic key that is used in a symmetric cryptographic algorithm.

Synchronous Digital Hierarchy
See SDH.

Synchronous Optical Network
See SONET.

synchronous transmission
Digital signals that are sent with precise clocking. Synchronous transmission signals have the same frequency, with individual characters encapsulated in start and stop bits, that designate the beginning and end of each character.

Synchronous Transport Signal level 1
See STS-1.

Synchronous Transport Signal level 3, concatenated
See STS-3c.

syslog
Type of message logged and sent to an external server to inform users of various reports in real time.

system-level acceptance testing
Practice of verifying if a network meets the business goals and design requirements. The results of system-level acceptance testing are recorded and are part of the documentation provided to the customer.

T1
Digital WAN carrier facility that transmits DS-1-formatted data at 1.544 Mbps through the telephone-switching network, with the use of AMI or binary 8-zero substitution coding.

T3
Digital WAN carrier facility that transmits DS-3-formatted data at 44.736 Mbps through the telephone switching network.

Tc
committed time

Calculated time interval that data takes to travel a specific distance.

T-carrier
Any of several digitally multiplexed telecommunications carrier systems.

TDM
time division multiplexing

Division of bandwidth to allow multiple logical signals to be transmitted simultaneously across a single physical channel. The signals are then seperated at the receiving end.

telecommunications room
Facility that contains network and telecommunications equipment, vertical and horizontal cable terminations, and cross-connect cables.

Also known as a riser, a distibution facility, or a wiring closet.

telecommunications service provider
See TSP.

telecommuting
Working from a location other than the centralized office.

teleconferencing
Method for a group of people to communicate in real time online.

telephony
Technology designed to convert audio to digital signals, and to transmit the signals over a network, especially packet-switched networks.

teleworker
Employee that works at a location other than the centralized office.

Teleworking
Employee that works at a location other than the centralized office location.

Telnet
TCP/IP protocol that allows a remote user to log on to a host on the network and issue commands remotely.

TFTP
Trivial File Transfer Protocol

Standards that allows files to be transferred from one computer to another over a network. TFTP is a simplified version of FTP .

three-way handshake
Series of synchronization and acknowledgments used by TCP to open a connection.

threshold
Acceptable level of errors on an interface.

threshold value
Maximum number of errors that a switch allows before it will go into store and forwarding switching to slow traffic and correct the problem.

time division multiplexing
See TDM.

time slice
Period of time during which a conversation has complete use of the physical media. Bandwidth is allocated to each channel or time slot. In standard TDM, if a sender has nothing to say, the time slice goes unused, wasting valuable bandwidth. In STDM, it keeps track of conversations that require extra bandwidth. It then dynamically reassigns unused time slices on an as-needed basis to minimize the use of bandwidth.

Time-based ACL
An ACL that permits and denies specified traffic based on the time of day or day of the week. Time-based ACLs are similar to extended ACLs in function, but they support access control based on a time range. A time range is created to define specific times of the day and week for controlling access. The time range relies on the router system clock, and the feature works best with Network Time Protocol (NTP) synchronization.

Top-down
See top-down approach.

top-down approach
Method for testing a network designed to support specific network applications and service requirements. When a design is complete, a prototype or proof-of-concept test is performed using the top-down approach approach to ensure that the new design functions as expected before it is implemented.

topology
Map of the arrangement of network nodes and media within an enterprise networking infrastructure. Topology can be physical or logical.

topology database
Location on a topology that stores SPF tree information.

topology table
One of three tables on an EIGRP router. The topology table lists all routes learned from each EIGRP neighbor. DUAL takes the information from the neighbor and topology tables and calculates the lowest cost routes to each network. The topology table identifies up to four primary loop-free routes for any one destination.

ToS
type of service

8-bit field used for frame classification located in the IP packet and used by a device to indicate the precedence or priority of a given frame. ToS is not used when a frame is received that contains an 802.1q frame tag.

traffic filtering
Control traffic in various segments of the network. Traffic filtering is the process of analyzing the contents of a packet to determine if the packet should be allowed or blocked.

traffic shaping
Using queues to limit surges that can congest a network. In traffic shaping, data is buffered and then sent into the network in regulated amounts to ensure that the traffic will fit within the promised traffic envelope for the particular connection. Traffic shaping is used in networks such as ATM and Frame Relay.

channel service unit
See CSU.

channel service unit/data service unit
See CSU/DSU.

CHAP
Challenge Handshake Authentication Protocol

Security feature supported on lines that use PPP encapsulation to prevent unauthorized access by identifying the remote user. CHAP is a three-way handshake with encryption and enables the router or access server to determine whether a user is allowed access.

child route
Subnet route on an EIGRP network.

CIDR
classless inter-domain routing

Technique based on route aggregation and supported by Border Gateway Protocol v4 that allows routers to group routes to reduce the quantity of information carried by the core routers. When using CIDR, multiple IP networks appear as a single, larger entity to networks outside of the group.

cipher string
Encrypted form of plain text.

CIR
committed information rate

Speed, measured in bits per second and is averaged over a minimum increment of time, that a Frame Relay network transfers information. CIR is a negotiated tariff metric.

circuit
Communication path between two or more points.

circuit switching
System in which a dedicated physical circuit path exists between sender and receiver for the duration of the connection. Circuit switching is often used in a telephone company network.

Cisco adaptive security appliance
See ASA.

Cisco Discovery Protocol
See CDP.

Cisco Enterprise Architectures
Combination of core network infrastructure with productivity-enhancing advanced technologies including IP communications, mobility, and advanced security. Cisco Enterprise Network Architecture divides the three-layer hierarchical design into modular areas. The modules represent different physical or logical connectivity. They also designate where different functions occur in the network. The modularity of the Cisco Enterprise Network Architecture allows flexibility in network design and facilitates implementation and troubleshooting.

Cisco Internetwork Operating System software
See Cisco IOS software.

Cisco IOS software
Cisco Internetwork Operating System software

Application that provides common functionality, scalability, and security for all Cisco products. Cisco IOS software allows centralized, integrated, and automated installation and management of internetworks, while ensuring support for a wide variety of protocols, media, services, and platforms.

Cisco Security Agent
Consists of host-based agents, deployed on mission-critical desktops and servers that report to the Cisco Management Center for Cisco Security Agents. The Management Center runs as a standalone application performing configuration of Cisco Security Agent deployments. Cisco Security Agents provide threat protection for servers, desktops, and laptops.

Cisco Security Device Management
See SDM.

Cisco switch clustering
Management of up to 16 switches simultaneously through a single IP address. To create redundancy in Cisco switch clustering, a network administrator assigns an IP address to a second switch. If the primary command switch fails, the backup or secondary command switch seamlessly takes over the management of the cluster. A user can still access the cluster through the virtual IP address.

Cisco switch clustering technology is featured in Catalyst 3500 XL, 2900 XL, 2955/2950, 2970, 3550, 3560, 3750, 4500, and Catalyst 1900/2820 Standard and Enterprise Edition switches.

Cisco Unified Communications Manager
IP-based PBX in an IP telephony solution. Cisco Unified Communications Manager acts as a call agent for IP phones and MGCP gateways. It can interact with H.323 or SIP devices using the protocols of the devices.

Cisco Unified Communications Manager is also known as Cisco Unified CallManager or CallManager.

CiscoView
GUI-based management application that provides dynamic status, statistics, and comprehensive configuration information for Cisco internetworking devices. In addition to displaying a physical view of Cisco device chassis, CiscoView also provides device monitoring functions and basic troubleshooting capabilities, and can be integrated with several SNMP-based network management platforms.

CiscoWorks
Series of SNMP-based internetwork management applications for monitoring router and access server status, managing configuration files, and troubleshooting network problems. CiscoWorks applications are integrated on several platforms including SunNet Manager, HP OpenView, and IBM NetView.

class-based weighted fair queueing
See CBWFQ.

classful
Type of subnetting that uses the extension of the subnet mask. An example of classful subnetting is IPv4.

classful boundary
Designation of subnets as a single Class A, B, or C network by protocols such as RIP and EIGRP.

classful routing
Selecting a path on a network without including subnet mask information. In classful routing, variable-length subnet masks are not supported.

classless inter-domain routing
See CIDR.

classless routing
Feature of a protocol where the subnet mask is sent with all routing update packets. Classless routing protocols include RIPv2, EIGRP, and OSPF.

Classless Routing Protocol
Standard that instructs data to send a subnet mask with all routing update packets. A classless routing protocol is necessary when the mask cannot be assumed or determined by the value of the first octet. Classless routing protocols include RIPv2, EIGRP, and OSPF.

CLI
command line interface

Ability to interact with the operating system that requires the user to enter commands and optional arguments on a command line.

client
Device requesting services or information.

client-to-client
From one end station to another end station on a network.

client-to-distributed server
From an end station to the server.

client-to-enterprise edge
From an end station to the perimeter of the enterprise before entering the Internet.

client-to-server farm
From an end user to a location with a number of servers.

clocking
Rate at which data moves onto the local loop.

clocking signal
Indicator of the rate at which data moves onto the local loop.

cluster
Network of servers used as a single unit. The redundancy of technology that occurs when clustering improves performance because of load balancing and failover among devices.

clustered
See cluster.

CO
central office

Strategically located environment that accommodates vital devices on a network topology.

coding
Electrical technique used to convey binary signals.

collapsed backbone
Physical media system in which all network segments are interconnected by an internetworking device. An example of a collapsed backbone is a virtual network segment that exists in a device such as a hub, router, or switch.

collision

Result when two or more devices transmit frames simultaneously which impact and become damaged when they meet on the physical media.

collision domain

Network area in Ethernet where frames that have collided are propagated. Repeaters and hubs have collision domains. LAN switches, bridges, and routers do not.

co-located

To also be present at a site. A secondary server may be co-located at the same SP for backup.

command line interface

See CLI.

committed burst

See Bc.

committed information rate

See CIR.

committed time

See Tc.

composite metric

Method used on an EIGRP network to calculate the best route for loop-free routing and rapid convergence.

Configuration Builder

Microsoft Windows application that enables the administrator to configure multiple routers at once. Configuration Builder automatically detects the model, software version, image type, and the number and type of installed interfaces on the router being configured. It quickly imports predefined priority queuing lists, access lists, and filters into multiple configuration files.

configuration register

16-bit, user-configurable value in Cisco routers that determines how the router functions during initialization. The configuration register can be stored in hardware or software. In hardware, the value for each bit position is set using jumpers. In software, the values for bit positions are set by specifying a hexadecimal value using configuration commands.

congestion

Traffic in excess of network capacity.

Consultative Committee for International Telegraph

See CCITT.

content addressable memory

See CAM.

content networking

Infrastructure that delivers static, streaming, and dynamic content to an end user in a reliable, scalable, and secure manner. Content networking offers efficient bandwidth management and content distribution for complex, high-bandwidth content, and the flexibility to accommodate new content and services.

Content networking is also known as content delivery networking or Internet content networking.

contiguous

Location of a neighboring device. Contiguous means adjacent or next.

control plane

Collection of processes that run at the process level on the route processor. Control plane processes collectively provide high-level control for most Cisco IOS functions.

converged

Condition where the speed and ability of a group of internetworking devices running a specific routing protocol agree on the topology of the internetwork after a change in the topology.

converged network

A network capable of carrying voice, video and digital data.

convergence

Condition where the speed and ability of a group of internetworking devices running a specific routing protocol moves towards agreement on the topology of the internetwork after a change in the topology.

convergence time

Condition where the speed and ability of a group of internetworking devices running a specific routing protocol react after a change in the topology. The faster the convergence time, the quicker a network can adapt to the new topology.

Core Layer

Layer in a three-layer hierarchical design with the Access Layer and Distrubution Layer. The Core Layer is a high-speed backbone layer between geographically dispersed end networks.

core router

Router in a packet-switched star topology that is part of the backbone. The core router serves as the single pipe through which all traffic from peripheral networks must pass on the way to other peripheral networks.

cost
Value, typically based on hop count, media bandwidth, or other measures, that is assigned by a network administrator and used to compare various paths through an internetwork environment. Costs are used by routing protocols to determine the most favorable path to a particular destination. The lower the cost, the better the path.

Cost is also known as path cost.

count to infinity
Situation in which routers continuously increment the hop count to particular networks when routing algorithms are slow to converge. Typically, an arbitrary hop-count limit is imposed to prevent count to infinity.

CPE
customer premises equipment

Terminating equipment, such as terminals, telephones, and modems, supplied by the telephone company, installed at a customer site, and connected to the telephone company network.

CQ
custom queuing

Method that guarantees bandwidth for traffic by assigning space to each protocol.

CRC
cyclic redundancy check

Store and Forward error checking technique that counts the number of packets the checksum generates by far end device and compares it to the checksum calculated from the data received. A CRC error may indicate noise, gain hits, or transmission problems on the data link or interface.

CRM
customer relationship management

Software used to help organizations attract and retain customers for their growth and expansion.

crossover cable
Style of connecting switches and hubs to be able to send and receive data.

cryptography
Process of transforming plain text into scrambled cipher text.

CSU
channel service unit

Digital interface device that connects end-user equipment to the local digital telephone loop. Often referred to with DSU, as CSU/DSU.

CSU/DSU
channel service unit/data service unit

Network devices that connect an organization to a digital circuit.

custom queuing
See CQ.

customer premise equipment
See CPE.

customer relationship management
See CRM.

cut-through packet switching
Process where data is streamed through a switch so that the leading edge of a packet exits the switch at the output port before the packet finishes entering the input port. Cut-through packet switching enables a device to read, process, and forward packets as soon as the destination address is looked up, and the outgoing port determined.

Cut-through packet switching is also known as on-the-fly packet switching. Contrast with store and forward packet switching.

cut-through switching
Process where data is streamed through a switch so that the leading edge of a packet exits the switch at the output port before the packet finishes entering the input port. Cut-through packet switching enables a device to read, process, and forward packets as soon as the destination address is looked up, and the outgoing port determined.

Cut-through packet switching is also known as on-the-fly packet switching. Contrast with store and forward packet switching.

cycle
Process that is repeated.

cyclic redundancy check
See CRC.

data center
Central management location that monitors all network resources.

A data center is also known as a NOC.

data communications equipment
See DCE.

Data Encryption Standard
See DES.

data integrity
Process, strategy, and technology that ensures data is unchanged from creation to reception.

data service unit
See DSU.

data terminal equipment
See DTE.

datagram
Unit of information on a network that contains the source and destination addresses.

A datagram is also known as a message, packet, segment, or frame.

data-link connection identifier
See DLCI.

DCA
dynamic channel assignment

Open radio frequency that is selected when an access point identifies an unused channel on a WLAN.

DCE
data communications equipment

Physcal connection to a communications network in an EIA expansion environment. The DCE forwards traffic, and provides a clocking signal used to synchronize data transmission between DCE and DTE devices. Examples of DCE devices include a modem and an interface card.

DCE is also known as data circuit-terminating equipment when used in an ITU-T expansion environment.

DE
discard eligible

Designation of a packet in Frame Relay networking. A packet with the DE bit set will be dropped first when a router detects network congestion. The DE bit is set on oversubscribed traffic, which is traffic that was received after the CIR was set.

de facto standard
Format, language, or protocol that becomes a standard because it is widely used. De jure standard, in contrast, is one that exists because of approval by an official standards body.

dead interval
Period of time, in seconds, that a router will wait to hear a Hello from a neighbor before declaring the neighbor down.

dedicated LAN
dedicated local area network

Network segment allocated to a single device. Dedicated LAN technology is used in LAN-switched network topologies.

dedicated line
Bandwidth on a communications line that is indefinitely reserved for transmissions rather than switched when transmission is required.

dedicated local area network
See dedicated LAN.

default gateway
Path of a packet on a network used by default, or as the gateway of last resort, when the destination hosts are not listed in the routing table.

default route
Path of a packet on a network used by default, or as the gateway of last resort, when the destination hosts are not listed in the routing table.

delay
1) Length of time between the initiation of a transaction by a sender and the first response received by the sender. 2) Length of time required to move a packet from source to destination over a given path.

demarc
Indicated point between carrier equipment and CPE.

demilitarized zone
See DMZ.

demodulation
Process of returning a modulated signal to its original form. A modem performs demodulation by taking an analog signal and returning it to its digital form.

demultiplexing
Act of separating a common physical signal into multiple output streams.

denial of service
See DoS.

denies
Rejection of data on a network.

dense wavelength division multiplexing
See DWDM.

DES
Data Encryption Standard

Symmetric key cryptosystem that uses a 56-bit key to ensure high-performance encryption. DES is a cryptographic algorithm developed by the U.S. National Bureau of Standards. Today, DES is no longer considered a strong encryption algorithm by the U.S. government.

designated port
Interface on a device that forwards traffic toward the root bridge but does not connect to the least cost path.

designated router
See DR.

desirable mode
Designation of a port on a device as trunk port if the other end is set to trunk, desirable, or auto mode.

deterministic network
System that is designed for data transmission to follow a pre-defined path for an exact duration.

DH
Diffie-Hellman

Public key exchange method that provides a way for two peers to establish a shared secret key over an insecure communications path.

DHCP
Dynamic Host Configuration Protocol

Standard used by a software utility that requests and assigns an IP address, default gateway, and DNS server address to a network host. DHCP allocates an IP address for a host dynamically so the address can be reused when hosts no longer needs it.

dial backup
Feature on a Cisco router that provides protection against WAN downtime by allowing the network administrator to configure a backup serial line through a circuit-switched connection.

dial-up line
Communications circuit that is established by a switched-circuit connection using a telephone company network.

Differentiated Services Code Point
See DSCP.

Diffie-Hellman
See DH.

diffusing update algorithm
See DUAL.

digital signal level 0
See DS0.

digital signal level 1
See DS1.

digital signal level 3
See DS3.

digital subscriber line
See DSL.

Dijkstra's Algorithm
Process used in a SPF to dentify all paths to each destination and the total cost of each path.

discard eligible
See DE.

discarding
State of a port in an RSTP network where the server does not send a reply. A solid amber LED signifies discarding is in process.

discontiguous
Address on a network that is separated by a network or subnet from other subnets.

discontiguous network
Networking system with non-adjacent subnets, or subnets that are separated from other subnets by other networks.

discontiguous subnet
Address on a network that is separated by a network or subnet from other subnets.

distance vector

Type of routing protocol that periodically informs directly-connected routers of changes on the network.

Distance Vector Multicast Routing Protocol

See DVMRP.

distance vector protocol

Type of standards that uses distance to select the best path. Examples of a distance vector protocol include RIP, IGRP, and EIGRP.

distance vector routing algorithm

Mathematical process that uses the number of hops in a route to find the shortest path to a destination. Distance vector routing algorithms call for each router to send its entire routing table in each update, but only to its neighbors. Distance vector routing algorithms can be prone to routing loops, but are computationally simpler than link-state routing algorithms.

distributed collaborative information system

Database and application programs that support online asynchronous collaborative activities.

Distribution Layer

Layer in a hierarchical design between the Access layer and Core layer. The Distribution layer interconnects access layer hosts and switches, and provides security and traffic management for the Core Layer.

divide-and-conquer

Troubleshooting technique to resolve a network issue by breaking down the problem into smaller parts that are more manageable.

DLCI

data-link connection identifier

Layer 2 address that is required for each virtual circuit to reach a destination on an NBMA network. The DLCI is stored in the address field of every frame transmitted. The DLCI usually has only local significance and may be different at each end of a virtual circuit.

DMZ

demilitarized zone

Area in a network design that is located between the internal network and external network, usually the Internet. The DMZ is accessible to devices on the Internet, such as a web server, FTP server, SMTP server, and DNS.

DNS

Domain Name System

System used in the Internet for translating names of network nodes into IP addresses

domain

Portion of the naming hierarchy tree that refers to general groupings of networks based on the type of organization or geography.

Domain Name System

See DNS.

DoS

denial of service

Attack by a single system on a network that floods the bandwidth or resources of a targeted system, such as a web server, with the purpose of shutting it down.

dot1q

See IEEE 802.1Q.

downtime

Percentage of time in which a network is unavailable because of administrative shutdown or equipment failure.

DR

Router that is designated by the OSPF Hello protocol on an OSPF network that has at least two attached routers. A designated router generates LSAs. It enables a reduction in the number of adjacencies required which reduces the amount of routing protocol traffic and the size of the topological database.

DRAM

dynamic random access memory

This non-permanent working memory on a Cisco router includes primary DRAM used for holding routing tables and the running configuration, and shared DRAM used for supporting packet buffering.

DROther

Any router on an OSPF network that is not the DR or BDR.

DS0

digital signal level 0

Framing specification when transmitting digital signals over a single channel at 64-kbps on a T1 facility.

DS1
digital signal level 1

Framing specification when transmitting digital signals at 1.544-Mbps on a T1 facility in the United States, or at 2.108-Mbps on an E1 facility in Europe.

DS3
digital signal level 3

Framing specification when transmitting digital signals at 44.736-Mbps on a T3 facility.

DSCP
differentiated services code point

Field in an IP packet that enables different levels of service to be assigned to network traffic. DSCP can be assigned by the router or switch. The first six bits in the ToS byte in the header is the DSCP.

DSL
Public network service that delivers high bandwidth at limited distances over the copper wiring of conventional telephone lines that run between the CPE and the DSLAM of a SP. DSL incorporates technology that enables devices to immediately connect to the Internet when they are powered on. DSL is a physical layer transmission technology similar to dial, cable, or wireless technologies.

DSU
data service unit

Digital transmission device that adapts the physical interface on a DTE to a transmission facility such as T1 or E1. The DSU is also responsible for functions such as signal timing. Often referred to with CSU, as CSU/DSU.

DTE
data terminal equipment

Physical connection to the user end in an EIA expansion environment. The DTE serves as a data source, destination, or both. It connects to a data network through a DCE device, such as a modem, and typically uses clocking signals generated by the DCE. Examples of DTE devices include computers, protocol translators, and multiplexers.

DUAL
diffusing update algorithm

Mathematical process used in EIGRP that provides loop-free operation at every instant throughout a route computation. DUAL allows routers involved in a topology change to synchronize at the same time, while not involving routers that are unaffected by the change.

dual stack
Two similar protocol systems operating concurrently on one device. For example, a strategy for IPv4 transitioning to IPv6 is to run both protocol stacks on the same device. This enables IPv4 and IPv6 to coexist.

DVMRP
Distance Vector Multicast Routing Protocol

Internetwork gateway protocol largely based on RIP that implements a typical dense mode IP multicast scheme. DVMRP uses IGMP to exchange routing datagrams with its neighbors.

DWDM
dense wavelength division multiplexing

Process that assigns incoming optical signals to specific frequencies or wavelengths of light. DWDM can amplify these wavelengths to boost the signal strength. It can multiplex more than 80 different wavelengths or channels of data onto a single piece of fiber. Each channel is capable of carrying a multiplexed signal at 2.5 Gbps.

Dynamic ACL
An ACL that requires a user to use Telnet to connect to the router and authenticate. An extended ACL initially blocks traffic through the router. Users that want to traverse the router are blocked by the extended ACL until they Telnet to the router and are authenticated. The Telnet connection then drops, and a single-entry dynamic ACL entry is added to the existing extended ACL. This entry permits traffic for a particular time period; idle and absolute timeouts are possible. Dynamic ACLs are sometimes referred to as "lock and key" because the user is required to login in order to obtain access.

dynamic channel assignment
dynamic channel assignment

Open radio frequency that is selected when an access point identifies an unused channel on a WLAN.

Dynamic Host Configuration Protocol
See DHCP.

dynamic NAT
dynamic network address translation

Network Address Translation process that converts a local IP address to a global IP address by assigning the first available IP address in a pool of public addresses to an inside host. The host uses the assigned global IP address for the length of a session. When the session ends, the global address returns to the pool for use by another host.

dynamic network address translation
See dynamic NAT.

dynamic routing
Process of finding a path that adjusts automatically to network topology or traffic changes.

Dynamic routing is also known as adaptive routing.

E1
Wide-area digital transmission scheme used predominantly in Europe that carries data at a rate of 2.048 Mbps. E1 lines can be leased for private use from common carriers.

E2
Route outside of the OSPF routing domain, redistributed into OSPF.

E3
Wide-area digital transmission scheme used predominantly in Europe that carries data at a rate of 34.368 Mbps. E3 lines can be leased for private use from common carriers.

ECNM
Enterprise Composite Network Model

Cisco network design that divides the network into functional components while still maintaining the concept of Core, Distribution, and Access layers. The functional components are the Enterprise Campus, Enterprise Edge, and Service Provider Edge.

edge device
Filter on the perimeter of an enterprise network where incoming packets are passed. Examples of edge devices include firewall and DMZ. Edge devices may be equipped with IDS and IPS to examine and block unwanted traffic.

EGP
Exterior Gateway Protocol

Standards for exchanging routing information between autonomous systems. EGP is an obsolete protocol that was replaced by Border Gateway Protocol.

EIGRP
Enhanced Interior Gateway Routing Protocol

Proprietary Cisco routing protocol that combines distance vector routing protocol standards and link-state routing protocol standards. EIGRP uses the DUAL algorithm to determine routing.

EIGRP is also known as Enhanced IGRP.

EIR
excess information rate

Average rate above the CIR that a VC can support when no network congestion exists.

electromagnetic interference
See EMI.

electronic mail
See email.

email
electronic mail

1) Widely used network application in which mail messages are transmitted electronically between end users over a network using various network protocols. 2) Exchange of computer-stored messages by network communication.

Email is also written e-mail.

EMI
electromagnetic interference

Disturbance in an electronic circuit from an external electrical source.

Encapsulating Security Payload
See ESP.

encapsulation
Transmission of one network protocol within another. Tunneling is the basis of several IP security systems, including IPsec used in VPNs.

encoder
Device that modifies information into a required transmission format.

encoding
Process used to represent bits as voltages in wires or pulses of light in fiber optics.

encryption
Application of a specific algorithm that protects data by scrambling the information as it is sent and unscrambling the data when it is delivered.

end of transmission
See EOT.

Enhanced Interior Gateway Routing Protocol
See EIGRP.

Enhanced Rapid Spanning Tree Protocol
See RSTP+.

enterprise
Corporation, business, or other entity that uses computers in a networked environment. An enterprise usually refers to large companies or organizations with complex networks.

Enterprise Composite Network model
See ECNM.

enterprise network
Network that integrates all systems within a company or organization. An enterprise network differs from a WAN because it is privately owned and maintained.

Enterprise Network Architectures
See enterprise network.

EOT
end of transmission

Character that signifies that the transfer of data has ended.

equal cost
See equal cost load balancing.

equal cost load balancing
Packet distribution technique supported by EIGRP to prevent overloading a network route.

ESP
Encapsulating Security Payload

Security protocol that encapsulates data to be protected. ESP provides a framework for encrypting, authenticating, and securing data. ESP offers data privacy services, optional data authentication, and anti-replay services.

EtherChannel
EtherChannel allows multiple physical Ethernet links to combine into one logical channel. This allows load balancing of traffic among the links in the channel as well as redundancy in the event that one or more links in the channel fail. EtherChannel can support Layer 2 or Layer 3 LAN ports.

Ethernet
Baseband LAN specification invented by Xerox Corporation and developed jointly by Xerox, Intel, and Digital Equipment Corporation. An Ethernet network uses the Carrier Sense Multiple Access/Collision Detection method and runs on cable types of 10 Mbps or more. Ethernet is similar to the IEEE 802.3 series of standards.

EUI-64
extended universal identifier-64 address

IPv6 address format created by taking an interface of the MAC address, which is 48 bits in length, and inserting another 16-bit hexadecimal string, FFFE, between the OUI, first 24 bits and the unique serial number, last 24 bits, of the MAC address. To ensure that the chosen address is from a unique Ethernet MAC address, the seventh bit in the high-order byte is set to 1 to indicate the uniqueness of the 48-bit address.

excess burst
See Be.

excess rate
Traffic on a network that is greater than the insured rate for a given connection. Excess traffic is delivered only if network resources are available, and may be discarded during periods of congestion. The excess rate equals the maximum rate minus the insured rate.

exit interface
Location on a router that the data passes through to move closer to the destination.

extended ACL
Type of access control list that filters source IP addresses, destination IP addresses, MAC addresses, protocol, and port numbers. The identification number assigned to an extended ACL can be from 100 to 199 and from 2000 to 2699.

extended star
Star topology that is expanded to include additional networking devices.

extended universal identifier-64 address
See EUI-64.

Exterior Gateway Protocol
See EGP.

external traffic
Data communication to and from a private network.

extranet
Network that provides access to information or operations of an organization to suppliers, vendors, partners, customers, or other businesses. Extranet is a private network using Internet protocols and the public telecommunication system to share internal resources. It may be considered an extension of an intranet.

faceplate
Protective component usually installed in the front of a device.

failover
Occurance of a redundant network device performing the load or function of another device automatically if the initial device fails. The failover scheme creates a backup system for mission-critical hardware and software. The objective is to reduce the impact of system failure to a minimum by actively monitoring and identifying system failure.

failure domain
Area of a network that is affected when a networking device malfunctions or fails. A properly designed network minimizes the size of failure domains.

Fast Ethernet
100BaseT-type Ethernet specification that offers speed 10 times greater than the standard 10BASE-T Ethernet specification while preserving such qualities as frame format, MAC mechanisms, and MTU. Based on an extension to the IEEE 802.3 specification.

fast switching
Feature developed by Cisco that uses a high-speed switching cache to expedite packet switching in IP routing. Destination IP addresses are stored in the cache to accelerate the packet forwarding process.

fast-forward
Cut-through switching method where the switch forwards the frame before all of frame is received. Using the fast-forward method, the switch forwards the frame out of the destination port immediately when the destination MAC address is read. The switch does not calculate or check the CRC value. The fast-forward method has lowest latency but may forward collision fragments and damaged frames. This method of switching works best in a stable network with few errors.

FCS
frame check sequence

Characters added to a frame for error control purposes. FCS is used in HDLC, Frame Relay, and other Data Link Layer protocols.

FD
feasible distance

Most desireable EIGRP metric along the path to the destination from the router.

feasible distance
See FD.

feasible successor
Backup route identified in a topology table. A feasible successor becomes a successor route if a primary route fails. The feasible successor must have a lower reported distance than the feasible distance of the current successor distance to the destination.

Feature Navigator
Web-based tool on Cisco website that helps to determine which features are supported by a specific IOS software image. Feature Navigator can also be used to find which IOS software images support a specific feature.

FECN
forward explicit congestion notification

Signal in a Frame Relay network to inform DTE that is receiving the frame that congestion was experienced in the path from source to destination. The DTE that receives the FECN signal can request that higher-level protocols take flow-control action as appropriate.

fiber-optic cable
Physical medium capable of conducting modulated light transmission. Compared with other transmission media, fiber-optic cable is more expensive and is capable of higher data rates, but is not susceptible to electromagnetic interference.

Fiber-optic cable is also known as optical fiber.

file transfer
Network application used to move files from one network device to another.

File Transfer Protocol
See FTP.

filter
Process or device that screens network traffic for certain characteristics such as source address, destination address, or protocol, and determines whether to forward or discard traffic based on the established criteria.

firewall
One or more router or access servers designated as a buffer between any connected public networks and a private network. A firewall router uses access lists and other methods to ensure the security of the private network.

firewall rule set
Set of configuration commands put into an access list on a Cisco security appliance or Cisco router that perform firewall functions. Source and destination IP addresses, protocols, or functions of a protocol can be affected by firewall rules.

first mile
Section of physical medium leading from the location of the customer to the central office of a service provider.

fixed configuration
Rules that are set and cannot be altered. An example of fixed configuration is a Layer 2 switch that has the number of ports and type of ports, such as FastEthernet and gigabit Ethernet, that are preconfigured in the factory.

flapping
Problem in routing when an advertised route between two devices alternates between two paths due to intermittent failures on a network.

flash memory
memory used to store and run the Cisco IOS software. When a router is powered down, the contents of flash memory are not lost. Depending on the router model, flash memory can be implemented on erasable programmable read-only memory (EPROM) chips, or in external compact flash memory cards. (It is called flash memory, since the contents of the EPROMs can be upgraded by "flashing" the chip.)

flash update
Routing information sent asynchronously in response to a change in the network topology.

flat network
System where all stations can be reached without having to pass through a device such as a router.

floating static route
Path that is manually configured and entered into the routing table that has an administrative distance set greater than the administrative distance of a dynamic route. This route is only used if the existing dynamic route becomes unavailable.

floods
Technique used by switches to pass traffic that is received on an interface to all other interfaces of the device except the interface on which the information was originally received.

flow control
Ability to maintain the rate of activity on a network.

form factor
Physical size and shape of computer components. Components that share the same form factor are physically interchangeable.

forward explicit congestion notification
See FECN.

forwarding
Process of sending a frame out of a port toward the destination by way of an internetworking device. Examples of devices that forward frames are hosts, repeaters, bridges, and routers.

fractional E1
Portion of a high-bandwidth E1 connection offered to a customer by a service provider.

fractional T1
Portion of a high-bandwidth T1 connection offered to a customer by a service provider.

FRAD
Frame Relay access device

Network device that provides a connection between a LAN and a Frame Relay WAN. A FRAD adds and removes headers and trailers for incoming packets.

fragment
Piece of a packet that has been broken down to smaller units.

fragmentation
Process of breaking a packet into smaller units when transmitting over a network medium that cannot support the size of the packet.

fragment-free
A switching technique that forwards a frame after the first 64 bytes are received. Fragment-free switching has a higher latency than fast-forward switching.

frame check sequence
See FCS.

Frame Relay
Industry-standard, switched, WAN standard that operates at the Physical Layer and Data Link Layer of the OSI Reference Model. Frame Relay handles multiple virtual circuits using HDLC encapsulation between connected devices. It is more efficient than the X.25 protocol that it replaced.

Frame Relay access device
See FRAD.

Frame Relay access support
See FRAS.

Frame Relay bridging
Technique described in RFC 1490 that uses the same spanning-tree algorithm as other bridging functions, but allows packets to be encapsulated for transmission across a Frame Relay network.

frame tagging
Method used by a Cisco Catalyst switch to identify the VLAN a frame belongs to. When a frame enters a switch it is encapsulated with a header that tags it with a VLAN identification.

FRAS
Frame Relay access support

Cisco IOS software feature that allows SDLC, Token Ring, Ethernet, and Frame Relay IBM devices to connect to other IBM devices across a Frame Relay network.

FTP
File Transfer Protocol

Defined in RFC 959, set of standards for transferring files between network nodes. FTP is commonly used to transfer webpages and download programs and other files to a computer.

full mesh
Network topolgy where each device connects to all others using either a physical or virtual circuit. Full mesh provides redundancy in the functionality of the network. It is usually reserved for network backbones because of the high cost of implementation.

gateway
Device that performs an application layer conversion of information from one protocol stack to another. An example of a gateway is the device that connects a traditional PSTN or analog phone to an IP network in VoIP.

Gateway Discovery Protocol
See GDP.

Gateway of Last Resort
Final stop on a route within an enterprise for packets that cannot be matched. Information about the packets appears in the routing tables of all routers.

GDP
Gateway Discovery Protocol

Cisco standard that allows a host to dynamically detect the arrival of a new router as well as determine when a router disconnects. GDP is based on UDP.

Generic Routing Encapsulation
See GRE.

Gigabit Ethernet
Data transmission bandwidth of 1000Mbps on a LAN. Gigabit Ethernet is the standard for high-speed Ethernet, approved by the IEEE 802.3z standards committee in 1996.

global unicast address
Unique IPv6 unicast address that can be routed worldwide with no modification. A global unicast address shares the same address format as an IPv6 anycast address. A global unicast address is assigned by IANA.

GMT
Greenwich Mean Time

Time zone located at 0 degrees longitude that sets the standard for all time zones.

GRE
Generic Routing Encapsulation

Cisco tunneling protocol used to encapsulate different protocols into a standard Internet protocol for transmission.

Greenwich Mean Time
See GMT.

hash
One-way encryption algorithm that takes an input message of arbitrary length and produces unique, fixed-length output text.

hash-based message authentication code
See HMAC.

Hashed Message Authentication Code-Message Digest
See HMAC-MD5.

Hashed Message Authentication Code-Secure Hash Alg
See HMAC-SHA-1.

HCC
horizontal cross-connect

Wiring closet where the horizontal cabling connects to a patch panel which is connected by backbone cabling to the main distribution facility.

HDLC
High-Level Data Link Control

Bit-oriented synchronous Data Link Layer protocol developed by ISO. HDLC specifies a data encapsulation method on synchronous serial links using frame characters and checksums.

header
Control information placed before data when the data is encapsulated for network transmission. Examples of a header information are the IP addresses of the sender and recipient.

hello interval
Period of time, in seconds, that a router keeps a Hello packet from a neighbor.

hello packet
Packet that is multicast to detect devices on a network and to test the connections. A hello packet is used by a router to determine the best connection available.

Hello Protocol
Standard used by OSPF systems for establishing and maintaining neighbor relationships. The Hello Protocol is an interior protocol that uses a routing metric based on the length of time it takes a packet to make the trip between the source and the destination.

helper address
Router configuration used to forward broadcast network traffic from a client computer on one subnet to a server in another subnet. A helper address is configured on an interface.

heterogeneous network
System of dissimilar devices that run dissimilar protocols and may support various functions or applications that are able to work together.

hexadecimal
Base 16 numbering system. Hexadecimal is a number representation using the digits 0 through 9, with their common meaning, plus the letters A through F to represent hexadecimal digits with values of 10 to 15. In a hexadecimal system, the right-most digit counts ones, the next counts multiples of 16, such as $16^2=256$.

hierarchical design model
Representation of a network featuring an access layer, a distribution layer, and a core layer.

hierarchical network
Design technique that divides the network into layers to prevent congestion and reduce the size of failure domains. The Cisco hierarchal design model uses core, distribution, and access layers.

hierarchical network design
See hierarchical network.

hierarchical routing
Transfer of data on a system that assigns network addresses based on the role or position of the network device or host.

hierarchical star topology
System on a network where a central switch or router is connected to other switches or routers. The layout of a hierarchical star topology is similar to the hub and spoke of a wheel.

High-Level Data Link Control
See HDLC.

High-Speed Serial Interface
See HSSI.

high-speed WAN interface card
See HWIC.

hijacking
When a hacker illegally gains access to a system through an authenticated connection.

HMAC
Algorithm using cryptographic hash functions to encrypt code. HMAC can be used with any iterative cryptographic hash function, such as MD5 or SHA-1, in combination with a secret shared key.

HMAC-MD5

hashed message authentication code-message digest 5

Algorithm that uses a specific cryptographic hash function called MD5, with a secret key. The output is a 128-bit hash string that can be used to verify the data integrity and the authenticity of a message simultaneously.

HMAC-SHA-1

hashed message authentication code-secure hash algorithm 1

HMAC-SHA-1 computes a Hash-based Message Authentication Code (HMAC) using the SHA1 hash function. The output is a 160-bit hash string that can be used to verify the data integrity and the authenticity of a message simultaneously.

hold time

Length of time that a router treats a neighbor as reachable.

holddown

Placing a router in a state that will neither advertise nor accept routes for a specific length of time, called the holddown period. Holddown is used to remove bad information about a route from all routers in the network. A route is typically placed in holddown when a link in that route fails.

Holddown is also known as a holddown period.

holddown period

See holddown timer.

Holddown timer

Timers that a route is placed in so that routers neither advertise the route nor accept advertisements about the route for a specific length of time (the holddown period). Holddown is used to flush bad information about a route from all routers in the network. A route typically is placed in holddown when a link in that route fails.

hop

Transfer of a data packet between two network devices, such as routers.

hop count

Routing metric that tracks the number of legs that a data packets traverses between a source and a destination. RIP uses hop count as its sole metric.

horizontal cross-connect

See HCC.

host number

Section of an IP address that designates the node on the subnetwork is being addressed.

A host number is also known as a host address.

Hot Standby Router Protocol

See HSRP.

hot-swappable

Ability for a component to be installed or removed without having to turn off the power first. Installing or removing a hot-swappable component will not disturb the operation of other components in a device.

HSRP

Hot Standby Router Protocol

Standard that provides the ability to communicate on an internetwork if a default router becomes unavailable. HSRP provides high network availability and transparent network topology changes.

HSSI

High-Speed Serial Interface

Protocol that establishes the codes and electrical parameters that the router and the CSU/DSU use to communicate with each other.

HTTP

Hypertext Transfer Protocol

Standard used to transfer or convey information on the World Wide Web. HTTP is a communication protocol that establishes a request/response connection on the Internet.

HWIC

high-speed WAN interface card

Optional module for a series of Cisco routers that provides high-speed WAN connectivity.

hybrid network

Internetwork made up of more than one type of network technology, such as a LAN and WAN.

Hypertext Transfer Protocol

See HTTP.

LLQ

low latency queueing

Strict-priority ordered list that allows delay-sensitive data such as voice to be taken out of sequence and sent first. A voice packet is sent to the priority queue part where it has a fixed bandwidth allocation and is served first. A data packet enters the CBWFQ system directly and is assigned priority to determine how the data is treated. LLQ provides strict priority queuing to CBWFQ.

LMI

Local Management Interface

Standard that enhances the basic Frame Relay specification. LMI includes support for a global addressing, and support for keepalive, multicast, and status mechanisms.

load

Amount of traffic on a network.

load balances

See load balancing.

load balancing

Ability of a router to distribute traffic over all network interfaces that are the same distance from the destination address. Load balancing increases the use of network segments which improves bandwidth. A load-balancing algorithm may use both line speed and reliability information.

local access rate

Clock speed, or port speed, of the local loop connection to the Frame Relay cloud.

local area network

See LAN.

local area network switch

See LAN switch.

local loop

Physical line from the premises or demarcation point of a telephone subscriber to the edge of the carrier or telephone company central office.

A local loop is also known as a subscriber line.

Local Management Interface

See LMI.

logging

Process to recording and accessing details about packets on a network that have been permitted or denied.

logical topology

Map of the flow of data on a network that shows how devices communicate with each other.

loop

Route on a network where a packet never reaches its destination. A loop carries data repeatedly through a constant series of network nodes.

loopback interface

Connection between devices that share the same type of routing.

Low Latency Queuing

See LLQ.

LSA

link-state advertisement

Broadcast packet used by a link-state protocol. An LSA contains information about neighbors and path costs. It is used by the receiving routers to maintain routing tables.

A LSA is also known as link-state packet.

LWAP

lightweight access point

Access point used in the Cisco Unified Wireless Network architecture. LWAPs depend on a Cisco WLAN controller for configuration and security information.

LWAPP

Light Weight Access Point Protocol

LWAPP is a draft protocol standard that defines how lightweight access points communicate with a centralized WLAN intelligence. LWAPP is used to manage security, mobility, QoS, and other functions essential to WLAN operations over an entire wireless enterprise.

MAC address

Media Access Control Address

Standardized data link layer address that is required for every port or device that connects to a LAN. Other devices in the network use these addresses to locate specific ports in the network and to create and update routing tables and data structures. MAC addresses are 6 bytes long and are controlled by the IEEE.

MAC address is also known as a hardware address, a MAC-layer address, or a physical address.

main cross-connect
See MCC.

main distribution facility
See MDF.

manageability
Ability of a system to be administered.

management domain
Information included on a message that each switch advertises on its trunk ports.

management information base
See MIB.

management virtual local area network
See management VLAN.

management VLAN
management virtual local area network

VLAN1 on a switch. The IP address of VLAN1 is used to access and configure the switch remotely and to exchange information with other network devices.

manual summarization
Feature on an EIGRP route where the administrator determines which subnets on which interfaces are advertised as summary routes. Manual summarization is done on a per-interface basis and gives the network administrator complete control. A manually summarized route appears in the routing table as an EIGRP route sourced from a logical interface.

maximum transmission unit
See MTU.

MCC
main cross-connect

Wiring closet that serves as the most central point in a star topology. An MCC is where LAN backbone cabling connects to the Internet.

MCU
multipoint control unit

Device used to support multiple-party conference calls. Members of the conference call can send media to the MCU which mixes the media and then sends it to all participants.

MD5
Message Digest 5

Method of authentication that requires that each router has a unique key and key ID. The router uses an algorithm that processes the key, the OSPF packet, and the key ID to generate an encrypted number. Each OSPF packet includes that encrypted number. The key is never transmitted.

MDF
main distribution facility

Primary communications room for a building. An MDF is the central point of a star networking topology where patch panels, hubs, and routers are located. It is used to connect public or private lines coming into the building to internal networks.

Media Access Control Address
See MAC Address.

media converter
Data Link Layer process on a router that changes a frame to Ethernet if it is on a LAN and to a WAN interface if it exits the LAN and enters the Internet.

mesh
Network topology where devices are organized in a segmented manner with interconnections strategically placed between network nodes.

metric
Information a routing algorithm uses to determine the best route on a network. Metrics are stored in a routing table. Metrics include bandwidth, communication cost, delay, hop count, load, MTU, path cost, and reliability.

Metro Ethernet
Network system based on Ethernet technology that covers a metropolitan area.

MIB
management information base

Database of network management information that is used and maintained by a network management protocol such as SNMP or Common Management Information Protocol, also known as CMIP. The value of a MIB object can be changed or retrieved using SNMP or CMIP commands. MIB objects are organized in a tree structure that includes public, or standard, and private, or proprietary, branches.

microprocessor
Chip that contains the central processing unit for the device.

microsegment
See microsegmentation.

microsegmentation
Division of a network into smaller segments, usually with the intention of increasing aggregate bandwidth to network devices.

Microsoft Visio
Diagramming application software published by Microsoft.

mission-critical
Type of network or computing process that is vital to an organization. Mission-critical applications that are halted often or for too long may have negative consequences.

Mobile Internet Protocol
See mobile IP.

Mobile IP
Mobile Internet Protocol

IETF standard for IPv4 and IPv6 which enables a mobile device to move without breaking the connection. Mobility is a feature of IPv6.

modem
Device that converts digital computer signals into a format that is sent and received over an analog telephone line. Modem is the common term for modulator-demodulator.

modular block diagram
Illustration of the major functions of a network in modular form. A modular block diagram helps a designer determine the underlying architecture on which the network is built.

modulated
See modulation.

modulates
See modulation.

modulation
Process where the characteristics of an electrical signal is transformed to represent information. Types of modulation include amplitude modulation, frequency modulation, and pulse amplitude modulation.

MOSPF
Multicast Open Shortest Path First

Intradomain multicast routing protocol used in Open Shortest Path First networks. An extension is applied to the base OSPF unicast protocol to support IP multicast routing. Multicast information is included in OSPF link-state advertisements. MOSPF builds a distribution tree for each group and computes a tree

for active sources sent to the group. The tree state is cached and must be recomputed when a link-state change occurs or when the cache times out.

MOSPF is also known as multicast OSPF.

MPLS
Multiprotocol Label Switching

Standard used to increase the speed of traffic flow on a network. The MPLS process marks each packet with the path sequence to the destination instead of using a routing table. Packet switching is done at Layer 2 of the OSI Reference Model. MPLS supports protocols such as IP, ATM, and Frame Relay.

MS Visio
Diagramming application software published by Microsoft.

MTU
maximum transmission unit

Maximum packet size, in bytes, that a particular interface can handle.

multi-access
Type of network that allows multiple devices to connect and communicate simultaneously.

multicast
Single packets copied by the network and sent to a specific subset of network addresses. Multicast addresses are specified in the destination address field.

Multicast Open Shortest Path First
See MOSPF.

multilayer switch
Device that filters and forwards packets based on MAC addresses and network addresses. A layer 2/layer 3 switch is a multilayer switch.

multilayer switching
Device that filters and forwards packets based on MAC addresses and network addresses. A layer 2/layer 3 switch is a multilayer switch.

multiplexing
Scheme that allows multiple logical signals to be transmitted simultaneously across a single physical channel. The signals are then seperated at the receiving end.

multipoint control unit
See MCU.

Multiprotocol Label Switching
See MPLS.

NAC
network admission control

Method of preventing a virus from infecting a computer by controlling access to a network. NAC uses protocols and software products to assess a host that tries to log onto a network. NAC determines the condition, called the posture, of the host,. An infected host may be placed in quarantine. A host with outdated virus protection will be directed to obtain an update. An uninfected host with virus protection will be allowed on the network.

Network admission control is also known as network access control.

NACL
named access control list

Standard or extended format that are referenced by a descriptive name rather than a number. When configuring a NACL, the router IOS uses a NACL subcommand mode.

NACL is also known as named ACL.

named access control list
See NACL.

NAS
network attached storage

High-speed, high-capacity data storage that groups large numbers of disk drives that are directly attached to the network and can be used by any server. A NAS device is typically attached to an Ethernet network and is assigned its own IP address.

NAT
Network Address Translation

Standard used to reduce the number of IP addresses necessary for all nodes within the organization to connect to the Internet. NAT allows a large group of private users to access the Internet by converting packet headers for only a small pool of public IP addresses and keeping track of them in a table.

NAT overload
Dynamically translates multiple inside local addresses to a single public address so more than one client can access the connection to the Internet.

native VLAN
Special VLAN that accomodates untagged traffic. Trunk links carry untagged traffic over the native VLAN. On Cisco Catalyst switches, VLAN1 is the native VLAN.

NAT-PT
Network Address Translation-Protocol Translation

Mechanism located between an IPv6 network and an IPv4 network to translate IPv6 packets into IPv4 packets and vice versa.

NBAR
Network Based Application Recognition

Cisco utility that conducts audits and traffic analysis. NBAR is a classification and protocol discovery tool that identifies traffic up to the application layer. It provides interface, protocol, and bi-directional statistics for each traffic flow that traverses an interface. NBAR does sub-port classification, which include looking and identifying beyond application ports. NBAR recognizes web-based and other protocols that use dynamic TCP and UDP port assignments.

NBMA
non-broadcast multi-access

Network that does not support broadcasting, such as X.25, or broadcasting is not possible, such as a SMDS.

NCP
Network Control Protocol

Standard that routes and controls the flow of data between a communications controller, in which it resides, and other network resources.

negotiate parameter
Parameter on a switch that automatically detects the encapsulation type of the neighbor switch.

neighbor
Routers that have interfaces to a common network in OSPF. On a multi-access network, neighbors are dynamically discovered by the OSPF Hello protocol.

neighbor table
One of three interconnected EIGRP router tables. The neighbor table collects and lists information about directly connected neighbor routers. A sequence number records the number of the last received hello from each neighbor and time-stamps the time that the packet arrived. If a hello packet is not received within the hold time, the timer expires and DUAL recalculates the topology. Other router tables include topology and routing tables.

neighboring routers
Routers that have interfaces to a common network in OSPF. On a multi-access network, neighbors are dynamically discovered by the OSPF Hello protocol.

NetFlow
Accounting tool used to analyze and provide details about traffic patterns in a network. NetFlow can be used to capture the traffic classification or precedence associated with each flow.

network access control
Limit access to the physical components of a network.

Network Address Translation
See NAT.

Network Address Translation-Protocol Translation
See NAT-PT.

network admission control
See NAC.

network analyzer
Monitoring device or software application that maintains statistical information about the status of the network and each device attached to it. Some network analyzers are able to detect, define, and fix problems on the network.

network attached storage
See NAS.

network backbone
Core network architecture for an enterprise. Network backbone connects all LAN segments of a system and provides fast switching between subnets.

Network Based Application Recognition
See NBAR.

network baseline
Process that involves monitoring network performance and behavior over a certain period of time to create a point of reference for future network evaluations. Network baseline is used by network administrators to monitor the network and troubleshoot if there is a problem.

network boundary
Location where route summarization occurs on a boundary router.

Network Control Protocol
See NCP.

network diameter
Maximum number of hops between any two end stations in the network. Network diameter is the maximum number of links that must be traversed to send a message to any host along a shortest path.

network discovery
Result of dynamic routing protocols enabling a router to share information about reachability and status, and also to add remote networks to the routing table.

network infrastructure diagram
Illustration of the topology of a network that shows the location, function, and status of devices. A network infrastructure diagram may represent either a physical or logical network.

A network infrastructure diagram is also known as a topology diagrams.

network maintenance plan
See NMP.

network management system
See NMS.

network modularity
Network modularity refers to organizing a network from smaller subsystems or modules that can be designed and implemented independently. The modules can represent areas that have different physical or logical connectivity. They also designate where different functions occur in the network. Modularity allows flexibility in network design, and facilitates implementation and troubleshooting. As network complexity grows, designers can add new functional modules.

network monitoring plan
Information used by a network administrator to evaluate the condition of a network.

network operations center
See NOC.

next hop
Interface on a connected router that moves the data closer to the final destination.

NMP
network maintenance plan

Ensures business continuity by keeping the network running efficiently. Network maintenance must be scheduled during specific time periods, usually nights and weekends, to minimize the impact on business operations.

NMS
network management system

System or application that is used to monitor and control managed network devices, such as CiscoWorks.

NOC
network operations center

Organization responsible for maintaining a network.

non-broadcast multi-access
See NBMA.

non-stub area
OSPF area that carries default, static, intra-area, interarea, and external routes. An non-stub area can have virtual links configured across it and can contain an ASBR.

Null0 interface
EIGRP installs a Null0 summary route in the routing table for each parent route. The Null0 interface indicates that this is not an actual path, but a summary for advertising purposes.

NVRAM
non-volatile random access memory. NVRAM is used as the storage location for the startup configuration file for a Cisco router. After the router loads its IOS image, the settings found in the startup configuration are applied.

OC
optical carrier

Series of physical protocols, such as OC-1, OC-2, OC-3, defined for synchronous optical network optical signal transmissions.

OC signal levels put synchronous transport signal frames onto fiber-optic line at different speeds. The base rate of an OC signal level is 51.84 Mbps for OC-1. Each signal level thereafter operates at a speed multiplied by that number. For example, OC-3 runs at 155.52 Mbps (51.84 x 3 = 155.52).

Open Shortest Path First
See OSPF.

open standard
Protocol or rule available to the public to be applied to a network. An open standard is not proprietary.

optical carrier
See OC.

organizational unique identifier
See OUI.

OSPF
Open Shortest Path First

Routing algorithm for a link-state, hierarchical Interior Gateway Protocol that replaces Routing Information Protocol. OSPF features include least-cost routing, multipath routing, and load balancing.

OUI
Three octets assigned to the hardware manager by the IEEE in a block of 48-bit LAN addresses.

outbound
One of two directions a packet will travel on a network through an interface. An outbound packet is exiting a device.

out-of-band
Transmission using frequencies or channels outside the frequencies or channels normally used for information transfer. Out-of-band signaling is often used for error reporting in situations in which in-band signaling can be affected by whatever problems the network might be experiencing.

outside global address
Public IP address of an external host, as it is referred to on the Internet.

outside global network
Network attached to a router that is external to the LAN and that does not recognize the private addresses assigned to hosts on the internal LAN.

outside local address
IP address of an outside host as it appears to the inside network.

Packet over SONET/SDH
See POS.

packet sniffer
Tool that analyzes traffic flows based on the source and destination of the traffic as well as the type of traffic being sent. Packet sniffer analysis can be used to make decisions on how to manage the traffic more efficiently.

packet switch
WAN device that routes packets along the most efficient path and allows a communications channel to be shared by multiple connections.

Packet switch is also known as a packet switch node.

packet switching

Networking method where nodes share bandwidth by sending packets to each other. Packet switching is a way to direct encoded information in a network from a source to a destination.

packet-switched network

See PSN.

PAP

Password Authentication Protocol

Standard used by PPP peers to authenticate each other on a network. A remote router sends an authentication request when attempting to connect to a local router. PAP passes the password and host name or username. PAP does not prevent unauthorized access, but identifies the remote user. The router or access server then determines if the user is allowed access.

parent route

When default summarization is disabled, updates include subnet information. The routing table installs entries for each of the subnets and also an entry for the summary route. A parent route is announced by the summarizing router as long as at least one specific route in its routing table matches the parent route.

The parent route is called the summary route and the child route is called the subnet route.

partial mesh

Network where devices are organized in a mesh topology with network nodes that are organized in a full mesh, and network nodes that connected to one or two other nodes in the network. A partial mesh does not provide the level of redundancy of a full mesh topology and is less expensive to implement. They are generally used in the peripheral networks that connect to a fully meshed backbone.

Password Authentication Protocol

See PAP.

PAT

Port Address Translation

Standard used to reduce the number of internal private IP addresses to only one or a few external public IP addresses. PAT enables an organization to conserve addresses in the global address pool by allowing source ports in TCP connections or UDP conversations to be translated. Different local addresses then map to the same global address, with PAT providing the unique information. PAT is a subset of NAT functionality.

patch panel

Assembly of pin locations and ports which can be mounted on a rack or wall bracket in the wiring closet. A patch panel acts like a switchboard that connects workstation cables to each other and externally.

PBX

private branch exchange

Digital or analog telephone switchboard located on the subscriber premises and used to connect private and public telephone networks.

PDM

protocol dependent module

Used by EIGRP making decisions about specific routing tasks. Each PDM maintains three tables.

per VLAN Rapid Spanning Tree Plus

See PVRST+.

permanent virtual circuit

See PVC.

permanent virtual path

See PVP.

permits

Allows a process to occur.

physical addressing

See MAC address.

physical topology

Layout of devices on a network. The physical topology shows the way that the devices are connected through the cabling and how cables are arranged.

pilot installation

Small implementation of a new network technology used to test how well the technology meets the design goals.

PIM

Protocol Independent Multicast

Standard for a routing architecture that enables the addition of IP multicast routing on an existing IP network. PIM is unicast routing protocol independent. It can be operated in the dense mode and sparse mode.

PIM dense mode
Protocol Independent Multicast dense mode

When a receiver affected by PIM standards processes large amounts of traffic. Packets are forwarded on all outgoing interfaces until pruning and truncation occurs. It is assumed that the downstream networks will receive and use the datagrams that are forwarded to them. PIM dense mode is driven by data and resembles typical multicast routing protocols.

PIM sparse mode
Protocol Independent Multicast sparse mode

When receivers affected by PIM standards are widely distributed, PIM sparse mode tries to constrain data distribution so that a minimal number of routers in the network receive it. Packets are sent only if they are explicitly requested at the rendezvous point. It is assumed that downstream networks will not necessarily use the datagrams that are sent to them.

plain old telephone service
See POTS.

PoE
Power over Ethernet

Powering standard of network devices over Ethernet cable. IEEE 802.3af and Cisco specify two different PoE methods. Cisco power sourcing equipment and powered devices support both PoE methods.

Point-of-Presence
See POP.

Point-to-Point Protocol
See PPP.

Point-to-Point T1
WAN connectivity that offers control over the quality of service available.

Point-to-Point Tunneling Protocol
See PPTP.

poisoned reverse
Routing update that indicates that a network or subnet is unreachable, rather than implying that a network is unreachable by not including it in updates. Poison reverse updates are sent to defeat large routing loops. The Cisco IGRP implementation uses poison reverse updates.

policy routing
Scheme that forwards packets on a network to specific interfaces based on user-configured policies. An example of policy routing is that it may specify that traffic sent from a particular network should be forwarded from one interface, while all other traffic should be forwarded from another interface.

POP
Point of Presence

Physical connection between a communication facility provided by an ISP or local telephone company, and an organization's main distribution facility.

port
1) Interface on a networking device, such as a router or a switch. 2) Upper-layer process that receives information from lower layers. 3) Female plug on a patch panel.

Port Address Translation
See PAT.

port density
Amount of ports per RU on a switch.

PortFast
Enhancement to STP that causes an access port to enter the forwarding state immediately, bypassing the listening and learning states. Using PortFast on access ports that are connected to a single workstation or server allows those devices to connect to the network immediately,

POS
Packet over SONET/SDH

Type of networking supported by SONET and SDH that moves large amounts of voice and data over great distances through fiber-optic cable.

POST
power-on self test

A process used to test the device hardware after the power is turned on.

POTS
Plain old telephone service. See PSTN.

Power over Ethernet
See PoE.

power-on self test
See POST.

PPDIOO
prepare, plan, design, implement, operate, and opt

Six-phase Cisco Lifecycle Services approach to support evolving networks. Each phase defines the activities required to successfully deploy and operate Cisco technologies. PPDIOO details how to optimize performance throughout the lifecycle of a network.

PPP
Point-to-point Protocol

Standard that provides router-to-router and host-to-network connections over synchronous and asynchronous circuits.

PPTP
Point-to-Point Tunneling Protocol

Point-to-Point Tunneling Protocol (PPTP) was developed by Microsoft. It is described in RFC2637. PPTP is widely deployed in Windows client software to create VPNs across TCP/IP networks.

PQ
priority queing

Feature in routing in which the characteristics of a frame, such as packet size and interface type, are used to determine the order the frame is sent.

prefix address
Pattern that matches the bits of an IP address. For example, 130.120.0.0/16 matches the first 16 bits of the IP address 130.120.0.0, which is 130.120. In another example, 12.0.0.0/12 matches 12.0.2.3, 12.2.255.240, and 12.15.255.255, but does not match 12.16.0.1.

prefix length
Identifies the number of bits used in the network.

A prefix length is also known as a network prefix.

prepare, plan, design, implement, operate, and opt
See PPDIOO.

priority queuing
See PQ.

Private addresses
Type of IP address that is reserved for internal use. A private network address is not routed across the public Internet. In IPv4, the range of private network addresses are 10.0.0.0 to 10.255.255.255, 172.16.0.0 to172.31.255.255, and 192.168.0.0 to 192.168.255.255.

Private Branch Exchange
See PBX.

private network address
Portion of an IP address that is reserved for internal use. A private network address is not routed across the public Internet. In IPv4, the range of private network addresses are 10.0.0.0 to 10.255.255.255, 172.16.0.0 to172.31.255.255, and 192.168.0.0 to 192.168.255.255.

proactive maintenance
Method for a network administrator to ensure uptime by monitoring network functionality and taking corrective action immediately. Proactive maintenance is performed on a regular basis to detect weaknesses prior to a critical error that could bring down the network.

process switching
Operation that occurs when a router evaluates the route and per packet load balancing across parallel links before sending a packet. In process switching, a router performs a table lookup for each packet, selects an interface, and looks up the data-link information. Because each routing decision is independent for each packet, all packets going to the same destination are not forced to use the same interface.

proof-of-concept
Proving that a design functions as expected.

propagation delay
Amount of time required for data to travel over a network, from the source to the destination.

proprietary
Device or software that cannot be used with devices or software from other vendors.

Protocol Dependent Module
See PDM.

Protocol Independent Multicast
See PIM.

Protocol Independent Multicast dense mode
See PIM dense mode.

Protocol Independent Multicast sparse mode
See PIM sparse mode.

PSN
packet-switched network

Network that uses packet-switching technology for data transfer.

PSTN
Public Switched Telephone Network

General term referring to the variety of telephone networks and services in place worldwide.

PSTN is also known as plain old telephone service, or POTS.

public network address
IP address that is unique and routable across the public Internet.

Public Switched Telephone Network
See PSTN.

punchdown
Spring-loaded tool used to cut and connect wires in a jack or on a patch panel.

punchdown block
A device that connects telephone or data lines to each other. The solid copper wires are punched down into short open-ended slots to establish connectivity.

PVC
permanent virtual circuit

Connection that saves bandwidth because the circuit is established ahead of time.

PVP
permanent virtual path

Passage that consists of permanent virtual circuits.

PVRST+
Per VLAN Rapid Spanning Tree +

Cisco implementation of one instance of RSTP per VLAN.

Q.922A
ITU-T specification for Frame Relay encapsulation.

QoS
quality of service

Standard for monitoring and maintaining a level of transmission performance and service, such as available data transmission bandwidth and error rate.

QoS policies
Procedures defined and used in the QoS process.

quad zero route
Route where the network address and subnet mask are both specified as 0.0.0.0. The command uses either the next-hop address or the exit interface parameters.

quality of service
See QoS.

query packet
Message used to inquire about the value of some variable or set of variables.

rack unit
See RU.

radio frequency
See RF.

radio frequency interference
See RFI.

RAM
random-access memory

Type of memory that allows any byte of memory to be accessed without affecting preceding bytes. RAM is used for temporary storage by programs. When the computer is shut down, all data stored in RAM is lost.

random-access memory
See RAM.

Rapid Spanning Tree Protocol
See RSTP.

Rapid Transport Protocol
See RTP.

RD
reported distance

Distance to a destination as reported by a neighbor.

read-only memory
See ROM.

Real-Time Transport Control Protocol
See RTCP.

Real-Time Transport Protocol
See RTP.

receiver signal strength indicator
See RSSI.

recursive lookup

Two steps necessary to determine the exit interface. First a router matches the destination IP address of a packet to the static route. Then the router matches the next hop IP address of the static route to entries in its routing table to determine which interface to use.

redirector

Software that intercepts requests for resources on a remote computer and then sends the requests to the appropriate host to process the transaction more efficiently. The redirector creates a remote-procedure call that is sent to lower-layer protocol software that can satisfy the request.

redistribution

Process of including routing information discovered through one routing protocol in the update messages of another routing protocol.

redlined

Marks on blueprints showing changes in the design.

redundancy

1) Duplication of components on a network, such as devices, services, or connections, for the purpose of maintaining operability if any tool fails. 2) Portion of the total information contained in a message that can be eliminated without losing the context.

redundant link

Secondary connection between network devices to ensure network availability if the primary link fails.

reference bandwidth

Parameter related to the OSPF cost metric which is used to calculate interface cost. The bandwidth value calculation of each interface uses the equation 100,000,000/bandwidth, or 10^8/bandwidth.

Reflexive ACL

An ACL that allows IP packets to be filtered based on upper-layer session information. They are generally used to allow inbound traffic into the network in response to sessions that originate on an inside interface of the router. This mechanism can help reduce exposure to spoofing and denial-of-service attacks. Reflexive ACLs function similarly to the "established" keyword used in extended ACL statements, except that reflexive ACLs can also inspect UDP and ICMP traffic in addition to TCP.

release notes

Documentation that accompanies software when it is distributed. Release notes include the most recent information, such as a user guide.

reliability

Ratio of expected-to-received keepalives from a link. If the ratio of keepalives is high, the line is reliable. Relibility is used as a routing metric.

Reliable Transport Protocol

See RTP.

remote login

See rlogin.

remote monitoring

See RMON.

remote shell protocol

See rsh.

remote-access virtual private network

See remote-access VPN.

remote-access VPN

Connectivity option used to augment or replace a traditional remote access strategy, such as the use of a dial-up link.

remote-access VPN is also known as remote-user VPN.

remote-procedure call

See RPC.

replay attack

Malicious process that allows a hacker to gain access to a router using information that is saved and replayed by the hacker as proof of identity.

reply packet

Information sent when a query packet is received. A reply packet helps DUAL to locate a successor route to the destination network. Queries can be multicast or unicast. Replies are always unicast.

reported distance

See RD.

Request for Proposal

See RFP.

Request for Quotation

See RFQ.

request message

When a router is started, message sent out by each RIP-configured interface requesting that all RIP neighbors send their routing tables.

response message

Reply to a message sent out by each RIP-configured interface requesting that all RIP neighbors send their routing tables.

RF

radio frequency

Electromagnetic waves generated by AC and transmitted to an antenna within the electromagnetic spectrum. Radio, cable TV, and broadband networks use RF technology. WLAN uses RF to transmit data.

RFI

radio frequency interference

Noise that interferes with information being transmitted across unshielded copper cabling.

RFP

request for proposal

Formal documentation presented to potential vendors by an organization asking for information on the type of services or products to be provided.

RFQ

request for quotation

Formal documentation presented to vendors by an organization asking for a bid or quotation of the cost of providing services or products. An RFQ is issued when the specifications have been determined.

RIP

Routing Information Protocol

Distance vector routing standard that uses hop count as a routing matrix.

RIPng

Routing Information Protocol next generation

Distance vector routing standard with a limit of 15 hops that uses split-horizon and poison reverse to prevent routing loops. It is based on IPv4 RIPv2 and similar to RIPv2, but uses IPv6 for transport. The multicast group address FF02::9 identifies all RIPng enabled routers.

RIPv2

Routing Information Protocol version 2

Distance vector routing standard based on RIPv1 with additional extensions to conform to modern routing environments. RIPv2 supports VLSM, authentication, and multicast updates. RIPv2 is defined in RFC 1723 and supported in IOS versions 11.1 and later.

Rivest, Shamir, and Adleman

See RSA.

rlogin

remote login

Terminal emulation program that is offered in most UNIX implementations to access a device remotely, such as Telnet.

RMON

remote monitoring

Management information base agent specification described in RFC 1271 that defines functions to remotely monitor networked devices. RMON provides monitoring, problem detection, and reporting capabilities.

rogue switch

Unidentified switch on a network.

ROM

read-only memory

ROM is typically used as the memory area from which a Cisco router begins the boot process, supports the Power-On-Self-Test, and supports the ROM Monitor diagnostic environment.

root bridge

Designated packet forwarding device in a spanning-tree implementation that receive topology information and notifies all other bridges in the network when topology changes are required. A root bridge prevents loops and provides a measure of defense against link failure.

Root bridge is also known as root switch.

root port

STP designated port that provides the least cost path back to the root bridge.

root switch

See root bridge.

route

Path between the source and destination devices.

route aggregation

See route summarization.

route map

Method to control and modify routing information on a network. A route map is a complex access list that allows some conditions to be tested against the route in question. If the conditions match, some actions can be taken to modify the route.

route poisoning

Setting the metric for a route to 16 to stop traffic on the route. RIP sends a triggered update immediately, poisoning the route.

route redistribution

Default route is propagated from the edge router to other internal routers.

route summarization

Consolidation of advertised addresses in a routing table. Route summarization reduces the number of routes in the routing table, the routing update traffic, and overall router overhead.

Route summarization is also known as route aggregation.

router

Network layer device that uses one or more metrics to determine the optimal path along which network traffic should be forwarded. Routers forward packets from one network to another based on network layer information.

router ID

IP address determined by a value configured with the router-id command, a value of the highest configured IP address on a loopback interface, or a value of the highest IP address on any active physical interface.

router-on-a-stick

Configuration on the router that determines that if the destination VLAN is on the same switch as the source VLAN, the router forwards the traffic back down to the source switch using the subinterface parameters of the destination VLAN ID.

routing

Process to find a path to a destination host. Routing is complex in large networks because of intermediate destinations a packet might traverse before reaching the final destination host.

routing algorithm

Mathematical formula for procedures used to determine the best route to forward traffic from source to destination.

routing domain

Group of end systems and intermediate systems that operate under the same set of administrative rules. Within each routing domain there are one or more areas, each uniquely identified by an area address.

Routing Information Protocol
See RIP.

Routing Information Protocol next Generation
See RIPng.

Routing Information Protocol version 2
See RIPv2.

routing metric

Standard of measurement that is used by a routing algorithm that determines that one route is better than another. Routing metrics are stored in routing tables and may include bandwidth, communication cost, delays, hop count, load, maximum transmission unit, path cost, and reliability.

routing prefix

Pattern to match some routes in a routing table.

routing protocol

Standard that makes use of the routing algorithm. Examples of routing protocols include EIGRP, OSPF, and RIP.

routing table

Table stored on a router or other internetworking device that keeps track of routes to network destinations and metrics associated with those routes.

Routing Table Protocol
See RTP.

routing update

Message sent from a router to check network access and associated cost information. A routing update is sent at regular intervals and after a change in network topology.

RPC

remote-procedure call

Communication from a local program to a remote program to request temporary use of services available on the remote program.

RSA

Rivest, Shamir, & Adleman

Algorithm for public key asymmetric encryption. RSA was the first algorithm suitable for signing as well as encryption. It was one of the first great advances in public key cryptography.

rsh

remote shell protocol

Standard that allows a user to execute commands on a remote system without having to log in to the system. For example, rsh can be used to remotely examine the status of access servers on a network without having to connect to each communication server to execute the command.

RSSI
receiver signal strength indicator

Measurement of received RF signal strength in WLAN application.

RSTP
Rapid Spanning Tree Protocol

Update to Spanning Tree Protocol standards that reduces the time for connections to be established to switch ports.

RSTP+
Enhanced Rapid Spanning Tree Protocol

Type of spanning tree protocol with increase convergence speed.

RTCP
Real-Time Transport Control Protocol

Control standard for RTP that monitors and provides feedback on the QoS of a transmission link.

RTP
Routing Table Protocol

VINES routing standard based on RIP that is used to distribute network topology information and assist VINES servers to find neighboring clients, servers, and routers. RTP uses delay as a routing metric.

Rapid Transport Protocol

Standard that provides pacing and error recovery for data as it crosses the APPN network. With RTP, error recovery and flow control are conducted end-to-end rather than at every node. RTP prevents congestion.

Real-Time Transport Protocol

Standard commonly used with IP networks that provides end-to-end network transport functions for applications transmitting real-time data, such as audio, video, or simulation data, over multicast or unicast network services. RTP provides such services as payload type identification, sequence numbering, timestamping, and delivery monitoring to real-time applications.

RU
rack unit

Standard form factor measurement for the vertical space that equipment occupies. A rack unit is equal to the height of 1.75 inches (4.4cm). A device is measured in RUs. If a device is 1.75 inches tall, it is 1RU. If it is 3.5 inches tall, it is 2RU.

runt
Frame that is less than 64 bytes, usually the result of a collision. In fragment-free switching, the switch reads the first 64 bytes of the frame before it begins to forward it out the destination port. Checking the first 64 bytes ensures that the switch does not forward collision fragments.

SAN
storage area network

Data communication platform that interconnects servers and storage at Gigabaud speeds. By combining LAN networking models with server performance and mass storage capacity, SAN eliminates bandwidth issues and scalability limitations created by previous SCSI bus-based architectures.

scalability
Ability of a network design to develop to include new user groups and remote sites. A scalable network design should support new applications without impacting the level of service delivered to existing users.

SDH
Synchronous Digital Hierarchy

European standard that defines a set of rate and format standards that are transmitted using optical signals over fiber. SDH is similar to SONET, with a basic SDH rate of 155.52 Mbps, designated at STM-1.

SDM
Cisco Security Device Management

Web-based device-management tool for a Cisco IOS software-based router. Simplifies router and security configuration through smart wizards used to deploy, configure, and monitor a Cisco router without requiring knowledge of the CLI.

SDRAM
synchronous dynamic random access memory. A form of DRAM.

Secure Shell
See SSH.

security
Protection of data and hardware against unwanted access or damage.

security appliance
Device that protects data and hardware against unwanted access or damage.

security policy
Description of the system, physical, and behavioral protection measures implemented in an organization.

segment
1) Section of network that is bounded by bridges, routers, or switches. 2) Continuous electrical circuit in a LAN using a bus topology, that is often connected to other segments with repeaters. 3) Single, logical transport layer unit of information.

A segment that is a logical unit of information may also be known as a datagram, frame, message, or packet.

segmented data
Small, uniform parts of data that switch quickly and efficiently between nodes.

Serial Line Address Resolution Protocol
See SLARP.

serial transmission
Method of data transmission in which the bits of a data character are transmitted sequentially over a single channel.

serial tunnel
See STUN.

server
Software program or node that provides data or services at the request of clients.

See also back end, client, and front end.

server farm
Collection of servers located in a central facility and maintained by the central group to provide server needs for organizations. A server farm usually has primary and backup server hardware for load balancing, redundancy, and fault tolerance purposes. Server farm architecture provides the operation and maintenance of servers.

service level agreement
See SLA.

service provider
See SP.

Service Set Identifier
See SSID.

setup mode
Interactive menu to create an initial configuration file for a new networking device, or a device that has had the startup-config file from NVRAM erased. Setup mode can also be used to modify an existing configuration.

shared secret
Password known between devices.

Shortest path first algorithm
See SPF algorithm.

Shortest Path Routing
See SPR.

silicon switching
High-speed, dedicated packet switching based on the silicon switching engine, not the silicon switch processor.

Simple Mail Transfer Protocol
See SMTP.

Simple Network Management Protocol
See SNMP.

simple password authentication
Method that offers basic securtiy to a router using a key to gain access.

site-to-site VPN
Connection between sites of an organization or between an organization and a partner site. Site-to-site VPN does not require IPSec client configuration on computer hosts because data is encrypted at the entry point of a site and decrypted at the exit point of the tunnel at the other site.

SLA
service level agreement

Binding contract between a network service provider and the end user who requires a certain level of service.

transceiver

Device that receives and forwards analog and digital signals.

transmit power control

Modify the RF transmission in a wireless LAN by increasing or decreasing the rate of power on a device to improve the link quality and signals received.

transmit queue

See TxQ.

transparent

Not visible or apparent. In networking, a lower layer protocol may make a decision that does not affect or include the upper layers, so the action is invisible, or transparent to the upper layers.

trial-and-error

Troubleshooting technique that relies on experience and testing to solve a problem.

triggered update

Message containing the routing table of a router that is sent to neighboring routers on a network when the router starts up.

triple data encryption standard

See 3DES.

Trivial File Transfer Protocol

See TFTP.

trunk

Point-to-point link that connects a switch to another switch, a router, or a server. A trunk carries traffic for multiple VLANs over the same link. The VLANs are multiplexed over the link with a trunking protocol.

trunk port

A port on a switch or router that connects a switch to another switch, a router, or a server through a trunk. A trunk carries traffic for multiple VLANs over the same link. The VLANs are multiplexed over the link with a trunking protocol.

TSP

telecommunication service provider

Vendor that is authorized by regulatory agencies to operate a telecommunications system and provide telecommunications service.

A telecommunication service provider is also known as a local exchange carrier, telecom carrier, or carrier.

tunnel

Secure communication path between two peers, such as two routers.

tunneling

Method of data transmission over networks with differing protocols. With tunneling, a data packet is encapsulated to form a new packet that conforms to the protocols used over intermediary networks.

two-way handshake

Authentication process used on a PAP. During the two-way handshake, a device looks up the username and password of the calling device to confirm the information matches what is stored in the database.

TxQ

transmit queue

Process of storing traffic on hardware and then sending the packets out in the order they were received.

type field

Extra field in a Cisco HDLC frame which allows multiple protocols to share the same link by identifying the type of protocol carried by the frame.

type of service

See ToS.

UDP

User Datagram Protocol

Standard for connectionless transmission of voice and video traffic. Transmissions using UDP are not affected by the delays caused from acknowledgements and retransmitting lost packets.

unequal cost

Additional bandwidth is needed to forward a packet on certain routes on a network. Some routes may have higher metric values than others.

unequal cost load balancing

Distribution of packets on more than one path using a specified variance in the metric. Distributing the traffic helps prevent a single path from being overloaded.

unicast

Type of message sent to a single network destination.

Unicast frames

Data packet that is addressed to a single destination.

uninterruptible power supply

See UPS.

untagged
Traffic with no VLAN ID that needs to cross the 802.1q configured link. Examples of untagged traffic include Cisco Discovery Protocol, VTP, and some types of voice traffic. Untagged traffic minimizes the delays associated with inspection of the VLAN ID tag.

update packet
Message about the network topology sent to a neighbor. The update packet is added to the topology table. Several updates are often required to send all of the topology information to a new neighbor.

uplink port
High-speed port that connects to areas that have a higher demand for bandwidth, such as another switch, a server farm, or other networks.

UplinkFast
STP enhancement to minimize downtime during recalculation. STP UplinkFast accelerates choosing a new root port when a link or switch fails, or when an STP is reconfigured. The transition of the root port to the forwarding state occurs immediately, without going through the normal STP procedures of listening and learning.

UPS
uninterruptable power supply

Continuous and reliable power source made available in the event of power failure. UPS is often provided to mission critical servers and network devices.

uptime
Period of time in which a network or a device is fully functional.

User Datagram Protocol
See UDP.

V.35
ITU-T standard describing a synchronous, physical layer protocol used for communications between a network access device and a packet network. V.35 is most commonly used in the United States and in Europe, and is recommended for speeds up to 48 Kbps.

variable-length subnet mask
See VLSM.

variance
Amount multiplied to a route to determine if it is within range of the maximum acceptable metric for use as a path. For example, If the variance value is 2,

the router balances the traffic load using any path for which the metric is less than two times the best metric.

VC
virtual circuit

Logical relationship created to ensure reliable communication between two network devices. A virtual circuit is defined by a virtual path identifier/virtual channel identifier pair, and can be either a permanent virtual circuit or switched virtual circuit. Virtual circuits are used in Frame Relay and X.25. In ATM, a virtual circuit is called a virtual channel.

vector
Data segment of an SNA message. A vector consists of a length field, a key that describes the vector type, and vector-specific data.

VID
VLAN ID

Identity of the VLAN inserted into an Ethernet frame as it enters a port on a switch.

video on demand
See VoD.

virtual circuit
See VC.

virtual local area network
See VLAN.

virtual path
Logical group of virtual circuits that connect two sites.

virtual path connection
See VPC.

virtual path link
See VPL.

virtual private network
See VPN.

Virtual Trunking Protocol
See VTP.

VLAN
virtual local area network

Group of devices on a network, typically end-user stations, that communicate as if attached to the same network segment even though they may be on different segments. VLANs are configured on workgroup switches. Switches with VLANs may interconnect using VLAN trunking protocols.

VLAN is also known as virtual LAN.

VLAN ID
See VID.

VLAN management policy server (VMPS)
See VMPS.

VLAN number
Number assigned to a VLAN when it is created. The VLAN number is any number from the range available on the switch, except for VLAN1. Naming a VLAN is considered a network management best practice.

VLSM
variable-length subnet mask

Technique used to specify a different subnet mask for the same major network number to identify different subnets. VLSM can help optimize available IP address space.

VMPS
VLAN management policy server

Server with a database that maps MAC addresses to VLAN assignments. When a device plugs into a switch port, the VMPS searches the database for a match of the MAC address and temporarily assigns that port to the appropriate VLAN.

VoD
video on demand

Type of system that allow a user to select and watch video content over a network as part of an interactive television system. A VoD system either streams content, allowing viewing while the video is being downloaded, or downloads the content entirely to a set-top box before viewing starts.

Voice over IP
See VoIP.

Voice/WAN interface card
See VWIC.

voice-enabled router
Device that converts analog voice from telephone signals to IP packets. The voice-enabled router forwards IP packets between locations.

VoIP
Voice Over Internet Protocol

Standard for transmitting voice data encapsulated in an IP packet on an already implemented IP network without needing its own network infrastructure. In VoIP, the digital signal processor divides the voice signal into frames which are paired in groups of two and stored in voice packets. The voice packets are transported using IP in compliance with ITU-T specification H.323.

VoIP is also known as Voice Over IP.

VPC
virtual path connection

Group of virtual channel connections that share one or more contiguous VPLs.

VPL
virtual path link

Group of unidirectional virtual channel links within a virtual path with the same end points. Grouping into a VPL reduces the number of connections to be managed, and as a result, decreases network control overhead and cost.

VPN
virtual private network

Network through which data is sent through a public telecommunication infrastructure while maintaining the privacy of the data by creating a tunnel through the public telecommunication infrastructure.

VPN concentrator
virtual private network concentrator

Gateway on a network that filters all VPN traffic.

VTP
Virtual Trunking Protocol

Cisco proprietary standard that maintains a consistent VLAN configuration across a common administrative domain.

VTP configuration revision number
VLAN Trunking Protocol configuration revision number

Numerical order of multicast messages on a network. The VTP configuration revision number begins at zero. As changes on the network occur, the configuration revision number increases by one. It continues to increment until it reaches 2,147,483,648. If a message has a higher VTP configuration revision number than the one stored in the database, the switch updates its VLAN database with this new information.

VWIC
voice/WAN interface card

Adapter that provides support for voice, data and integrated voice, and data applications. A VWIC facilitates the migration from data only, as well as channelized voice and data, to packet voice solutions which simplifies deployment and management.

WAN
wide area network

Data communication network that serves users across a broad geographic area and often uses transmission devices provided by common carriers. Examples of WAN technologies include Frame Relay, SMDS, and X.25.

WAN interface card
See WIC.

warranty
Guarantee that a product or service is free of defects and performs as advertised. A warranty is limited in duration and in the services provided.

WEP
Wired Equivalent Privacy

Optional security mechanism standard defined within the 802.11 standard designed to make the link integrity of wireless devices equal to that of a cable.

WIC
wide area network interface card

Adapter that connects a system to a WAN link service provider.

wide area network
See WAN.

wide area network interface card
See WIC.

Wi-Fi Protected Access
See WPA.

wildcard mask
32-bit quantity used in conjunction with an IP address to determine which bits in an IP address should be ignored when that address is compared with another IP address. A wildcard mask is specified when access lists are set up. A wildcard mask is used in in IPv4.

wire speed
Rate that packets are forwarded on a network.

Wired Equivalent Privacy
See WEP.

wireless access point
Physical sites connected on a network that transmit signals for wireless devices.

wireless LAN
See WLAN.

wireless LAN controller
Type of module that provides a secure enterprise-class wireless system. A wireless LAN controller enables a smaller organization to cost-effectively and easily deploy and manage a secure WLAN.

wiring closet
Specially designed room used to wire a data or voice network. Wiring closets serve as a central junction point for the wires and wiring equipment that is used to interconnect devices.

WLAN
wireless local area network

Connection between two or more computers without using physical media. WLAN uses radio communication to accomplish the same functionality as a LAN.

WLAN is also known as wireless LAN.

WPA
Wi-Fi Protected Access

Standard based on IEEE 802.11i that was developed to address security issues. WPA provides high levels of security in a wireless network. WPA uses the Temporal Key Integrity Protocol for data protection and 802.1X for authenticated key management.

zero CIR
Excess bandwidth that is discounted when it is available from a Frame Relay service provider. In Zero CIR, a user pays a small fee for the capability to transmit data across a PVC at speeds up to that of the access link. If there is congestion, all DE lableled frames are dropped. There is no guarantee of service with a CIR set to zero.

CCNA Discovery
learning resources

Cisco Press, the authorized publisher for the Cisco® Networking Academy®, has a variety of learning and preparation tools to help you master the knowledge and prepare successfully for the CCENT™ and CCNA® exams.

From foundational learning to late-stage review, practice, and preparation, the varied print, software, and video products from Cisco Press can help you with learning, mastering, and succeeding!

Learning Guides

Learning Guides provide the textbook and labs all together as one resource per course.

Networking for Home and Small Business, CCNA Discovery Learning Guide	1587132095 / 9781587132094
Working at a Small-to-Medium Business or ISP, CCNA Discovery Learning Guide	1587132109 / 9781587132100
Introducing Routing and Switching in the Enterprise, CCNA Discovery Learning Guide	1587132117 / 9781587132117
Designing and Supporting Computer Networks, CCNA Discovery Learning Guide	1587132125 / 9781587132124

Other CCENT and CCNA resources

Books, software, and network simulations to help you prepare

31 Days before your CCENT Certification	1587132176 / 9781587132179
31 Days Before your CCNA Exam, Second Edition	1587131978 / 9781587131974
CCNA Official Exam Certification Library, Third Edition	1587201836 / 9781587201837
CCNA Portable Command Guide, Second Edition	1587201933 / 9781587201936
CCNA 640-802 Network Simulator (from Pearson Certification)	1587202166 / 9781587202162
CCNA 640-802 Cert Flash Cards Online	1587202212/9781587202216

For more information on this and other Cisco Press products, visit www.ciscopress.com/academy

Cisco Press

Learning is Serious Business. **Invest Wisely.**